12,17,22

To G...
Me
from an...
enjoyed journalism.
mu... love, Paul and
Emalett

The BALLANTINES

BUILDING COMMUNITY ISSUE BY ISSUE

JOHN PEEL

HAMILTON BOOKS
an imprint of
ROWMAN & LITTLEFIELD
Lanham • Boulder • New York • London

Content editor: Elizabeth A. Green
Copy editor: Tracy Boyd Pope
Design: Lisa Snider

Published by Hamilton Books
An imprint of The Rowman & Littlefield Publishing Group, Inc.
4501 Forbes Boulevard, Suite 200, Lanham, Maryland 20706
www.rowman.com

86-90 Paul Street, London EC2A 4NE, United Kingdom

British Library Cataloguing in Publication Information Available

Library of Congress Cataloging in Publication Data Available

ISBN 978-0-7618-7377-8 (cloth : alk. paper)
ISBN 978-0-7618-7376-1 (pbk. : alk. paper)
ISBN 978-0-7618-7383-9 (electronic)

♾™ The paper used in this publication meets the minimum requirements of
American National Standard for Information Sciences—Permanence of Paper
for Printed Library Materials, ANSI/NISO Z39.48-1992.

praise for
THE BALLANTINES:
BUILDING COMMUNITY ISSUE BY ISSUE

The saga of a family and the small-town newspaper the Ballantines have loved and stewarded for three generations. A fascinating account of a world that is rapidly disappearing, and a great argument for saving it.

– Alex S. Jones
Pulitzer Prize-winning *New York Times* reporter
biographer of Bingham and Ochs/Sulzberger newspaper families
and himself from a four-generation small-town newspaper family

✦

Filled with amusing anecdotes and revealing stories, John Peel's book *The Ballantines: Building Community Issue by Issue* traces family history across generations for a well-written account of a family dedicated to a free press and grassroots community building. Rarely do business and family histories have this deep level of insight and cultural context. The Ballantines understand the struggle to maintain local, independent journalism in a digital age. Peel tells their story with masterful research, enlightening, incisive interviews and editorial excerpts. This book is a family history but also a business history of one of America's great media-owning families still committed to rigorous, award-winning journalism.

– Andrew Gulliford
Professor of History, Fort Lewis College, Durango

✦

The Ballantines: Building Community Issue by Issue shines a bright light on the larger-than-life families whose love of the West and newspapers created the fiercely independent *Durango Herald*. The book is a love letter to the transformational influence of good journalism on a small town.

– Lynne Perri
Journalist in Residence, American University School of Communication

John Peel takes the reader on a behind-the-scenes look at the life and family of Arthur and Morley Ballantine whose reach and influence was national in scope as they set about creating a legacy of award-winning small-town newspapering through honest, compassionate, hard-hitting journalism that continues to this day. Their lasting impact on the Durango, Colo., region through the news and editorial columns of *The Durango Herald* is matched by their committed involvement in all things Durango and their charitable giving back. Morley Ballantine's words spoken in 1992 ring very true today: "For democracy to function successfully, its citizens need to have information about the wide variety of topics important to their government. They need complete information and they need accurate information. It's a newspaper's responsibility to provide this information."

John Peel has done a delightful job of capturing the Ballantine story.

– Gary M. Hook
Director (retired), USA Today
former board member Ballantine Communications Inc.

✦

John Peel's book is a revealing story – and a very readable one – about one of Durango's first families. Durango has always had its movers and shakers, from the 19th century founders who ensured their city would be dominant in Southwest Colorado, to those who picked up the torch in the 20th century to maintain and grow that status. The list of people and families who worked to make Durango a special place is long, but few on that list had a loftier vision for or exerted more power and influence in making Durango a progressive city than the Ballantines. Their presence in Durango marks nearly half the city's history. To a great extent, their history is our history.

– Robert McDaniel
founding Director, Animas Museum,
La Plata County Historical Society

Contents

Preface

Seventy years ago this summer, our parents took a chance on a small town and two newspapers. Our mother came from a newspaper family, and our father had grown to love the profession as well. Three generations of our family have now been a part of the continued publication of *The Durango Herald*. That's an achievement worth celebrating.

Growing up in Durango as part of a newspaper family gave me and my siblings a unique perspective. Our house was always filled with people, including strangers and distant relatives. We were encouraged to listen, learn stories, and report back gossip that might show up in the newspaper. No one else was quite like us.

The optimism and open nature of Westerners shaped our views. We children attended school, enjoyed community events, wandered around Durango in the freedom of another era, and enjoyed many good times with our friends. One of my proudest moments as a teenager was carrying the banner of the Goldenaires, the American Legion marching band, in the annual August Spanish Trails Fiesta Parade. We children knew what was important to Durango: more tourists to grow the economy, clean water, good schools, the new ski area, saving the train, and above all, good journalism.

Dozens of editors, salesmen, writers, pressmen, accountants, and janitors became family friends. In a small town, it's easy to be friends with a wide range of people, to share ideas and embrace possibilities together. The mayor or a county commissioner might be a neighbor. You might see your children's teacher at church or while dining at a local restaurant. Our parents loved that about Durango, as do we.

The newspaper plays a vital role in bringing people together, keeping them informed, and fostering the exchange of ideas. In many ways, it becomes the anchor of a small town. It is the primary disseminator of information and the keeper of our stories, both as individuals and as a community.

This book is the product of some of the people who worked at *The Durango Herald,* or other media companies. They share the toil, the vision; they understand first-hand the triumphs and failures of the initiatives recounted in this book.

The author, John Peel, has been a sports editor, columnist, and outdoor writer for *The Durango Herald* for more than thirty years. He employed his prodigious research and writing skill to tell the rich story of seven decades of editorials, columns, board service, and philanthropy reflected in the Ballantines' engagement with Southwest Colorado. We family members have learned many new facts, thanks to his skillful work.

Mike Wegner is a veteran *Des Moines Register* reporter and editor. He helped to edit the story of the Cowles family, their media properties, their politics, and cultural and business heritage in Iowa and Minnesota – a factor in Morley and Arthur's lives.

Beth Green is a former reporter and editor for other newspapers, and an award-winning editor for the Durango Herald Small Press (DHSP). A tireless, indefatigable editor, she has smoothed the prose and brought buried concepts to life for the reader. Lisa Snider is also a veteran of *The Durango Herald* and was the award-winning designer for DHSP. As our designer, she created the format and graphics for this book. Finally, our ace copy editor is Tracy Pope, an experienced broadcast journalist, who now serves as grants executive for the Community Foundation serving Southwest Colorado.

In an era when local, family-owned newspapers are going out of business, or being gobbled up and gutted by hedge funds, the story of *The Durango Herald* stands out for its enduring success. Our family remains committed to all it stands for: good journalism, solid reporting, support for the institutions and organizations that contribute to people's quality of life, and advocacy for Durango and the Four Corners region.

Many thanks to my family members – especially my siblings – who demonstrated confidence in this project, reading and correcting portions. History repeats itself as once again their personal lives are material for storytelling – just as they were in the 1950s, seven decades ago.

– **Elizabeth Ballantine**

Acknowledgments

Elizabeth Ballantine was the driving force behind this project, and she is a very steady and determined driver, as those who know her will attest. Much of the credit for this book coming to fruition must go first to her. As a veteran journalist herself, she brought an important perspective to documenting her family's history. Starting in her teens, she wrote for *The Durango Herald* and later reported for *The Des Moines Register*. Her love and deep regard for responsible journalism, inspired by her parents, is at the heart of this story.

An author is only as effective as his sources allow, and I was especially fortunate to be given full access to the Ballantine family's extensive collection of personal correspondence, papers, and photographs. Re-reading the seventy-year accumulation of *The Durango Herald* and *Durango Herald-News* stories, columns, and opinion pieces painted a lively picture of Morley and Arthur Ballantine as journalists, business owners, parents, and citizens.

This book would not have been possible without the help of many people. Their eagerness to reminisce about Morley and Arthur Ballantine and their family has demonstrated the breadth and depth of their impact in Durango, the state of Colorado, and the nation. The list of people I was able to interview in person is long, and I am grateful to each of them for sharing their personal and professional experiences: Mary Jane Clark, Jim Foster, Jackson Clark II, Antonia Clark, Sherry Manning, Gail Klapper, Dan Ritchie, Doug Bennett, Sarah Healy-Vigo, Helen Healy, Katherine Healy Dougan, Richard Ballantine, Mary Lyn Ballantine, Bill Ballantine, Elizabeth Ballantine, Russell Cowles, Bill Roberts, Pam Patton, Stephanie Moran, Andrew Gulliford, Karen Zink, Bob Lieb, Ellen Roberts, Don Mapel, Sheri Rochford Figgs, Linda Mannix, Jeff Mannix, Diane Wildfang, Katherine Barr, Robert C. "Bobby" Duthie III, Joanne Spina, Deborah Uroda, Susan Lander, Steve Short, Beth Lamberson, Jim Morehart, Barbara Eggleston Conn, and Pat Rustad. Thanks also to those who wrote about their memories of the Ballantines by email: Sherry Manning, Nancy Whitson, James Rousmaniere, Sarah Leavitt, and Barry Smith. To Tilly Grey, thanks for taking the time to talk with me several times by phone. And to the others who one way or another helped me gather the personal touches and information that bring the Ballantine story to life: Herbert Strentz, Briggen Wrinkle, Gary Hook, Robert McDaniel, and Judith Reynolds. To all the others who were consulted and might have been missed in this list, I thank you.

– John Peel
Durango, Colorado

Introduction

Durango in 1952 was a gritty, rural town of almost 8,000. This relatively isolated southwestern Colorado burg was bounded by Native American reservations to the south and a mountainous mining district to the north, from which a narrow-gauge steam-powered train carried iron ore to Durango and beyond. The San Juan National Forest and Animas River provided a beautiful backdrop, but the town was frequently sullied by the dust and noise of mining commerce and coal-burning furnaces.

It was the kind of town where Hollywood came to film Western movies. Tourists were just beginning to discover the charms of the Four Corners, which included the spot where four states converge and you can place one appendage in Arizona, New Mexico, Utah, and Colorado; and Mesa Verde National Park, once home to Puebloan people who built thriving, spectacular communities on the mesas and in the cliffs. Denver, the closest major city, was at least seven hours away by car on seasonally hazardous roads.

It was not the type of place you'd expect a young Minneapolis couple – he, a New York-raised, Ivy League-educated lawyer; and she, the daughter of a prominent Midwestern newspaper publishing family – to pack up and relocate with their four young children. By 1952 Minneapolis had paved its streets. Durango had not. Minneapolis boasted respected public and private universities. Durango, in 1952, offered one failing junior college seventeen miles away.

Minneapolis had thriving fine arts institutions. Durango had next to none.

What Durango did have that Minneapolis didn't was two newspapers for sale that a husband-wife team eager to make their mark on the world could afford to purchase. And that's what Arthur Ballantine Jr. and Morley Cowles Ballantine did. They bought and merged the two papers, and set out to change the local media for good.

The Ballantines employed their considerable skills and hard work to win over skeptics and to make their publication one of the journalistic best in Colorado. They were committed to honesty and integrity and willing to face the blowback. Commercial success followed, helping them to settle into the community and to befriend those who shared their dreams. Over the years, they served on countless committees and boards that contributed to a better Durango. And frequently it was their ideas, editorial prodding, and seed money that got new projects off the ground.

When it became obvious, decades later, that the wealth-producing days of newspapering had passed, the Ballantines held to the ideals of a family-owned paper. They were unwilling to take the instant profit from a sale to a media chain – a sale that would hasten the almost-certain dismantling of an award-winning newsroom and decrease the value of a community asset they'd worked so diligently to create.

Durango has been good to the Morley and Arthur Ballantine family. The Ballantines over the course of seventy years have been even better to Durango. Primarily through their stewardship of *The Durango Herald*, Arthur and Morley, and later their son Richard, had a guiding hand in many changes that have turned Durango and the surrounding area into a thriving part of the American Southwest.

The story – of a newspaper family with a vision to help inform and improve its community – begins with Arthur and Morley Ballantine, but the full picture can't be properly drawn without including the roles played by their ancestors, their children, and a complementing cast of journalists, governors, members of Congress, presidential candidates, academics, and leaders of business. It is a tale of hard work, some good luck, some sorrow, and no small amount of accomplishment. At its soul, it is a story about how a newspaper – even a small local one – can, with the right leadership, improve the lives of those in their region and beyond.

"The first thing a reporter must learn is
that unlike the editorial writer or columnist
his personal opinions have no place in his work.
Regardless of whether he likes what he finds out,
his task is to find out. …"

— **Arthur Ballantine Jr.**

"For democracy to function successfully,
its citizens need to have information about
the wide variety of topics important
to their government.
They need complete information
and they need accurate information.
It's a newspaper's responsibility to provide
this information."

— **Morley Ballantine**

Ballantine & Cowles Family Tree

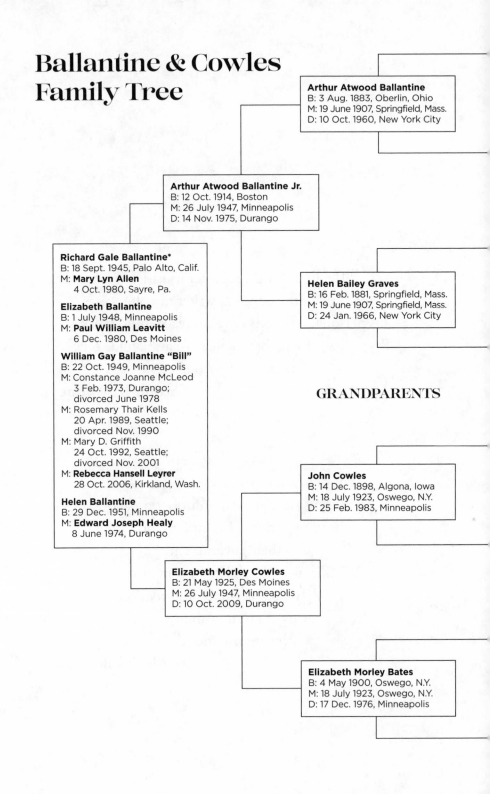

Arthur Atwood Ballantine
B: 3 Aug. 1883, Oberlin, Ohio
M: 19 June 1907, Springfield, Mass.
D: 10 Oct. 1960, New York City

Arthur Atwood Ballantine Jr.
B: 12 Oct. 1914, Boston
M: 26 July 1947, Minneapolis
D: 14 Nov. 1975, Durango

Richard Gale Ballantine*
B: 18 Sept. 1945, Palo Alto, Calif.
M: **Mary Lyn Allen**
    4 Oct. 1980, Sayre, Pa.

Elizabeth Ballantine
B: 1 July 1948, Minneapolis
M: **Paul William Leavitt**
    6 Dec. 1980, Des Moines

William Gay Ballantine "Bill"
B: 22 Oct. 1949, Minneapolis
M: Constance Joanne McLeod
    3 Feb. 1973, Durango;
    divorced June 1978
M: Rosemary Thair Kells
    20 Apr. 1989, Seattle;
    divorced Nov. 1990
M: Mary D. Griffith
    24 Oct. 1992, Seattle;
    divorced Nov. 2001
M: **Rebecca Hansell Leyrer**
    28 Oct. 2006, Kirkland, Wash.

Helen Ballantine
B: 29 Dec. 1951, Minneapolis
M: **Edward Joseph Healy**
    8 June 1974, Durango

Helen Bailey Graves
B: 16 Feb. 1881, Springfield, Mass.
M: 19 June 1907, Springfield, Mass.
D: 24 Jan. 1966, New York City

GRANDPARENTS

John Cowles
B: 14 Dec. 1898, Algona, Iowa
M: 18 July 1923, Oswego, N.Y.
D: 25 Feb. 1983, Minneapolis

Elizabeth Morley Cowles
B: 21 May 1925, Des Moines
M: 26 July 1947, Minneapolis
D: 10 Oct. 2009, Durango

Elizabeth Morley Bates
B: 4 May 1900, Oswego, N.Y.
M: 18 July 1923, Oswego, N.Y.
D: 17 Dec. 1976, Minneapolis

William Gay Ballantine
B: 7 Dec. 1848, Washington D.C.
M: 17 Aug. 1875
D: 10 Jan. 1937, Springfield, Mass.

Elisha Ballantine
B: 11 Oct. 1809, Schodack, N.Y.
D: 20 Apr. 1886, Bloomington, Ind.

Betsey Anne Watkins
B: 29 Nov. 1812, Oldham, Va.
D: 4 Apr. 1873, Bloomington, Ind.

Emma Frances Atwood
B: May 1857, Waupun, Wis.
M: 17 Aug. 1875
D: 1919, Springfield, Mass.

Almon Atwood
B: 2 Apr. 1823, Rutland, Vt.
D: 25 Oct. 1889, Fond du Lac, Wis.

Lovina M. Wheeler
B: 16 Sept. 1833, New Haven, Vt.
D: 22 Feb. 1904, Waupun, Wis.

Charles Asaph Graves
B: 21 Dec. 1846, Springfield, Mass.
M: 17 May 1877, Springfield, Mass.
D: 4 Jan. 1893, Springfield, Mass.

Francis Sidney Graves
B: 20 Aug. 1816, S. Hadley, Mass.
D: 13 Nov. 1872, Springfield, Mass.

Fidelia Baker
B: 2 Apr. 1817, Hawley, Mass.
D: 5 July 1864, Springfield, Mass.

Henrietta Fowler
B: 7 Apr. 1852, Windsor, Vt.
M: 17 May 1877, Springfield, Mass.
D: 18 Dec. 1938, Springfield, Mass.

John Fowler
B: approx. 1825, England
D: 7 Feb. 1894, Windsor, Vt.

Jane "Jennie" Fowler
B: approx. 1827, England
D: 9 Feb. 1898, Hartland, Vt.

GREAT-GRANDPARENTS

Gardner Cowles
B: 28 Feb. 1861, Oskaloosa, Iowa
M: 3 Dec. 1884, Algona, Iowa
D: 28 Feb. 1946, Des Moines

Rev. William Fletcher Cowles***
B: 11 May 1819, Cortlandville, N.Y.
D: 14 July 1899, Burlington, Iowa

Elizabeth Maria La Monte
B: 4 Jan. 1836, Charlotteville, N.Y.
D: 3 Aug. 1873, Keokuk, Iowa

Florence M. Call
B: 28 Aug. 1861, Algona, Iowa
M: 3 Dec. 1884, Algona, Iowa
D: 23 Mar. 1950, Des Moines

Ambrose Call
B: 9 June 1833, Ohio
D: 22 Oct. 1908, Algona, Iowa

Nancy E. Henderson
B: Dec. 1843, Illinois
D: 10 Sept. 1922, Algona, Iowa

Norman Lawrence Bates**
B: 23 June 1865, Oswego, N.Y.
M: 26 Jan. 1899, Oswego, N.Y.
D: 19 May 1923, Oswego, N.Y.

Byron W. Bates
B: 21 July 1839, Oswego, N.Y.
D: 11 Sept. 1921, Hutchinson, Kans.

Harriet Richardson
B: 14 Dec. 1842, New York
D: 3 Aug. 1908, New York

Florence Morley
B: 8 June 1878, Marine City, Mich.
M: 26 Jan. 1899, Oswego, N.Y.
D: 25 Dec. 1945, Manhattan, N.Y.

William Bissell Morley
B: 18 Jan. 1832, Pultneyville, N.Y.
D: 15 June 1891, Rochester, N.Y.

Elizabeth Preston
B: 29 Mar. 1838, Sodus, N.Y.
D: 11 July 1904, Sodus, N.Y.

*Richard Gale Ballantine's father was Richard P. Gale (1924-1946). After Richard Gale's death, Morley married Arthur Ballantine Jr.

**Norman Bates was an only child. His father, Byron W. Bates (1839-1921) left their family. The Bates marriage was dissolved Dec. 20 1886 in New York.

***Rev. William Fletcher Cowles was previously married to Alexina Eliza Blanchard (1828-1855), and had at least three children with her before she died. He married Elizabeth Maria La Monte in 1857.

Part I

BEFORE
DURANGO

Arthur

Arthur Ballantine Jr. was born in 1914 in Boston, the third of five children and the son of a man destined to become one of the country's most accomplished lawyers.

Arthur Ballantine Sr. (1883-1960) was a 1904 Harvard classmate of Franklin Delano Roosevelt, where they were rivals on *The Harvard Crimson* newspaper. Though not best friends, Arthur Sr. knew FDR well enough to refer to him as "Frank" in a remembrance article he wrote for the *Crimson* in 1953. Their paths would cross frequently in their post-Harvard years, primarily because of Arthur Sr.'s expertise in banking and tax law.

Just four years after the 16th Amendment established a federal income tax in 1913, Arthur Sr. became a legal adviser interpreting the War Revenue Act. The 1917 act increased income tax to pay for US efforts in World War I. It was work that would establish him as a tax and federal revenue authority and result in his appointment as assistant secretary of the Treasury in 1932. In that role he was advising President Herbert Hoover on reconstruction from the Great Depression.

Roosevelt, after defeating Hoover in a landslide in 1932, began cleaning house of cabinet and high-ranking officials upon his March 4, 1933, inauguration. But new Treasury Secretary William Woodin asked Arthur Sr. to stay on, at least temporarily. Arthur had urged Hoover to declare a "bank holiday," to determine which banks were

Arthur Jr., left, with his father and siblings Barbara and John "Jack", at their Oyster Bay home, ca. 1929.

solvent enough to reopen, and now FDR was following that advice. And several sources, including Arthur Jr., said it was Arthur Sr. who drafted much of Roosevelt's first renowned Fireside Chat delivered via radio on March 12, 1933.

Young Arthur was eighteen in 1933 and recalled later the banking crisis and his father's involvement "quite well. Dad changed from meeting with Herbert Hoover daily" to meeting with FDR, he remembered.

Historians credit Arthur Sr.'s efforts at the outset of FDR's reign as being instrumental in the reconstruction of the nation's battered banking system. Arthur Sr. stayed on with the Roosevelt administration another few months to help solve the immediate crisis, then returned to his law practice in New York City, the old-line Root, Clark, Buckner & Ballantine, located at 40 Wall Street in Manhattan. The family had moved from Boston to New York in 1919.

While his father was helping Hoover battle the Great Depression, Arthur Jr. was working his way through Milton Academy, a well-known preparatory boarding school in Milton, a few miles south of downtown Boston. Arthur graduated from Milton in 1932 and then headed for Harvard University just a few miles away in Cambridge, across the Charles River from Boston. Arthur began to develop his journalism skills as an editor of *The Harvard Crimson* in 1934. The work forced him to learn about the university. "The chance to talk with the faculty, officials, coaches, and students interested in a variety of activities, combined with the necessity of taking editorial positions, gave me a picture of Harvard I will always value and carry with me."

He wrote in 1948, after two years at the *Minneapolis Tribune*:

> I ... have frequently called upon the experience I had at the *Crimson* in 1934-35. The jobs of reporting, writing editorials, putting the paper together, delivery, circulation, and advertising are basically the same on all newspapers. The chief lesson I have learned since is that we did not pay enough attention in those days to the less romantic side of newspapering, circulation and advertising. It does not do much good to put out the best newspaper in the world if it is not going to be read and make its own way.

Those lessons were paramount to his and Morley's success later in Durango. His brother John was also a *Crimson* editor several years later. Arthur Sr. later wrote: "I think that my two sons, Arthur A. Ballantine Jr. (class of 1936) and John W. Ballantine (class of 1942) really got more discipline from the (*Crimson*) than they did later on from the Navy."

Arthur, following his 1936 graduation, headed to law school at Yale. Perhaps this was the first sign that Arthur Jr. wished to divert from the path taken by his father, a Harvard man through undergrad and law school. He earned his Yale law degree in 1939, passed the New York State Bar, and joined the elite New York law firm Sullivan & Cromwell. But his experience at Sullivan & Cromwell determined for him early on that he was not cut out to be a corporate lawyer.

In 1940, he went to Washington, D.C., as assistant to Nelson Rockefeller, future New York governor and US vice president.[1] At the time, Rockefeller was head of the Office of the Coordinator of Inter-American Affairs, State Department. The office oversaw relations with Latin American countries, its goal being to raise their standard of living, improve overall relations, and counter the growing Nazi and communist influences. Arthur was never shy about sharing his opinion. In his short tenure there, a friend wrote of Arthur, "I remember a delightful but not wholly popular memorandum in which he advised one of the leaders of that office that he 'should not try to build structures of steel with girders of jelly'."[2]

Arthur then worked at the State Department's Division of World Trade Intelligence, which Roosevelt organized in July 1941 to prepare a list of companies that had ties to the Axis nations (Germany, Italy, Japan) with whom the US did not want to do business.[3] Specifically, he was working on blacklisting Latin American newspapers.[4]

Arthur Jr. married Sue Barbara Headington on Oct. 4, 1941. Barbara grew up in the Flushing area of Queens, about twenty miles or so from Oyster Bay, where Arthur had spent much of his youth at the family's second home. Barbara was a Smith College graduate, age twenty-four when the marriage took place in Manhattan. Arthur was a few days shy of twenty-seven. The new couple settled in Washington, D.C.

Whatever future this couple might have had together would become a casualty of the war. For the US, war began just two months after the marriage, when Japanese planes bombarded Pearl Harbor on December 7, 1941, and Congress declared war the next day. Arthur was commissioned an ensign in the Navy in March.[5] His first assignment was as an aide to Admiral Jules James, then commander of a naval base in Bermuda.

After leaving Bermuda, on November 2, 1942, Ensign Ballantine was assigned to the USS *Migrant*, in port in Boston.[6] The *Migrant*, a 223-foot converted luxury schooner, patrolled the country's eastern seaboard.

A few months later he headed for Miami's Sub Chaser Training Center and joined the crew aboard the *Sub Chaser-691* on March 15, 1943.[7,8] The wooden craft and its crew of twenty-eight soon left for North Africa. The 110-foot ship arrived at Mostaganem, Algeria, in early May 1943.[9]

"These sub chasers … proved to be no help searching for modern day submarines," Arthur later divulged.[10] "So we were used mainly to lead landing craft to the shore and then to lay smoke screens around the anchorage area. We only had one dress rehearsal off the coast of Africa before we started into Sicily."

On July 8 the sub chaser, under the command of William G. Crenshaw with Arthur as executive officer, left "North African Waters" ominously heading toward "Dangerous Waters," according to Navy records.[11] This was the start of the allied invasion of Sicily, or Operation Husky, which began late on the night of July 9.

"I remember that it was very hard for me to believe that I was actually participating in an invasion," Arthur wrote. The chaos of war made this a seat-of-the-pants operation. *SC-691* guided landing craft to shore. "You would just get in front and start leading them into shore. If you became uncertain of a point, this didn't make any difference. You felt the point was to get to shore. We did that all night long."[12]

Arthur served as an officer in the Navy from March 1942 to October 1945.

The battle lasted more than a month before the US and its allies took Sicily from the Italian and German forces. It is worthy of noting that the Allied campaign on Axis-controlled Europe actually began July 9, 1943, not eleven months later at Normandy. And Arthur Ballantine Jr. played a supporting role.

Yet, it was one of the most unnecessary and horrific incidents of the war that left the longest-lasting impression on Arthur. On the night of July 11, 1943, more than 300 US paratroopers were killed or wounded by friendly fire as they descended over the Sicily battle zone in a second attack wave. A nervous American gunner on the beach is believed to have started the firing, and nearly the entire invasion fleet joined in. Arthur's crew on the *SC-691* watched, uncertain of what they were witnessing.

"We were naturally worried," he said in an interview decades later.[13]

"We sometimes didn't know whether we were in range or not because we were inexperienced. Our guns, as a practical matter, wouldn't fire that high. I don't think we realized on the *691* what had happened until the next morning. In fact, we may first have heard it in the broadcast coming from the United States."

The Sicily battle led to the collapse of Italian leader Benito Mussolini's government and disarray in the government that replaced him. But with German help, the Italians kept fighting.

In August, newly promoted Lt. Junior Grade Arthur A. Ballantine took command of *SC-691*. And then came one of the war's biggest battles, as US and British forces landed at Salerno, Italy, and fought the dug-in German troops and remaining Italians September 9-18, 1943. Progress was slow but steady, and the Allies prevailed.

"In August I became skipper of a 110-foot sub chaser," Arthur wrote at the time. "We have participated in the landings at Gela, Sicily, and in the Gulf of Salerno, Italy – the latter being the tougher proposition."[14]

In a December 1943 letter, he expressed confidence that the tide of events would lead to ultimate victory and praised his crew. "I am most impressed by the courage and initiative of the average American boy who knows what it is all about and still does his job calmly and efficiently." He went on to describe frequent air attacks in the Gulf of Salerno, which landed bombs in our vicinity [and patrols] of the anchorage area and mine-swept channel," including under cover of smokescreens at night.

By early October 1943 the Allies had captured all of southern Italy. In November, on another front, the Allies began heavy bombing of Berlin.

Meanwhile, his parents and wife wrote frequently, telling him about their doings and frequent gin rummy card games. Arthur Jr. wrote them back when able.

"Another large wave of optimism has swept the country this week with the three-day bombing of Berlin," Barbara wrote on November 26. She was keeping busy, working for Red Cross Army Relief and other causes. "Many say that all will be ended in Europe by the first of the year. ... All my love darling, B."[15]

Arthur Sr. wrote to his son, "This war will indeed become history, yet it will change the course of most men's lives, as it already has yours. So far, I am inclined to believe you have derived a positive benefit from it, in spite of the vast sacrifice."[16]

And from his mother, Helen: "Of course we pray every day that you are on your way home – sometimes I just can't stand it – it has been so many months."[17]

In January 1944 the *SC-691* participated in a major battle at Anzio, which ultimately led to the fall of Rome. Arthur Jr. called the work at Anzio "strenuous." German midget submarines were captured or hit, and the sub chaser hauled several enemy soldiers out of the water.

"You're also indoctrinated – 'the enemy is terrible' – but to see these poor, scared, German boys was really quite moving. So, we gave them a hearty breakfast and delivered them to the flagship."[18]

Later the sub chaser fought off southern France in an invasion Arthur described as "routine" after the Italian battles. Arthur found the strain of command difficult in many ways, but the crew held him in high regard. A fine writer with deep insight into both people and politics, Arthur kept a journal that illuminates his day-to-day struggles.

"Whenever anything is wrong, a man wants some kind of transfer," Arthur wrote in April 1944, the same month he'd been promoted to full lieutenant. "You next have to find out what the matter is. This time the trouble is between Mansfield and Jacobs. ... Eddie LaVorgna is another rather difficult personality as things upset his temperament easily."[19]

The men represented several regions of the US, hailing from Hollywood, Calif., to Queens, N.Y., and places in between – Cleveland; Essington, Pa.; Nashville; Kansas City; Oklahoma City.

Arthur did his best to keep the crew happy and in line. During lulls, one of his projects was the creation of a periodical distributed to the crew called "News Buoy." In early May 1944 he alluded to a bout of homesickness, noting in his diary that he missed the New York spring; it was his third straight May away from North America.

Helen and Arthur Sr., still active as a lawyer, supported the war effort as they could. That included a visit to the West Coast to hang out briefly with industrialist Henry J. Kaiser (1882-1967), without whom it is questionable whether the US could have turned the tide of World War II. His seven Kaiser Shipyards – in the Bay Area; Vancouver, Wash.; and Portland, Ore. – churned out Liberty and Victory cargo ships at an unprecedented rate as America militarized at a staggering pace in 1942-45.[20]

In July 1944, Helen and Arthur joined Henry Kaiser on a sightseeing tour of his shipyards. While there, Helen was asked to christen one of the Victory cargo ships. She did a fine job smashing the champagne bottle on the ship, Arthur Sr. wrote, but most of the spray managed to hit her "trigger man," Arthur Sr.[21]

By September 1944, Arthur Jr. and his *SC-691* were off the coast of France, preparing to hand over the sub chaser to the French navy. The ship's inventory that Arthur and crew prepared gives insight into their jobs and dangers.[22,23] A very partial list:

> Instruction manuals for auxiliary and main engines, fire and bilge pumps, radar, and sounding devices; provisions including egg powder, tomato puree, canned stew, beef and salmon, 1,000 potatoes, and a coffee urn; narcotics including ipecac opium, morphine tartrate, and phenobarbital; ammo such as .30 rifle, .45 pistol and machine gun, depth charges, smoke, 40mm armor-piercing anti-aircraft; tools and spare parts for every conceivable use, including a small sea clamp; twenty-seven life preservers; and three life rafts.

Once Arthur signed the ship over to French commanding officer Etienne Luquet, the crew went ashore at Toulon, France, and raised as much hell as possible without disturbing the peace.

Around midnight several police kicked them out of a local drinking establishment.[24] They caught a transport ship back to the United States, relieved but perhaps a bit uncertain of what would come next in their lives. In all, Arthur spent twenty months overseas.

The final entry in his journal was written Saturday, October 21, 1944.[25] He recalled how depressed he'd been in Salerno, Italy, in August 1943. And he was gratified to be returning with the rest of the crew, finding it almost surprising that "the only hard part is to lose their companionship." He noted "a distinctly paternal feeling about all of the men, which is not superficial."

> I seemed to be carried along on an irresistible tide which will carry me to Fifty-Second Street (in Manhattan, where he lived), regardless of my actions. Tomorrow at this time Barbara and I will probably be sitting in a bar following an excellent Sunday lunch with the family almost as if it never happened.

Arthur continued with the Navy and was sent to Princeton University to learn Japanese in preparation for a planned landing on Formosa (Taiwan). He continued his studies at Stanford University in the Bay Area before the Japanese quickly surrendered after two atomic bombs were dropped in early August 1945. Arthur was discharged in October.[26]

Arthur and Barbara divorced shortly after his return. That may have been painful emotionally, but it freed Arthur to leave the Northeast. He certainly could have stayed in New York at a prestigious law office. The firm he'd been working for, Sullivan & Cromwell, included partner John Foster Dulles, later to become Secretary of State (1953-59) under President Eisenhower. But the corporate law he'd been practicing – and his father still practiced – no longer appealed to him.

"I simply didn't like the environment of Wall Street," Arthur Ballantine told an interviewer in 1974.[27] "I felt that I was leading a rather narrow, sheltered life in the environment in which I was situated."

He also could have returned to the State Department in D.C. But still a young man, he had an idea that he would resurrect in a few years: Go West. Many of his friends were making similar moves. His interest in journalism while at Harvard, which continued apparently with "News Buoy," guided his next career move into the newspaper business. Possibly with the help of family connections, he secured a job with the Cowles newspapers.[28] His choice: Minneapolis, or Des Moines?

"[With my] being bred an Easterner, Minneapolis sounded better to me than Des Moines, Iowa," Arthur said in 1974. "[Morley and I] have laughed about that since. So, I took the job at Minneapolis." Arthur joined the *Minneapolis Star and Tribune* as a reporter by May 1946, making fifty dollars a week.[29]

He started as a general assignment reporter, doing whatever stories needed to be done. He gained some stature a few months later when he began writing about the city's polio outbreak and an institute established a few years earlier by a controversial and outspoken Australian nurse, Elizabeth Kenny.

While the medical establishment had long believed that polio patients should be placed in plaster casts to keep their limbs from contracting, Kenny believed that patients' affected parts should be kept warm and limber. Polio had ravaged US cities since around 1910, fatal to some and leaving others scarred or paralyzed. Outbreaks occurred primarily during the summers. By the time Arthur began writing his stories, many of Kenny's practices were widely accepted, but she and the institute remained controversial. Minneapolis became Kenny's base in 1940 due to its proximity to the Mayo Institute in Rochester, Minn.

"It was really about the struggle between the doctors and Sister Kenny as to whose views were going to prevail at the General Hospital," Arthur recalled.[30]

After his series of stories about the issues and personalities involved in this struggle, the city editor took note of Arthur's work and asked him what he wanted to do, which was to cover the state legislature. As 1947 began, his legislative experience was being touted in *Minneapolis Morning Tribune* ads: "Art Ballantine, a graduate of Yale Law School, is right at home among the lawyers of the legislature. He was a skipper of a Navy sub-chaser during his twenty months overseas."[31]

Morley

Elizabeth Morley Cowles was born May 21, 1925. Early in her life she was called Morley, her maternal grandmother's last name, and it stuck. Morley spent her first thirteen years in Des Moines, Iowa, where the Cowles family was establishing a media empire.

The progenitor of the empire was Morley's grandfather, Gardner Cowles, who with his friend and partner Harvey Ingham built the *Des Moines Register* into a newspaper that over its history would win fourteen Pulitzer Prizes and be listed by *Time* magazine in 1983 as one of the ten best in the country. The family would also build the *Minneapolis Star and Tribune* into one of the country's best newspapers and establish *LOOK* magazine, among other journalistic endeavors.

Harvey Ingham and Gardner Cowles had become friends in Algona, in northwest Iowa, where they had once owned competing newspapers. Harvey was a terrific editor. Gardner was a terrific businessman who at one point controlled ten banks in northern Iowa. Harvey had moved to Des Moines in 1902 to become editor of the *Des Moines Register and Leader*.

Gardner had studied the newspaper business closely while in Des Moines during his two terms in the Iowa legislature, so when Harvey told him they had a chance to buy the paper, Gardner put up most of the money. In 1903 the two became owners of the *Register and Leader*.

Of Gardner's six children, it was Morley's father, John, and Gardner

Jr. (Mike), who most fully embraced the family business. In December 1922, just months before his marriage to Elizabeth "Betty" Morley Bates, John took the title of associate publisher at the Des Moines Register and Tribune Company.

During their honeymoon in Europe, twenty-four-year-old John took off on a solo tour that included a visit to the newly formed USSR. The trip expanded John's worldwide view – he wrote a fourteen-part, front-page series titled "Soviet Russia Today" – and it also gave Betty a firm idea how integral work and knowledge were to her husband.

For Morley, being born to a successful newspaper publisher had its perks and pressures. To the unaided eye, the perks are the most obvious. For better or worse, Morley Cowles was always in the limelight. The company's success meant her father was away from home a lot and that she continued to move into bigger houses and began to rub elbows with the country club set.

The Great Depression was in full swing in 1933 when John and Betty Cowles moved their family of five into a spacious residence at 50 Thirty-Seventh Street in Des Moines. It had been the home of two former US secretaries of agriculture.[32] It was also just a couple houses away from Gardner and Florence Cowles, Morley's grandparents, who lived at 100 Thirty-Seventh.

Morley had a multitude of activities to keep her busy, and her education was taken seriously. At just ten years old in May 1935, she took part in a Greenwood Elementary school production of "Peter Rabbit," performed in French.[33]

Morley was eleven when Marian Anderson came to town and made a big impact on her worldview. Anderson, an African-American contralto, had risen to world acclaim and was touring with the St. Louis Symphony. John and Betty were boosters and fund raisers deeply involved with the Des Moines Civic Music Association, which brought Anderson to the city in March 1937.[34] John and Betty took Morley to Anderson's evening performance at the Hoyt Sherman Place auditorium.[35] Anderson, though greatly appreciated in Des Moines for her talent, nonetheless experienced discrimination.

"I remember my father being upset that a great artist of her caliber had to use the servants' elevator in the hotel," Morley recalled in a 2005 interview.[36] "This was long before the civil rights movement, and I remember Miss Anderson, her beautiful voice, and my parents' concerns."

John Cowles encouraged his daughter's writing talents, praising her thank-you notes. One of Morley's favorite things to do with her father was to walk with him to the office, then attend an afternoon football game with him.[37]

When John and Mike Cowles purchased the *Minneapolis Star* in 1935, *Time* took notice and placed John Cowles on the cover of the country's most influential magazine.[38] *Time* reported that as a youth, John would "perch himself on the desk of his father's secretary [and] spout a stream of questions: 'What does so-&-so do?' … 'What is that voucher for?' … 'How much does newsprint cost?'"

This "intelligent inquisitiveness," as *Time* put it, was passed on to his children. Morley would exhibit this quality repeatedly during her own newspaper career. She also caught her father's travel bug and the desire to educate others through descriptions of her journeys.

The family's fortunes and destinations were inextricably linked to the Cowles media expansion. So when the Cowles brothers purchased the *Star* in 1935, it led to a big family adjustment. The family decided John would oversee the Minneapolis paper and Mike would be in charge in Des Moines.

Betty and John Cowles continued to make Des Moines their main home for another three years, perhaps partly not wanting to displace the children. Also, in early 1936, Betty became pregnant with their fourth child, son Russell, born in October in Des Moines. But over time, it became apparent that John needed to reside in Minneapolis if he and his newspaper wished to be accepted by the public.

In 1938 the Cowleses packed up and left Des Moines, where John, now thirty-nine, had lived since he was five. That summer they were splitting time between two homes in the Twin Cities – the main home in downtown Minneapolis, and a rented summer home at Crystal Bay, on the shores of Lake Minnetonka, a large lake west of downtown. The children set about making new friends.

Morley, at age thirteen, won standing dive in her age group at the

Woodhill Country Club annual swimming tournament.[39] Woodhill is in Wayzata, a suburb just west of Minneapolis. During summers she competed in tennis tournaments at Woodhill and yachting races at Lake Minnetonka. In 1940, Morley competed in the Andrews Cup series, piloting a one-person X boat – a sixteen-foot sailing dinghy called *Lucky*.[40] In the winter months, Morley enjoyed toboggan rides at the Minikahda Club snow slide and ice skating at the Northrop Collegiate school rink.[41]

Whether she enjoyed it or not, Morley was taught to dance. Arthur Murray dance classes were popular, and the Cowleses pitched in by hosting those classes a time or two. Morley is pictured doing the "London Bridge dance" in a photo that appeared in the *Minneapolis Star* in January 1940 – along with a group of equally perplexed (or maybe just camera shy?) teenagers.[42] She was among a group of juniors at Woodhill Country Club planning a series of junior dances.[43]

In the early 1940s, the Cowles family began to spend part of each summer at their large spread at Glendalough, a retreat and game farm located among west-central Minnesota's Battle Lakes, a three-hour drive northwest of Minneapolis. The property's six lakes include more than nine miles of shoreline. The land had been developed into a private family summer retreat in 1903, and then sold to F.E. Murphy, owner of the *Minneapolis Tribune*, in 1928. Murphy renamed the land Glendalough after a monastery in Ireland, expanded the retreat, and added a game farm.[44] When the Cowles Media Company bought the *Tribune* in 1941, it acquired Glendalough as part of the deal. John Cowles eventually expanded Glendalough to 2,000 acres in Otter Tail County, northeast of the town of Battle Lake.

Though raised in comfort, the Cowles children – Morley (born in 1925); Sarah, or Sally (1926); John Jr. (1929); and Russell (1936) – learned the value of money through small but regular allowances.[45] The 1930s were not kind to many Americans, but the Cowleses had positioned themselves in the right place, and in the right business, to prosper. Impacts of the Great Depression as well as religious influences – Gardner Cowles' father was a stern Methodist minister and the church-going tradition was passed down – kept the children from being spoiled. As they grew, they took on summer wage-paying jobs. Morley may not have known poverty intimately, but throughout her life she never shied from labor, and continued to push causes that helped the underprivileged. These were values she learned from previous generations and responsibilities she embraced.

As Russell recalled, "There were these beliefs that my mother and father had about how people ought to live together and cooperate with each other to help."

So the privileges were obvious. But the pressures were just as real for Morley. How was she supposed to live up to the achievements of her parents, grandparents, and other family that preceded her? What was emphasized to the children was the importance of perseverance, hard work, and long hours.

Morley spent her high school years at Rosemary Hall, a private girls prep school in Connecticut.

"It was just sort of taken for granted that if you were going to be good at something you had to put in a lot of effort at it," said John Cowles Jr. in a 1994 interview.[46]

"Different things were expected of a boy than of a girl," Sally Cowles said, also in a 1994 interview, "and yet at the same time standards were very high for all of us. I know I grew up feeling that always I should do my best in everything that I did. And sometimes the best might not even be good enough."[47]

Morley's doings were constant news in the society columns and pages of the *Des Moines Register* and later the Minneapolis papers. Does it make you feel special or just under the microscope when you are fifteen and the paper lets everyone know you are in town visiting your old Des Moines friend Miss Jean Shuler on Foster Drive?[48] Morley grew accustomed to it, and decades later she never shied from writing about her own family's doings and vacations while publisher at *The Durango Herald*.

In the fall of 1938, Morley enrolled at Northrop Collegiate School, a private girls prep school designed to prepare students for elite colleges in the Northeast.[49] She spent two years there, and in the fall of 1940, at age fifteen, was enrolled at Rosemary Hall, a girls boarding school in Greenwich, Conn. Her mother, Elizabeth Bates Cowles, was a Rosemary graduate.

Morley served as editor-in-chief of *The Rosemary Question Mark*, a quarterly, bound publication, in 1941-42. She didn't shy away from the big issue of the day. For the December edition, likely written before the Pearl Harbor bombing, Morley, as the "Roving Reporter," asked classmates and teachers the "question that was not only bothering her but the whole civilized world as well: 'Do you think that the United States should enter now into actual warfare against the Axis powers?'"[50] While eleven said yes, eleven said no and fourteen were undecided.

"Your reporter also discovered something about how a person's mind functions when a question is popped at them. It seems that there are very few who have thought this question through previously and could answer directly without evasion. Now we wonder if Mr. Roosevelt could do any better," she wrote.

Decades later, after she had moved to Durango and established herself as an eminent journalist and publisher, Morley was given the school's prestigious Annual Alumnae Award, "presented each year to a Rosemarian who has distinguished herself in some special field of endeavor."[51] She would also serve as a Rosemary Hall trustee.

After three years in Connecticut, shuttling back to Minneapolis during school breaks, in the fall of 1943 she continued on her mother's path, heading for Smith College in Northampton, Mass. She joined the freshman choir, singing at Sunday vespers and special occasions.[52] That winter, to help the war effort, she became a nurse's aide in Northampton, as her mother was doing at General Hospital in Minneapolis.[53] Morley had completed a National Red Cross course the previous summer in Minneapolis for the Nurse's Aide Corps.

In mid-May of 1944, she returned to Minneapolis for a break between spring and summer classes. The expectation – at least from her parents – was that she'd continue at Smith in late May.[54] By this time she'd gotten serious with a young man named Richard Gale Jr., whom she'd met in social circles, possibly at Minikahda or Woodhill.[55] Or perhaps they had met through a connection between their parents.[56] Richard lived in Mound, just around Lake Minnetonka from Crystal Bay, about ten miles away.

Richard Pillsbury Gale Sr. (1900-1973) was a lifelong Minnesotan, born in Minneapolis in October 1900. At that time, the only larger town west of Minneapolis was San Francisco. His maternal grandfather, John Pillsbury, was co-founder of the Pillsbury Company in 1872 and governor of Minnesota from 1876-1882. John was a noted philanthropist, and Pillsbury Hall at the University of Minnesota is named in his honor.

Richard Sr., "Dick," was a 1922 Yale University grad. A doctor diagnosed him with diabetes and strongly suggested that going into law would quickly kill him.[57] So he returned to Minneapolis, undertook graduate work in agriculture at the University of Minnesota, and purchased the 250-acre Wickham farm west of Mound. For several decades he considered himself a "dirt farmer," raising beef cattle, sheep, pigs, and thoroughbred horses.[58]

Dick married Isobel Rising, a University of Minnesota graduate, before about 700 witnesses on August 8, 1923, in St. Paul.[59] They resided at Wickham, where Mrs. Gale was known as a fine horsewoman and hosted equestrian competitions at the farm.[60] The couple had two boys, Richard Jr., born in 1924, and Alfred, born in 1927. Dick, a Republican, was elected to the Minnesota House in 1939 and then to the US House of Representatives, where he served from 1941-1945, dates that coincided with World War II.

Richard Jr. was a student at Blake School, a preparatory school in Minneapolis, and then at Landon, a private school in Washington, D.C., after his father was elected to Congress.[61] In fall 1941 or 1942 Richard enrolled at Massachusetts Institute of Technology. But World

War II pulled him in, and he enlisted in the Army Air Corps, the precursor to the Air Force, on February 15, 1943, at Fort Devens in Massachusetts.[62] Because he had to wear glasses, Richard Jr. was not eligible to be a pilot or navigator, but ultimately became a "purser" serving on a cargo plane.

Richard and Morley saw each other during the summer of 1943 in Minneapolis before he began his active military service. Richard was six months older, but both were eighteen that summer. They wanted to get married, but Morley's parents weren't keen on the idea, and implored her to instead head to college.[63] By September 1943 Richard was sent to Iowa City for training.[64] Later, he was stationed in New Haven, Conn. With Morley at Smith College in Northampton, that fall and winter they were only a couple hours apart and Morley "spent every free moment" with him.[65]

In June 1944, John and Betty Cowles agreed that they'd go along with Morley's wedding wishes. "Betty and I finally acquiesced because Morley was so insistent," John Cowles wrote to his mother.[66] "Both Betty and I are happy about having him as son-in-law."

After a quick formal engagement – they'd considered themselves engaged for a year and a half – Morley and Richard, both nineteen, were married at Gethsemane Episcopal Church in Minneapolis on a Saturday evening, July 1, 1944. A reception at the Cowles home followed.[67] That night the new couple stayed at the new Hotel Lowry in St. Paul. They paid six dollars and fifty cents for their room.[68]

Richard was transferred to the 1503rd Army Air Corps Base at Hamilton Field in the Bay Area, and Morley went to California with him, moving into a place near the air base in San Rafael.

She first stayed busy by getting a job as retail clerk at Woolworth's in San Rafael. Then, with some prodding from Father, Morley enrolled at Stanford University, which she attended for two quarters.[69] She worked as a waitress at the student union, which was short of help, and started babysitting for couples around the university. Wages were "exorbitant" for such work due to the labor shortage, and Morley stowed her earnings, exerting her independent streak, her father believed.[70] At about the end of that second quarter at Stanford, she became pregnant.

Hamilton Field, off San Pablo Bay, was about ten miles north of San Rafael, so when Richard was stationed at Hamilton or on leave, he had not been far from Morley.[71] At other times he was off flying missions over the Pacific battle zones. Private First Class Gale served as a purser on a C-54, which worked a wide area of Pacific Asia – the Philippines, New Guinea, Australia, and Japan. The C-54 was a cargo, or transport, plane used often for long-range missions. It could hold as many as fifty people, and often transported injured soldiers, of which there were many. A purser's roles were many and varied, including filling out paperwork, assuring that safety measures were followed, keeping track of ship supplies, and even acting in a medical role.

There's no record or detail of what Pfc. Gale saw during the war, but the Pacific theater was notorious for long, draw-out battles, and island landings and occupations with extremely high casualty rates.[72] An unrelenting enemy committed acts that were inhumane to a Western view, to wounded soldiers, civilians, and even themselves as they conducted so-called Banzai-style suicide charges into certain death rather than surrendering. Poor living conditions and tropical diseases led to many more US casualties.

Richard would have witnessed the effects that these conditions could impose on a man's body and soul. He would have met and talked to many of the wounded as well as escaped prisoners of war during transports.[73] Plus, he apparently was in the thick of conflict at times, or nearby, as he earned an Asiatic-Pacific ribbon and three battle stars – an Air Medal, Philippine Liberation, and Good Conduct.[74] When he returned to California from the western Pacific just before Christmas 1944, he had apparently spent time in Saipan or thereabouts.[75] US forces captured Saipan in July 1944, after a particularly brutal ground campaign and instances of mass suicides by Japanese soldiers and Saipan citizens, some of which were committed by daylight in front of US soldiers. Japanese planes bombed American bases there and on other Mariana Islands between November 1944 and January 1945.

The war against Japan ended officially on September 2, 1945, and Morley's baby entered a war-free world on September 18, 1945, at

Stanford University Hospitals.[76] He was named Richard.

Richard Gale Jr. was honorably discharged on December 20, 1945, and with his wife and son drove home to Minneapolis to celebrate Christmas and show off their three-month-old boy.[77] For a year that seemed to be so promising – the war was over, the young couple seemed happy, life could return to normal – 1946 was just the opposite.

The bad run really started on Christmas Day, when Morley's grandmother, sixty-seven-year-old Florence Morley Bates (1878-1945), died after suffering a stroke in a Manhattan hotel. She'd gone to New York to take care of her sick daughter, Sally Bates (1903-1985), who had contracted pneumonia. Sally recovered.

In February 1946, Richard and Morley left for Cambridge, Mass., where Richard would resume studies at MIT. Not long after that, another of Morley's grandparents, the media legend Gardner Cowles (1861-1946), died in Des Moines on February 28. His death was not a shock at age eighty-five, but it was certainly emotional to lose the family patriarch.

Richard, age twenty-one, began classes at the Business and Engineering Administration School on March 4, and Morley, twenty, started nearby at Radcliffe College, a women's liberal arts school that later was integrated into Harvard University. Radcliffe students were said to be intellectual, literary, and independent-minded. A housing crunch was making it difficult to find a place to live – little Richard was staying in Minneapolis with the baby nurse Hilda, known as "Fraulein," until a suitable place could be found. Otherwise, all seemed well and good. But things were about to take a tragic turn.

Richard Jr. suffered bouts of depression, something all too common among returning veterans trying to readjust to a life that seemed detached from what they'd experienced – and being told to forget what they'd seen, buck up, and get on with life. The brutality of the Pacific fighting was horrifying for everyone involved – particularly for an innocent teenager from the Midwest.

Richard didn't return home one Monday night after his studies at MIT. His body was found the next day, April 9, 1946, in a car in the woods near Wilmington, about fifteen miles from Boston.[78] He had taken a hose and siphoned the car's exhaust into the car's cabin.

Grief-stricken, Morley returned to Minneapolis within days, with a six-month-old child still to look after. A letter John Cowles, her father, wrote to his mother on April 16 indicated that Morley was staying at the Gales' downtown dwelling with "Fraulein."

"Morley is getting along beautifully," he wrote. "(She) … came over and slept at our house last night. She feels lonely staying at the Gales' house nights."[79] He added that his daughter was planning to spend a good deal of time at Glendalough during the coming summer.

Richard Jr.'s parents, Richard Sr. and Isobel, supported Morley and continued for the remainder of their lives to be involved in their grandson's life. The Gales befriended their daughter-in-law's next husband, Arthur Ballantine Jr., and the Ballantine family as it grew. Richard Gale Ballantine recalls that he felt somewhat fortunate to have three sets of grandparents spoiling him as he grew up.

Morley's old room at the Cowles house was fixed up, and she returned to live there. She spent time at Glendalough, where the next tragedy occurred on June 25. The family baby nurse, Hilda "Fraulein" Schratt, who was helping to raise Richard, wanted to go on a horse ride. She'd had a little experience, so insisted on a lively horse, and ended up on one that had thrown Morley's mother the year before.[80]

Nearing the stables on the return, the horse suddenly shied and threw off Hilda, who struck either a tree limb or a stone when she fell. She didn't think she was badly hurt but was apparently bleeding internally. She was rushed back to camp, and then, at Betty's insistence, to the family doctor in nearby Battle Lake. The doctor, before Hilda even left the car, realized the extent of the injuries and sent her on to the hospital in Fergus Falls, about twenty minutes away.

In the operating room she went into shock, and in those days, once that happened, surgeons would not operate and couldn't do much of anything. Hilda was given six blood transfusions, but still could not be saved. Betty, still in her tennis clothes, stayed at Hilda's side for the next twenty hours until Hilda succumbed.

Coming on the heels of so many other painful losses, Fraulein's death was particularly tough on Morley.[81] If Morley could withstand the challenges of this year, then what could possibly knock her down?

To help her recovery, Morley was invited to Mexico in August by the family of her longtime Minneapolis friend and bridesmaid, Lucia Heffelfinger. Lucia's two sisters and her mother joined on the trip.[82]

By September, Morley was back in school, attending classes at the University of Minnesota. It was the fourth time she'd enrolled at college – Smith, Stanford, Radcliffe, and now Minnesota. This urge to continue her education indicates not only her tenacity but her strong wish to achieve a higher degree – which she would achieve, but not for nearly three more decades.

Church and Faith

Both Arthur and Morley were descendants of Protestant theologians, two of whom – William Gay Ballantine and William Fletcher Cowles – were leaders in important religious and secular issues of the mid-nineteenth and early-twentieth centuries. William Ballantine waged battles using the scientific method to examine fundamentalist Christian theology, and William Cowles was a well-known preacher and slavery abolitionist in the Civil War era. Both practiced a progressive Christianity that, through family, would help shape Arthur's and Morley's personal lives and lay the foundation for their newspapering philosophy.

The Ballantines' long line of religious leaders began with John Winthrop – Arthur Jr.'s seventh great-grandfather – who led a group of Puritans in 1630 to create the Massachusetts Bay Colony, nine years after the Mayflower had landed at Plymouth Rock. Later, John Ballantine (1716-1776), who married Mary Gay, was a pastor for thirty-five years at the Church of Christ in Westfield, Mass., before his death.

The Rev. Elisha Ballantine (1809-1886), Arthur's great-grandfather, was both a teacher and preacher, serving for a time at Washington's historic First Presbyterian Church. He later moved the family to Bloomington, Ind., where he taught for thirty-two years at Indiana University. The ten-story Elisha Ballantine Hall, at one time the largest academic building in the world, was named for him.

**Arthur Ballantine Sr.
ca. 1904**

William Gay Ballantine (1848-1937), Elisha's son and Arthur's grandfather, grew up around the academic atmosphere at IU where his father taught languages and the Greek classics. After graduation from Marietta College in Ohio at age nineteen, William worked as a surveyor for two years then attended Union Theological Seminary in New York City from 1870-72 and did postgraduate study in theology at the University of Leipzig in Germany. After a half-year in Leipzig, in February 1873 he joined an American Palestine Exploration Society team as an assistant engineer for six months. The American society had joined British efforts in exploring and mapping the Holy Land. He worked primarily as a surveyor, making maps.

His time in the Holy Land made a deep impression. Young William later wrote: "Brought up as I had been in daily familiarity with all of the Bible stories and with undoubting faith in every detail of them all, that first day in the Holy Land in sight of all the biblical objects, camels, palm trees, long-robed patriarchal men – that radiant day on the very spot where Solomon's rafts had brought timbers for the temple, where Jonah had set sail, where St. Peter had raised the dead – was more like heaven than earth."[83]

He returned to the Midwest, first as professor of chemistry and natural science at Ripon College in Wisconsin from 1874-1876.[84] It was there he met and married Emma Atwood, one of his students. After a brief stint at Indiana, where he briefly joined his father on the faculty, he went to Oberlin Theological Seminary in Ohio where he was professor of Old Testament Language and Literature. In 1891, when he was just forty-three, Oberlin College trustees named him president.

He lasted five years before being forced out due to faculty politics.

His religious views were evolving and ultimately would lead him to publish a number of books, including in 1896, *Inductive Logic*, an examination of the principles behind scientific reasoning and how scientists ascertain conclusions without directly observable facts.

William spent the winter of 1896-97 traveling, with Athens, Greece, as his base. A former Oberlin student, L.L. Doggett, who had just been named the first full-time president at the International YMCA Training School in Springfield, Mass., implored William to move to New England to become a professor of the Bible.

He took to heart the now famous YMCA triangle – a philosophy combining physical (body), intellectual (mind), and religious (spirit) training – and thanks in part to his efforts, he wrote his sister, "the shackles of dogmatism were broken."

"I had a great part in the work of that group of men and I believe that I saved the day for intelligent religion."[85]

Intelligent religion? He taught students to be liberal and Christian, to think and to examine the Bible. William had watched the sciences blossom over the last several decades – Charles Darwin and evolution, Alfred Wallace and natural selection, Charles Lyell and geology, for example – and figured religion needed a kick in the pants, too. To the end of his life, William remained frustrated at the "glacial treatment" that the Christian public gave to "honest religious scholarship."[86] YMCA Training School president Ernest Best spoke about this at William's memorial service in 1937:[87]

> After coming to Springfield his thought grew by the application of the scientific method and the spirit of "higher criticism" to fundamentalist theological teachings. He insisted that common sense was at the base of Christ's teachings.

William retired from YMCA Training School after twenty-two years in 1921. In 1923, in one of the crowning achievements of his life, he completed his translation of the New Testament from the original Greek, and it was published by Houghton as *The Riverside New Testament*. It remains available, and in use, today.

The Cowles family tree has an equally principled and outspoken religious figure. The Rev. William Fletcher Cowles (1819-1899), Gardner Cowles' father, was a Methodist minister serving multiple eastern Iowa towns as an ardent abolitionist and renowned "political preacher."

Both he and his wife, Maria Elizabeth La Monte, were native New Yorkers. He was born in Cortland, N.Y.; she in Schoharie County, N.Y. They had two children, La Monte Cowles, who became a lawyer in Burlington, Iowa, and Gardner Cowles.

The family moved at the church's discretion from parsonage to parsonage every few years. William served Methodist churches in Oskaloosa, Keokuk, Muscatine, Mount Pleasant, and Burlington. According to the *Memorial Volume on Gardner Cowles* published in 1946 by the *Des Moines Register*, the family lived on a pay-as-you-go basis, with a budget of one dollar a week per person for food, clothing, and all necessities.

The Bible was often consulted in the home "to solve worldly as well as spiritual problems; prayers were said in a family circle twice daily; idleness was regarded as something akin to sin."

Gardner Cowles once said, "At an early age I knew that I would never have money given to me; that I never would be helped to get jobs; and that it was up to me alone if I succeeded in business."

William was a forceful presence in the pulpit, which made him a prominent figure both within church circles and in the political arena. The *Burlington Hawkeye* wrote after his death in 1899:

> He made a practice of espousing the abolition cause at all the great meetings of the church, usually the camp meeting then in vogue, and while he made hundreds of converts to the cause of the slave, he excited the enmity of many others, and his life was often threatened and in jeopardy. His advocacy of the cause that led to the war made him a prominent political figure, and he was largely instrumental in laying the foundation of the Republican party in Iowa [in 1856], being the friend and co-worker with Senators [James] Grimes and [James] Harlan.

His abolitionist views garnered the attention of President Abraham Lincoln, who in 1861 signed the Revenue Act. The act taxed imports and land, and imposed a three percent tax on individual incomes over $800. The difficulty was in collecting taxes. In 1862 Lincoln and his government granted William a patent to collect taxes in Iowa's Fourth District, centered in Ottumwa. It left William, as one family member put it, "serving both God and Caesar."

Gardner Cowles Sr.

William Cowles, grandson Mike Cowles wrote, "argued that the nation could not endure half-slave and half-free. When he preached on the subject, his divided congregation sometimes turned into an angry mob and he needed the protection of armed guards."

So Gardner, the soon-to-be newspaper executive, grew up watching a man who believed it was fine to speak your mind. He also learned about withstanding abuse from those who didn't believe as he believed. This heritage would be inflected in later civil rights positions of Gardner, his sons John and Mike, and the Durango Ballantines. At the *Des Moines Register* the Cowleses imposed bans on advertising for cigarettes, gambling, and liquor. Later, their newspaper also forbid the portrayal of guns in advertisements, prompting one movie-theater operator to place an ad for a Clint Eastwood movie by replacing the gun in Eastwood's hand with flowers.

Descendants of Gardner Cowles eventually joined the Episcopal Church and the denomination was part of Morley's life from childhood.

A New Beginning

In a matter of months, Arthur could reflect on his decision to leave the legal profession in favor of a career in journalism. Readers and editors were taking note of his skills as a reporter for the *Minneapolis Tribune*.[88] Morley's life would change again when her father invited the new reporter to Sunday dinner. Morley and

Morley and Arthur Ballantine with son Richard.

Arthur Ballantine Jr. hit it off and the two began dating, although they kept the news staff from finding out how close their romance had become. On June 1, 1947, their engagement became public news.[89] She was twenty-two. He was thirty-three.

Their wedding was held July 26, 1947, at the Cowles home with about two dozen present. Morley and Arthur each had one attendant: Lucia Heffelfinger, for Morley, and John "Jack" Ballantine, for his brother. (Lucia and Jack apparently hit it off and were married almost exactly a year later.) Less than two weeks later newlyweds Morley and

Arthur Jr. ate a cozy dinner at the Ballantine home in New York with Arthur Sr. and Helen Ballantine and their close family friends, John and Janet Dulles. Arthur Sr. and John Foster Dulles were best friends and colleagues.

The next day, Morley and Arthur boarded the famed *Queen Mary*

express passenger liner and sailed to England, arriving August 13 in Southampton port and checking into the Grosvenor Hotel in London.[90] It was Morley's first trip overseas. They took in London and Paris, and then motored along France's Riviera coastline to Italy, where they visited Florence and Rome, among other sights.[91] On September 24 they arrived back in New York and headed for Minneapolis, where a week later they took possession of a house at 4724 Emerson Avenue South. The new place was about four miles south of downtown and just a couple of blocks from picturesque Lake Harriet. After the setbacks of 1946, in 1947 Morley had her life back on track.

Accompanied by her son Richard, Morley attends a November 1947 meeting of the Women's Action Committee for Lasting Peace which the newspaper notice said "seeks participation of American women in the building of a world of peace and justice."

The couple celebrated Arthur's first child, and Morley's second, on July 1, 1948. Elizabeth, called "Betty" during her younger years, was the first of three children born to them in Minneapolis. William Gay Ballantine was born October 22, 1949, and Helen Ballantine on December 29, 1951.

Morley was busy tracking children, but she had some help from a nanny, which freed her for some community work. She picked up one of her mother's causes, becoming a director of the Hennepin County League for Planned Parenthood in 1947.[92] In February 1949, Morley was one of six team captains for Hennepin Planned Parenthood's drive to raise

$18,660 to finance the league's clinic in the Walker Building.[93] She continued to serve on the board periodically.

By 1950 both Morley and Arthur Ballantine were stockholders of the Minneapolis Star and Tribune Company. Morley and her siblings held one percent or more; Arthur Jr. an undisclosed amount less than one percent. But owning and operating were completely different. Around mid-1951 they hatched a plan.

Arthur and Morley with children Richard, Elizabeth, and Bill, in 1949.

"After the war," Morley recalled in a 2005 interview, "everybody was looking for a place to make a life. If you've got newspapering in your blood, at some point you want to own your own paper."[94]

With that goal set, the question for Arthur and Morley became, "Where?" The time-honored phrase "Go West, young man" still held many adventurous Americans in thrall. It evokes visions of wide-open spaces, room to grow and establish your own turf and destiny. Indeed, the original phrase credited to newspaperman Horace Greeley in 1865 was linked to the American belief in Manifest Destiny, and continued expansion westward.

Many World War II veterans chafed at returning to the roles their fathers had laid out for them, roles they grew up assuming they would take. Seeing the world and facing death numerous times changed their outlook. As Arthur's friend at the Minneapolis papers, and fellow New York native and Ivy League graduate Otis Carney wrote, "I had one life. If I got back to live it (after the war), the hell with what the world said. I'd use it my way, my dream."[95]

Morley and Arthur scoured the country but focused on the West.

Several family connections had moved out that way, including John Cowles Sr.'s friend, foreign policy expert Stanley R. Resor, who would later serve as secretary of the army under Presidents Johnson and Nixon. The Resor family had established a vacation home and ranch in Jackson Hole, Wyo., in 1930.[96]

After checking out multiple newspapers and communities, Morley and Arthur narrowed the choices. "Arthur and I knew that California was out – too expensive. We looked around the West, and then the Durango papers came on the market."[97]

"In the end," Arthur Jr. recalled, "partially because the West was not only where we'd like to live but where we could buy a newspaper, we settled down finally between two places – the state of Washington in the Columbia Basin and here in Durango."[98]

In April 1952, Morley and Arthur jointly attended the 66th annual American Newspaper Publishers Association national convention in New York City. This was a large affair at the time, with 1,500-plus editors, writers, publishers, "and other celebrities" attending at the Waldorf-Astoria Hotel. Following the conference they flew from New York to Denver, as Morley's father put it, "to see some small paper in that region which might be for sale."[99]

They arrived in Durango and liked what they saw: a diverse community with farming and ranching, mining and logging, a growing oil drilling presence, a nearby two-year college that could use a boost, beautiful mountains all around, an Old West spirit, and lots of room to grow. They knew absolutely no one in the area. They would be the city slickers trying to fit in, but what they felt for certain: unlike staying in Minneapolis, their presence here could make a big difference.

Part II

GO
WEST

Settling In

On May 23, 1952, Arthur drove from Minneapolis to Durango and worked out the final details of the deal. He purchased both the daily *Durango Herald-Democrat*, and the tri-weekly *Durango News*, which were for sale by different owners, with the intention of merging them into one paper, the *Durango Her-*

The Ballantines' first Durango home was at 1689 West Third Avenue.

ald-News. With a circulation of approximately 4,500, it would be a six-days-a-week afternoon paper, skipping only Saturday.

As the deal went through, Morley arrived to pick out a suitable living space. They purchased a home from one of their first contacts, lawyer Fred Emigh, who had helped them with the newspaper transactions.[100] The two-story house at 1689 West Third Avenue included a large playroom upstairs. The children stayed for several weeks at Glendalough while the furniture was shipped from Minneapolis to Durango and the house was prepared.

Meanwhile, Morley and Arthur got to work, taking over the papers on June 1. They put off making big changes until they got to understand the community and the workings of the papers. They were business owners who understood the importance of making their newspaper profitable. That meant securing advertisers and subscribers, and making their investments in the paper worth their while.

Arthur believed it was essential to understand the business side, but fundamentally, he and Morley were journalists. They wanted to have a positive impact on Durango. They wanted people to read the newspaper, talk about it, and act on what they learned from it.

Between them, Morley and Arthur had plenty of ambition, and both were adventurous and resilient. They knew these qualities were essential to meld with a small, mostly rural populace.

"We come to Durango full of enthusiasm for the city and for the job ahead of us," Arthur wrote in June 1952. "We will do our best to fulfill our responsibility to our readers and to the community. We will do our utmost to cooperate with efforts to make this area grow as an agricultural, business, and recreational center, to develop its great natural resources, and to make Durango an even pleasanter city in which to live."[101]

At first Arthur naturally took the lead role, but Morley would begin to find her own voice, create her own role, and eventually assume that lead role. She foresaw correctly that the challenges of the 20th century – a Cold War and the nuclear threat at the top of the list – would take a steady hand. In a 1952 editorial titled "Calmness and Action," she wrote, "Our faith in the future tells us that we stand just inside the door of the greatest half-century known to mankind."[102]

As Arthur and Morley settled in Durango, they embraced their chosen task. It was in their favor to be curious people who would make friends, poke around, acquaint themselves with the movers and shakers, and operate a newspaper with ethical and journalistic integrity.

In Morley's case, she'd seen how her grandfather and father had done just that, getting to know the nooks and crannies of Iowa and then Minnesota. And how they'd used that knowledge – whether it was memorizing train schedules to systematically deliver newspapers or understanding the needs and beliefs of both city and rural dwellers – to not only run successful papers, but also to offer readers greater aware-

ness of the world around them. Although he had not come from a newspaper family, Arthur had a Yale law degree, newspaper experience both at Harvard and Minneapolis, a knack in social circles, and a father of utmost integrity who had introduced him to some of the country's greatest leaders.

The Ballantines enjoy a Minnesota summer day at Glendalough in 1954. From left, Richard (age nine), Elizabeth (six), Arthur (forty), Helen (two), Morley (twenty-nine), and Bill (five).

If they had any doubts about moving to a small town in Southwest Colorado, those quickly faded. They were charmed by the people and the landscape and captivated by the challenge of running a small-town paper. They grew to love the Southwest.

Upon arrival they faced more mundane issues, such as settling into a new home with their four rambunctious children, ages six months to seven years. Those experiences became useful column fodder, making them all the more relatable to their readers. Morley and Arthur enjoyed needling each other in print, while also presenting their human side to the community.

"This recent move of ours has exposed vividly an unfortunate quality in my husband," Morley wrote in August 1952, only two months after they began their new lives as newspaper publishers.[103] "Whenever asked to fix something, he pleasantly agrees that he will, and then quietly and promptly disappears for work. When he returns, he comments on, for example, how wobbly the table is, but does he then get out the glue? Six months later, maybe, he'll get around to it, but it's usually easier by then to do it myself." She concluded with a revelation: "His current streak of inefficiency is purely and simply to sabotage any future schemes of mine to have him repair anything at all."

Many husbands could relate to Arthur's response a few days later:[104]

> In the main she is right. The men on my side of the family always have evaded hanging pictures, fixing doors, hammering nails and like. My grandfather preferred to translate the New Testament from the Greek. My father even today never can be found when my mother is worried about some lamp fixture. I claim no credit for the various techniques I use daily in our house. They came to me by inheritance from skilled and intelligent men.

Readers could almost see his loving smirk when he concluded, "You ought to see how competently my wife handles these matters in which I am so deficient."

Morley and Arthur had some adapting to do. They had limited insight into rural living, and none into Western ranching lifestyle. One of the first big events they witnessed in Durango was the Spanish Trails Fiesta, a Western cultural gathering of rodeo, horse races, Native American dances, parades, and more, held in early August. It attracted thousands of outside visitors annually.

They tried to soak it all in, while simultaneously getting to know all the town's wheelers and dealers. That September, Morley wrote, "This has been the busiest week I've had since coming to Durango, including Fiesta. ... The pleasure of meeting Mayor [Robert] McNicholas, Councilmen [Samuel] Miller and [A.J.] Andrews, to mention just a few, for the first time, and of hearing Councilman [Noel] Fiorini play his accordion more than made up for an untidy house over the week-end."[105]

They met with Western Colorado Power Company executives, dealt with a washing machine catastrophe and "the baby," Helen, beginning to crawl "everywhere," and sent Richard to his new elementary school. "It is no wonder my husband feels I've not been tending to business properly at the paper. Today we are off for the first time on the train trip to Silverton."

As much as Morley and Arthur might have tried to bide their time before jumping into the morass of local issues and politics, it wasn't long before they did so in print. The issues for a small, slowly growing town adapting to technological changes and an ever-increasing pace of life were tricky and controversial. These topics were an endless supply of material for the publishers, who doubled as the editorial board. Morley's editorials were signed "MCB," and Arthur's "ABJr."

In the family traditions, they considered themselves progressive Republicans. This meant that although one might be hesitant to throw money at every problem, it was okay to invest in technology and other improvements and causes – to embrace that quickly changing future. It was a future that, in many aspects, Morley and Arthur had already seen in their large-city upbringings and wanted to champion in their new home. Durango felt it was competing with Farmington – a New Mexico town fifty miles south of Durango – for business opportunities, for residents, even for tourists. It needed to modernize, the Ballantines realized, and that needed to happen soon. Many of their fellow county residents – and Coloradans in general – were more conservative Republicans, so MCB and ABJr. faced some opposition.

Within the first year they'd targeted several important issues that needed attention or fixing. Durangoans had been complaining about poor water quality for a decade or more. Construction of a new water purifying and delivery system, as well as a new sewage treatment system was the top priority. San Juan Basin Public Health was in disarray, and Arthur and Morley emphasized, to anyone who would listen, the importance of a strong health department.[106]

By the spring of 1953 the Ballantines were all-in on a $380,000 City of Durango water bond headed to a public vote. Bond money would line the reservoir on what was then called Airport Hill (the mesa where Fort Lewis College is now) to prevent buildup of weeds and algae, and to fix the distribution system. A larger, automated chlorinator also was needed. At the time, many suspected that chlorinating water was a communist plot, which led a small, radical contingent to label the Ballantines as communists.

Morley had become active with the Durango League of Women Voters, which made an in-depth study of the bond issue and campaigned for it. Through the league, Morley was made available as a speaker.[107] Arthur, meanwhile, wrote an editorial warning that Farmington was getting ahead of Durango: "Defeat of the water bond issue would be a severe setback to civic improvement. It would be a triumph for those who do not want Durango to be ready for expected oil and natural [gas] expansion. The world does not wait for the timid and doubting."[108]

For several weeks starting in March and running up to the April 7, 1953, election, the editorial column was daily topped by such bold titles as "Let's Grow With Good Water," and always under that, "VOTE 'YES' APRIL 7" and "It is to the self-interest of every Durango property owner to vote for the $380,000 water bond issue."[109]

The vote passed resoundingly, but the Ballantines found themselves still cast by some as negative "outsiders." Still, they persisted. Nearly a year after the vote, Arthur chastised the "bogged down" city council in a February 1954 editorial titled "Failure in City Government."[110] He wrote, "The new council not only abandoned its fine plans for water but repudiated the paving program to which the former council had committed the city. The new city council does not have a single major accomplishment in its record."

City councilors, in particular Robert S. Ayres, took offense in a rebuttal printed in the *Herald-News* a day later:[111] Ballantine made a "poor choice" in criticizing the council, Ayres wrote, adding that the newspaper had shown a "lack of co-operation." He wrote:

> Apparently, it has become the policy of the *Herald-News* to discourage and divide the people of our city, and to drive future residents away by your constant references to high taxes,

your claims of impure water, our dusty streets, etc. … It could be said that the *Durango Herald-News* has "failed" the people of this community. … If your paper can become a booster for our city and tell us the news about our neighbors, I believe it will be successful, but I do not think it will be if it continues along its present path.

As journalists, Arthur and Morley explained to readers, they would never allow the paper to take the role of "booster," and neglect what they believed was their duty to keep the public informed on issues, controversial or benign.

Conflicts over water treatment continued. Another water bond issue, again supported by the *Herald-News* and League of Women Voters, came before the city in April 1954. This time it was for a filtration system and a concrete-covered storage facility, as recommended by the state health department. The Ballantines had gone so far as to persuade state health officials and legislators to visit and witness the dismal condition of the water system for themselves.[112] State engineers saw that Durango water hadn't met state bacteriological standards for half of 1953.

The issue polarized the town, relationships were torn asunder, and, as one reporter wrote later, "The Ballantines were not only resented for being outsiders, themselves, but were blamed for bringing other outsiders into the dispute."[113]

This time the bond was soundly defeated. The paper lost an estimated $10,000 in advertising revenue during the election turmoil, although circulation rose.[114] A new water treatment plant was completed in June 1956 but it took until 1974 to get the covered reservoir built.

Undaunted, the Ballantines engaged on myriad other topics as well. They advocated paving city streets to eliminate the omnipresent irritation of dust and gravel (only Main, East Second, and East Third avenues were paved); bringing part of Fort Lewis A&M to Durango; keeping alive the train for tourism; Native American interests; education; and many other causes. Sometimes these battles led to the loss of a subscriber, or an advertiser, or even, in Arthur's case, a pair of busted glasses in a dust-up with the mayor.

Richard and Elizabeth compete in the annual Winter Carnival on the Third Avenue Hill.

Their perspective as newcomers allowed Arthur and Morley to see things that locals might have come to accept over time. Yet while their observations led them to seek change, Arthur recognized it would require a "quiet approach" if they wanted to "help with these problems."

"We like the people a lot and know it will be a wonderful place to bring up our four children fishing, riding, winter sports, and plenty of expeditions," Arthur had written in July 1952 to former Minneapolis colleague Percy Villa, a writer at the *Minneapolis Spokesman*, a black-owned paper.[115]

He Added:

Durango has two of its own racial problems. Unfortunately, discrimination of some kind seems to exist wherever you go in the world. Here the minority groups are the Mexicans, or Spanish-American, and Indians. The community is satisfied that relations with the Spanish-Americans are proceeding smoothly. However, one hardly ever sees them in local restaurants. Many of their homes are substandard, their education poor, and few of them occupy responsible jobs.

The Indian problem is especially interesting because I have never run into it before. Many of the traditions of the tribes make it difficult for an Indian boy to leave his family and enter the mainstream of American life. ... The boys need encouragement, but when they do get away, they usually find an unfriendly reception.

Morley and Arthur filled many column inches writing about their intentions for the editorial page and news content. They wanted people to read the paper and engage in community affairs, and of course, they needed to be profitable.[116]

"My husband and I felt, when we came to Durango, that a six- or eight-page paper was too small to let one page go almost unread, or at best to be read only by one small segment of the community," Morley explained to readers and at the University of Colorado Newspaper Week in May 1953. "In order to have a paper that was effective in the community, we would have to put some life into the editorial page so that all people would read it."[117]

While the news staff of four – Managing Editor Bob White (who'd moved from the Minneapolis papers to Durango), Dick Cunningham, Jack Greene, and Nancy Elliott – worked diligently, it couldn't cover everything. The editorial page sometimes filled in gaps, Morley said. She talked about providing national and international opinions from various sources, stories on the state legislature from the Denver papers, and even borrowing news from the Cortez paper. She believed that a "strong and well-read editorial page" was "integral" to a good newspaper.

At the same conference, Arthur spoke about the importance of the publisher establishing roots and getting to know the community, and of the newspaper not only understanding but also being part of the town and county it serves.[118]

> Interest should be the first objective of a newspaper. If its readers do not read it, the newspaper will have no effect upon the community no matter how good the newspaper may be. Interest is created by news of local people and events, comics, features, women's page, sports, and local editorials. When subscribers really read the paper, you are then in a position to turn their attention to vital problems which, despite their importance, seem to have only limited interest in readership surveys.

Within the first year of Ballantine ownership the *Herald-News* had made tremendous gains, ABJr. wrote in an editorial May 31, 1953.[119]

"Here in Durango the *Herald-News* and radio station KIUP are the two chief ways merchants have of telling the public what they have to offer," he wrote. "That the merchants recognize the importance of these pipelines to the public is increasingly evident. The *Herald-News* has just finished the biggest advertising month in its history, May 1953, to roll up the biggest year in its advertising history."

The newspaper under Ballantine ownership sold one-third more advertising in the first twelve months than previous owners had in the preceding twelve months. For two fledglings in the business, that fantastic beginning was mighty satisfying.

The Paper Flourishes

The *Herald*, founded as a weekly in June 1881, was seventy-one years old when Morley and Arthur purchased it.[120] The printing press, an old flatbed eight-page machine, was fifty years old in 1952, Arthur said in an interview.[121] The *Herald* badly needed modernization, and the Ballantines were determined to move forward. But it would have to proceed one step at a time.

The newspaper office had been located at 1128 Main Avenue since 1928. The first step was to find a more suitable and larger building. Less than a year after the couple assumed ownership, in late May 1953, the *Herald-News* moved to 1022 Main Avenue. "We need new and modern quarters for the more efficient operation of both the *Herald-News* and the Durango Printing Co.," publisher Arthur Ballantine Jr. said.[122]

Morley and Arthur Ballantine, 1952

The Ballantines' commitment to good reporting was evident from the outset. Winning awards wasn't the motivation for writing good stories and operating an impactful business, but it was always a time for celebration when honors did come the newspaper's way.

After a twenty-year-old woman took a seventy-foot plunge off Twin Thumbs in the Needle Mountains in July 1952, the *Herald-News* was given a national citation by the Associated Press Managing Editors Association for its coverage of the three-day rescue.[123] The AP often depends on its local affiliates to provide the news it distributes nationally, and the story of a young woman's plight in the remote wilderness captured national attention. The *Herald-News* was cited for going far beyond its duties and responsibilities in providing photos and news reports. The paper's coverage involved a reporter taking the train up as far as Needleton, the work of several other reporters and editors, and Arthur taking a plane ride over the scene.

The climber was carried out several miles by stretcher and "taken to safety in a huge bucket dangling from a cable stretched across the boiling [Animas] River in a wild mountain canyon," the *Herald-News* said. After the woman arrived at Mercy Hospital in Durango, Arthur and a reporter gained permission to speak with her. "Her own account of her misadventure made a fresh lead on the dramatic story for newspapers all over the country."[124]

One of Morley's earliest individual awards was a first place for column writing at the Thirteenth Annual Colorado Press Women convention in April 1954.[125] The Ballantines never thought provincially. Morley and Arthur attended national as well as regional newspaper gatherings. MCB wrote often about family matters, women's issues, and travels, but one of her areas of expertise was foreign relations; no doubt this focus stemmed from her father's international interests.

In 1955 Morley garnered a first place for editorial writing at the National Federation of Press Women in New Orleans.[126] It was for a column she wrote in opposition of the Bricker Amendment, which apparently derived from a League of Women Voters discussion. US Sen. John Bricker, a Republican from Ohio, wanted to amend "the Constitution to decrease the president's powers in negotiating with other countries and increase that of Congress," Morley wrote.[127] She concluded:

> President Eisenhower feels this would make it impossible for him to move with either speed or secrecy, both of which are necessary to conduct properly our relations with other nations. Giving Congress such detailed authority over our foreign affairs would be greatly at variance with what the writers of the Constitution felt was best when they spelled out the checks and balances between the three arms of the federal government.

In 1956 the *Herald-News* was showered with seventeen awards, five going to Morley. At the Colorado Press Association meeting that February, the *Herald-News* was given the general excellence award for its circulation size, the award that most pleased the couple, who had been toiling for four years to improve the newspaper in every way possible.

"My wife and I feel that the staff of this newspaper is of high caliber and are delighted to see its work recognized," Arthur wrote in a *Herald-News* editorial.[128] "It is often hard for a local reader to tell how his newspaper compares with others. One of the best ways to judge is through the judgment of others."

This recognition justified the difficult work of pursuing difficult issues in a small community that did not always understand the benefits of an active press. The Ballantines persevered, believing in the improvements they espoused, and enjoyed the success they achieved. They loved their work, kept their standards high, and (in the mid-1950s) delivered papers to the doorsteps every afternoon for just thirty cents a week.

The Ballantines lent their strong backbone to the reporting staff whenever necessary. No worthy issue was swept under the rug, despite the political or economic pressure. In April 1956, managing editor Dick Cunningham became embroiled in a case that threatened to put him in jail. "At considerable personal risk," ABJr. wrote, Cunningham went to Cortez to buy bootleg liquor, thus providing evidence for a grand jury. The seller was sentenced to eight months in jail, after which the seller's sister wanted Cunningham to serve jail time for buying the liquor.

"Dick has kept faith with our readers through keeping faith with the traditions which make great reporters and great newspapers. ... We have great confidence that the high quality of Dick's service to the public will be recognized by all who know the facts," Arthur wrote. "The *Herald-News* is proud of Dick Cunningham."[129]

Cunningham went on to work at *The Boston Globe*, making the Ballantines even more proud. Over the years many other rookie *Herald* reporters stepped successfully into big-city roles. Arthur and Morley had a clear vision of what the newspaper's, and the reporter's, roles should be. Arthur wrote:[130]

> The reporter is the most important individual on an honest newspaper for his job is to present to you in understandable fashion the facts upon which you will form your opinions. The first thing a reporter must learn is that unlike the editorial writer or columnist his personal opinions have no place in his work. Regardless of whether he likes what he finds out, his task is to find out. ... Explaining so the interested laymen can understand is the mark of the good reporter, an essential of the profession he has undertaken. It is not enough for him to understand the maze of detail; he must be able to put it on paper in clear, simple language. ...
>
> As in the past many government agencies are shutting down on information they wish made available to the public. The reporter can become pretty certain of an action without being able to check upon his facts. Should he go ahead and use the story? ... The reporter has to use judgment and talent every step of the way. Thus the kind of person he is and the way he looks at things can't help but play a role in his job.
>
> When you find a reporter whose stories you find to be impartial, informative, and readable, you have come across quite an individual.

Even bigger recognition came later in 1956 when the *Herald-News* won two major prizes from the University of Colorado School of Journalism: the Arthur A. Parkhurst trophy for community service and the Ralph Crosman trophy for editorial writing.[131]

Dayton D. McKean presents the Ralph Crosman trophy to Arthur and Morley Ballantine in 1956.

"The *Durango Herald-News* has dealt outstandingly with local issues," the Parkhurst trophy presenters said. Dayton D. McKean, Dean of the CU Graduate School, who presented the award, said, "The judges were particularly impressed by the style and quality of the editorials on local issues."

The newspaper would go on to win the Crosman and Parkhurst several more times.[132] A dedicated staff worked long hours for livable but not extravagant wages, and the Ballantines tried their best to let the employees know they were valued. Awards helped.

"Durango has been good to the *Herald-News*," Arthur wrote on June 15, 1956, the fourth anniversary of the first edition of the combined *Herald-News*.[133] "We shall strive to put out an even better newspaper."

With their success, the Ballantines sought to expand their business. In the late 1950s, the *Cortez Sentinel*, a semi-weekly started by the Beaber family in 1928, came up for sale. At the time, bolstered by energy development in the area, Cortez's population was rapidly expanding. The town went from 2,680 inhabitants in 1950 to 6,764 in 1960. It was predominantly rural and very conservative.

If one was going to establish a newspaper empire in Southwest Colorado, it seemed, then this might be the beginning. Arthur and Morley made the purchase in April 1958, and optimistically turned the *Sentinel* into a daily, the first time Montezuma County had ever had a daily paper. *Herald-News* operations were coordinated with those of the *Sentinel*, and in June 1958 the papers started printing a joint Sunday edition.

Ownership of the Cortez paper proved unworkable and unsuccessful. After eleven months as a daily the *Sentinel* returned to a weekly format in October 1959. "General business conditions of the last year simply have not justified advertising budgets needed to support a daily," Arthur was quoted as saying.[134] The Ballantines sold the Cortez paper a couple years later. For now, it was an untenable arrangement, but nearly forty years later, the Ballantines would expand back into Cortez.

A Distinct Style

In the early days of their *Herald-News* ownership, Morley's columns and editorials were often about family issues, the challenges of raising children being a common theme. It was a smart and entertaining method that created a bond with a rainbow of readers from ranchers' wives to drugstore clerks. Using a sly sense of humor, she discussed the exasperation of disciplining children and the sometimes even more exasperating give-and-take with her husband.

Their family, seen here Thanksgiving 1953, was a frequent feature in Morley and Arthur's newspaper columns.

Arthur and the children had to live with the reckoning that every action – whether brave, embarrassing, or amusing – might appear in the local newspaper. There's this nugget from a 1954 column subtitled "Famous Last Words":[135]

Four-year-old [Bill], catching on fast, to his father: "When

I say no, I mean no."

Eight-year-old [Richard], confidentially to a friend: "I never ask if I can stay out for lunch, I always TELL my mother. That's what my dad does."

Recognizing the reader rapport engendered by her home-front musings, Morley expanded her writing role, creating the popular and ostensibly anonymous Señora San Juan. It began as a "Dear Abby" advice column for Durango readers and expanded to take on other pressing community issues. In the first column Señora San Juan invited "all *Herald-News* readers – men and women, boys and girls – to write her about any problems, emotional, domestic or otherwise," that were troubling them. She added, "Señora San Juan believes she has the only column of this nature with males on its advisory staff."

In December 1952 "Good Husband" wrote to the Señora that his wife didn't seem happy around the house but brightened up for a night on the town.[136] "She smiles and talks to all my friends and seems very interested in what they say, especially the men."

Rebutted Señora San Juan: "That's just exactly what you aren't – a good husband – as your wife's actions show. … Of course she thinks your men friends are wonderful. They treat her as a person instead of just someone to do the work. Why don't you pay her compliments once in a while or show her that you still like her? … Ask her for her opinions too, then she'll be more interested in what you say."

MCB ventured into the risqué with Señora San Juan. She allowed a male reader to offer this tip for dealing with phone solicitors of the opposite sex: "Anytime a young female voice calls me about an offer I try to make my voice just as glooey as possible and reply that of course I'm interested in having my picture taken or buying life insurance, and that I'll pick her up anywhere she says at 8 p.m. and we'll come over here and have a few drinks and talk over her ideas."[137]

Mostly it was the Señora giving advice, often on social etiquette. A sixteen-year-old was in a quandary because her mother wouldn't let her host a party. The teenager wasn't sure it was okay to attend numerous other parties without reciprocation, so her mother suggested she stay home. "I don't want to have to sit at home all summer – what can I do?" she wrote.

Señora suggested the girl ask her mother if she could bake cookies, make lemonade, and invite friends over to enjoy them: "It doesn't have to be fancy, as you know. ... All hostesses become tired, in time, of the freeloader who comes and comes to be entertained by others and never makes a contribution of his own to the group or to everybody's having a good time. ... Start thinking! And good luck!"[138]

Later, Arthur became involved in a Señora controversy. He wasn't afraid of speaking his mind and his editorials occasionally ruffled some feathers. His wife wasn't all sweet and innocent either. The trouble with Harry happened like this:

Harry J. Miller was mayor (then called president) of the Durango City Council for one year in 1957-58. Arthur and Morley did not perceive the *Herald-News* as an arm of the chamber of commerce. It was an independent, freethinking platform for hard news and thoughtful debate. Apparently, Mr. Miller wasn't quite ready for this, as Arthur wrote in an editorial September 20, 1957:[139]

> A coolness has developed between Harry Miller and the *Herald-News* since he became president of the city council last spring. This is to be regretted since Miller has excellent points in his favor. ... The problem facing Miller is that he seems to consider Durango a private business, a field in which he has had much experience, rather than as a public trust, a field in which he is a comparative newcomer. He appears to resent the raising of any criticism concerning the city council or its policies. ... He would accomplish a lot more if he remembered he voluntarily ran for public office and is thus accountable to those who voted in the election.

Things quickly deteriorated, and Señora San Juan got involved. She apparently called Miller for a reaction about a complaint against the city, which she had received. She refused to tell the council president the source of the complaint, which was a question of general interest, not a personal complaint against Miller.

Two weeks later, on October 3, Arthur wrote in an editorial, "City Council President Harry Miller and our Señora San Juan have had a quarrel. Although most would consider Miller entirely capable of handling such a matter single-handed, he apparently does not think so."

The editorial went on to report that Miller had sent his personal lawyer to visit Morley, and then at a council meeting "enlisted the support of two other council members, the entire city police department, the entire city fire department, the city manager, the city clerk, and everybody else on the city payroll to protect him against the Señora, really a lovable, motherly woman if you know her."

> By formal city council resolution, the Señora may no longer call our council president about a complaint unless she tells him the name and address of her informant. ... Frankly when one sees the action Miller has taken on Señora, one has sympathy with the reluctance of troubled taxpayers to make themselves known.

This was not the end of the incident. Perhaps fortunately for everyone involved, using guns to settle disputes in Durango had gone out of fashion since 1922, when *Durango Democrat* publisher Rod Day shot and killed *Herald* city editor William Wood after a back-and-forth dispute in their respective papers.

One evening, apparently not long after his editorials took Miller to task, Arthur was standing in front of his home on West Third Avenue, talking to Judge James Noland, a close family friend. According to Noland, Miller "stepped out from behind one of these trees and popped Arthur in the eye and broke his glasses and that was all."[140]

Arthur wasn't badly hurt and chose not to add more fuel to the fire. He told friend Don Schlichting, a *Herald* manager, that there was a seven-year statute of limitations on such assaults, and "I'll let Harry Miller stew for a while."

More often, Morley wrote outside her Señora San Juan persona. She was capable of both serious reporting and light-hearted musings. Part of an August 1953 MCB column was devoted to skirt lengths.[141]

> With Nancy Elliott on vacation and men running the
> women's page, it seems only appropriate to have a few words
> on the battle of women's fashions right here. As I understand
> it, Christian Dior started it by having his fall collection show
> skirts covering only the kneecap. … Eighteen or nineteen
> inches from the floor, as fashion reporters estimated Dior's
> skirts to be, is pretty short compared to last year's twelve. Un-
> less we stand firm, we're soon going to find ourselves doing a
> lot of hemming on last year's dresses.

Daily life at a newspaper forces a person to be aware of current
events. If Morley wanted to write just about skirt lengths and negligent
husbands – and there's no reason to think she did – that bubble would
pop on its own. She wrote news stories about fashion, cooking, and
skiing. But from the start she also took on bigger issues such as freedom, civil rights, politics, and women's causes. Morley wrote bylined
stories about vital local and regional issues, such as basin water distribution and school overcrowding.

In the fall of 1953, she attended her first League of Women Voters
state board meeting, and by 1954 she was a member of that board.[142]
She wrote of their board meeting, "Four hours was spent by twelve
women from all parts of the state discussing everything from the proposed Bricker constitutional amendment to a telegram from Sen. Ed
Johnson and a letter from President Eisenhower on the mutual security
administration program."

Morley noted pointedly that "No one mentioned children or recipes
more than once," adding, "Although it seems to be popular currently
to lambast the little woman, most of them are certainly doing a job of
trying to correct the wrongs of this complex world."

In December 1952, Morley joined the National Conference of Editorial Writers on an all-day tour of the Colorado-Big Thompson water
project, whose purpose was to divert water from the Western Slope for
irrigation on the Eastern Slope (through the Continental Divide). She

Arthur, Morley and Jay Walz, of *The New York Times* at the 1022 Main Avenue *Durango Herald-News* office, 1956 (now home to Carver Brewing Company). Walz was doing pre-election coverage that fall.

wrote an informative story discussing not only the project's history and status, but also its mushrooming costs and Western Slope residents' fears of losing their water – deep-rooted fears that continue to this day.[143]

Morley and Arthur were quickly coming to understand the arid West, its geography, its people, and its concerns. With time and maturity, Morley's writing evolved. She was just twenty-seven when the family moved to Durango, had never held a journalism job, and wasn't even a college graduate yet. A more complex style is evident in a January 1957 column that describes a Sunday afternoon when she was trying to relax with a fashion magazine but couldn't keep the real world from interrupting her reading.[144]

... Your figure, the article went on, seems to be as much a matter of posture as anything. I tried to see if I could carry a book on my head, without much success. Posture was a factor here, obviously.

"When are you going to take us skiing? We want to go right now," yelled another wet figure. "I have snow inside my overshoes."

"Well, you can't go skiing that way, and besides, Daddy can't get the car out of the driveway yet. I don't think he'll be able to get it out at all today. You go help him," was my cheery reply, although I'm as aware as the next mother that fathers frequently dislike help from the very young. They find it just too helpful sometimes.

The new suits seem primarily beige. Some are belted, others bloused. Jackets are shorter and in a particularly pretty flannel one of Dior, "the jacket is aligned with, but never touching" the figure. There are beige coats too and white camel's hair.

Sure enough. There was Father's voice, raised in anger. "Now look, I just finished shoveling there, and I do not want you to tunnel in the piles on the side and get it all right back on the driveway. Now go inside."

I put down the magazines and left the dream world to go and begin a realistic supper. It was the end of the quiet Sunday afternoon.

Travel stories were a common topic, and the Ballantines had plenty of adventures to share. Morley wrote about everything from international trips, to adventures in the San Juans, to visiting a renowned beauty spa. Morley's mother joined her for a week at the Greenhouse Spa near Dallas – "the beauty spa of Neiman-Marcus." MCB's three-part series in November 1966 was titled "Quest for Beauty."

"When we arrived we were each given a pair of light blue stretch leotards and a light blue stretch tank suit," she wrote with some chagrin. "This little costume mercilessly revealed every bulge."[145]

Eating – or rather, *not* eating – was a major theme in the spa series. The 850-calorie-per-day diet proved a challenge: "I missed drinking skim milk as much as anything, although the last night I dreamt vividly of chocolate roll smothered in whipped cream with a lot of thick chocolate sauce to pour over it."

As were many parents, Morley was recruited to help with school programs. She wrote about discussing *The Swiss Family Robinson* with a class of fifth graders at Needham Elementary, and about the annual school science fair.[146]

"Yes sir, it's that time of year again – science fair time – when numberless parents wish they could go to Phoenix for a couple of weeks or be launched into outer space or just simply vanish," MCB began a February 1962 column.[147] "Frankly, every parent we've talked to is hard at work on his child's science fair project."

MCB found plenty of serious topics, many times writing about social issues, and often taking the side of human rights. With her two eldest children in college by 1968, her attention turned to higher education. A May 1968 column discussed recent college student protests and presciently noted societal changes sweeping the nation.

"To a casual reader, or to one not concerned with the issues involved, it might seem that college students on campuses across the nation – and the world – are simply making trouble wherever they can with no firm goals in mind. This, however, is not the case," she wrote.[148] Students were, she explained, promoting Afro-American studies and handling their own discipline and dormitory regulations, and should be added to advisory boards, MCB asserted.

"By and large college students today are a serious group," Morley concluded. "No longer are they content with goldfish swallowing and panty raids. What they have to offer should be listened to. They know, by and large, what they're after. They want to help govern their society."

Her writing, always poignant and never evasive, developed a loyal and faithful following.

New Name, New Location

In July 1960, the Ballantines decided the *Herald-News* moniker seemed a bit lengthy. The newspaper became simply *The Durango Herald*.[149]

The Ballantines' greatest business expenditure occurred a few years later, when the *Herald* purchased its present location at 1275 Main Avenue, across from Buckley Park. The move, along with building construction and a modern offset printing press, cost the company $300,000 (about $2.5 million in today's currency).[150] At that point it was considered one of the best small-town newspaper plants in the country.[151] At 13,600 square feet, it doubled the size of the previous quarters.[152]

The Durango Herald relocated to its present headquarters at 1275 Main Avenue in 1965.

A dedication ceremony held October 8, 1965, was a grand affair. It included the Fort Lewis College marching band; an invocation by the Rev. Jerry McKenzie; remarks by Arthur's brother, John Ballantine, a teacher and consultant in labor-management relations; and a dedication speech by Morley's brother, John Cowles Jr., editor of the *Minneapolis Star and Tribune*. A program printed for the dedication said the *Herald's* paid circulation was 5,355 daily and 5,592 Sundays, and about 20,000 people read the paper each day.[153] It still cost a nickel.

"Hundreds of persons jammed the 1200 block of Main Avenue at noon today," wrote *Herald* reporter Bill Bogle.[154] State senators and representatives, newspaper publishers, and editors from Denver and Grand Junction, a variety of local officials, and a state Supreme Court justice attended. At a dinner that night at the Strater Hotel, the principal speaker was Colorado Gov. John Love.[155]

John Cowles Jr. said, "The investment of $300,000 in this new, completely modern plant seems to me to represent a considerable vote of confidence by Arthur and Morley in the prosperity and growth not only of Durango but of Southwest Colorado and indeed the entire Four Corners region of the American Southwest."[156]

Cowles' speech, however, was not universally well received by the rural-leaning audience. He applauded a recent court decision favoring "one man, one vote" legislative reapportionment, and called the current system "malapportionment." The audience felt it stood to lose legislative representation if Cowles' wishes were followed. Reapportionment under "one man, one vote" would focus power more on population centers and away from rural areas.

"I remember the crowd was a little cool toward this," Richard Ballantine recalled.[157]

The upgrade to offset printing can't be overstated. It was a huge shift that improved the *Herald's* look, allowed for better color and bigger sections, and sped up the press run.

Prior to 1965 the *Herald* printed photos infrequently, because the reproduction was poor. Images could turn out mostly black. Advertisements generally used sketches or drawings instead of photos. When the *Herald* moved into its new building, the old hot type that exposed workers to liquid lead and fumes was left behind. With offset printing, a chemical process applied ink to paper. The process was both cleaner and quieter.[158]

"The thing which offset printing does is to give you so much better reproduction, so much better pictures," Arthur explained in a 1974 interview.[159] "Back in 1965 there were already quite a few offset papers, but we made a very careful study of this. It took us a year and a half, but when I told our two neighbor publishers [in Grand Junction and Farmington] what we planned to do, they said they thought we were rather foolish. You could pick up on the market the old metal presses. That was the way they both went at the time. It's a great satisfaction to me to see that they have now turned to offset."

In 1967 the computer age reached *The Durango Herald*, well ahead of the curve. The newspaper began using "high speed electronic equipment to produce type, headlines, and advertising." Production times improved greatly, as the new "Quick" machines printed twenty lines a minute, compared to eight lines for the old linotype machines.[160] The $70,000 investment brought the total cost of the three-year modernization program to nearly a half million dollars. It was the result of Arthur and Morley and managers studying other newspapers around the country and attending conferences such as the American Newspaper Publishers Association.

The investment in faster, cleaner, quieter equipment paid dividends. The paper's circulation, like the town's population, grew slowly but steadily. By 1974 it was up to 6,300 daily and 6,800 on Sunday.[161] It had more than doubled since 1952.

The *Herald* expanded its building again in 1979, adding 9,400 square feet with a new wing on the south end. Gov. John Love and his wife, Ann, who championed women's causes alongside Morley, were among the few who attended both the 1965 and 1979 dedications. It was not unusual for state politicians to visit Durango, but Love was among the most frequent.

"I had forgotten how often he came here or to other Southwest Colorado communities until I looked through our files," MCB wrote in remembrance of Ann Love (1914-1999).[162] "Frequently, Ann Love came with him and their daughter, Becky, now a state Supreme Court judge."

When Arthur and Morley simultaneously bought both the *Herald-Democrat* and the *News*, they eliminated the daily competition. In the years that followed, several people tried to start weekly papers in Durango, and some seemed like legitimate threats, but all fizzled. Not because the *Herald* played hardball; it was just the opposite, according to Bill Wehrman, co-founder of *Today*, a free weekly published from 1975 to 1985. Wehrman sensed that Arthur "relished the competition for news stories."

"[Arthur Ballantine] seemed excited for us to be trying to launch a new newspaper. It was easy to see he had a romance with journalism, and that put us on common ground," Wehrman wrote. "When I talked of building a newspaper from the ground up, he was an enthusiastic listener who pointed out possible problem areas, pitfalls to watch for, but he didn't try to discourage the effort."

The weekly *Basin Star*, which pledged to present "fully, accurately, and objectively" news of the San Juan Basin, lasted from March 1959 to June 1962. Despite excellent reporting and photography, the market proved too small.[163] The weekly *Mountain Eagle, San Juan Journal* in 1979-80 (with ex-*Herald* editor Louis Newell as publisher), *Animas Journal,* and *The Trading Post* (mostly classified ads) all succumbed after short lives.

As Arthur told attendees at a statewide newspaper conference, "No one should publish a newspaper today unless he knows the business side. Newspaper costs, with the huge equipment investment, are among the highest in the country. The slim margin between black and red ink explains the steadily growing number of single-ownership towns."

Throughout, the *Herald* remained Durango's media centerpiece, other than the radio station (KIUP-AM). The Ballantines used that position not only to their advantage, but to the town's advantage as well. They could be a little more forceful in their editorial views, confident that most advertisers would choose to continue working with them rather than harming their own businesses by removing their ads from the only daily in town.

It could be said that the Denver papers – *The Denver Post* and *Rocky Mountain News*, which could both be purchased in Durango – were regional competition. In 1974, Arthur downplayed the Denver threat. "The *Post* is stronger (than the *News*) down here," he wrote. "I don't consider the *Post* real competition to us because I think that most of the *Post* readers take the *Herald* as well."[164]

As the paper grew, Arthur and Morley expanded the news staff. They took pains to keep the newsroom strong, hiring talented reporters, editors, and photographers, despite the bigger budget this entailed. This practice endured more than a half-century until economics and media delivery changes (the Internet and social media) finally forced alterations.

"We have a bigger newsroom than most people would have," Arthur said in 1974.[165]

> We have a number of things that some chain newspapers wouldn't. When they're making all the economics that they could, we try to get as much in-depth coverage as we can, to cover some of the subjects more than just what you're given.
>
> This is partly due to Morley's and my belief that giving people information is the most important function of a newspaper, and if you can get correct information for them, they're going to begin making and rendering decisions.

The newsroom was always a priority for the Ballantines, sometimes to the chagrin of other departments at the paper. Moreover, it was a newsroom that was free to pursue the controversial and impactful stories in the community, a newsroom that wasn't shy about seeking and bringing to light stories that might offend some of its readership.

Ian "Sandy" Thompson, associate editor of the *Herald* from 1970-1973, said, "What impresses me most about the Ballantines and the *Herald* is the willingness to allow the news/editorial staff a lot of autonomy in determining news/editorial content. I never had the feeling that any news story I was developing or any assignments I was making to reporters needed to be approved in advance by Arthur and Morley."[166]

The Ballantines backed the newsroom even to their economic detriment. When an eager summer intern from Harvard wrote a series on the low wages being paid by Durango's larger businesses, Thompson said, "a number of prominent business leaders came to the *Herald* demanding that the series be stopped and that I be fired. They threatened to pull their advertising if their demands were not met. ... The businessmen were told the series would continue and so would I. They pulled their advertising. That must have been difficult for the Ballantines; some of those advertisers were their close personal friends."[167]

Despite such setbacks, the paper grew – in both circulation and staff. And the *Herald* continued to garner plenty of awards. Morley and Arthur were extremely proud of an honor bestowed in 1967, when they were jointly honored by the University of Colorado's School of Journalism faculty, as Outstanding Journalists of Colorado for their newspaper work and participation in the community. Their award certificate stated several precepts that guided the Ballantines:

> The special job of the newspaper is to give a balanced, accurate picture to the reader of the issues important to him. ... The facts the newspaper finds worthy of publication are a major way in which it helps shape the scene around it. ... The newspaper influences policy through the contacts reporters, editors, and publishers have with those in authority. ... The newspaper has a part sometimes in shaping policies through the editorial, a tradition unfortunately abandoned today by many smaller newspapers.

The certificate said that through the Ballantines' "actions as editors and publishers based on these beliefs, they have produced a quality newspaper in news coverage, community participation, consistent taking of stands; and, by investing in equipment, constructing a new plant, switching to offset publication."[168]

In 1969 they earned a Governor's Award for services to the arts and humanities in Colorado. In 1970 Fort Lewis College awarded the couple a Distinguished Service Award.

Connections

Newspaper editors and pub-lishers are frequently immersed in politics – local, state, national, and world. But few families have had the deep connection with important political figures as have the Ballantine and Cowles families. The couple's associa-tions far beyond Durango pro-vided a link for their readers to

the entire country and world. Morley and Arthur's personal accounts of contacts with national figures helped bring the broader political scene to this small community.

Arthur Ballantine Sr. had an ongoing rivalry with Harvard classmate Franklin D. Roosevelt. Both men sought to be president of *The Harvard Crimson*. Arthur also was a trusted adviser to both Herbert Hoover and FDR. And he and Thomas Dewey, who lost to Harry Truman in the 1948 presidential elec-tion, later became partners in the Dewey Ballantine law firm in New York City.

Fellow Iowans Gardner Cowles and Herbert Hoover were political allies. Cowles served as director of the Reconstruction Finance Corporation under President Hoover in 1932.

Gardner Cowles Sr. also was a close friend of his fellow Iowan Herbert Hoover, and his sons were important advisors and advocates of Wendell Willkie, who ran against Roosevelt in 1940. In Minnesota, John and Betty Cowles hosted some of America's top movers and shakers at Glendalough, which the Cowleses grew into a 2,000-acre property encompassing five lakes.

Dwight Eisenhower, president from 1953-1961, was a guest several times. Richard Nixon stayed there. Other US cabinet holders and businessmen took their turns refreshing their spirits in Glendalough's open and uncrowded spaces.

One of Arthur Jr.'s best friends was Harvard undergrad and Yale Law classmate George Franklin Jr. (1913-1996), who became one of the country's leading experts on foreign affairs. Franklin also was executive director of the Council on Foreign Relations, an influential foreign policy group founded in the aftermath of World War I in 1921.

Franklin was named Bill Ballantine's godfather. Helen's godfather was Hadlai Hull (1914-2011), another Yale Law classmate of Arthur's. Hull served as chief financial officer for Minneapolis-based Dayton Company, which spawned Target stores, and then in Washington, D.C., as assistant secretary of the Army. His wife, Anne Hull, a friend of Morley Ballantine's from Minneapolis, was Elizabeth's godmother. Another friend of Arthur Jr.'s was Caspar Weinberger (1917-2006), a 1938 Harvard grad and *Crimson* editor. Weinberger served as President Reagan's secretary of defense in the 1980s.

And there was the Rockefeller connection. Arthur Jr. worked for Nelson Rockefeller as World War II began, but his closer friend was Nelson's brother, David Rockefeller (1915-2017), a banker and chief executive of the powerful Chase Manhattan Corporation from 1969-1980. Both Rockefellers were grandsons of Standard Oil tycoon John D. Rockefeller. Arthur and David both graduated from Harvard in 1936 and served together as *Crimson* editors.

The politics of both families can best be described as progressive republicanism, which Arthur Jr. described as socially progressive and fiscally conservative. That view is evident in private letters and in the editorials both Arthur and Morley wrote for *The Durango Herald*.

The *Durango Herald* endorsed the Republican candidate, Richard Nixon, for US president in the 1960 election. Arthur had attended the Republican convention in Chicago that summer as a delegate.

"I thought Nixon greatly increased his stature, both through his handling of the convention and by his excellent acceptance speech," Arthur wrote to his father.[169]

Nixon, however, lost that election to the young and captivating John F. Kennedy. Neither the Ballantine nor the Cowles families had much respect for the Kennedy family, particularly for the patriarch, Joseph Kennedy, a pre-World War II isolationist who wanted the US to stay out of what began as a European war.[170]

Arthur was a delegate to the 1960 Republican National Convention, where he met candidate Richard Nixon.

Arthur and Morley actually had more in common with Kennedy than with Nixon. Both Arthur Jr. and John Kennedy, who was three years younger, were Harvard graduates. Kennedy enrolled in 1936, mere months after Arthur Jr. had graduated. Both men had spent parts of their youth in Boston and New York City. Among the Cowleses, Ballantines, and Kennedys, there were many mutual acquaintances and friends. As one example, Arthur Jr. served as the escort to McGeorge Bundy, President Kennedy's assistant for national security, at a Harvard commencement ceremony in 1961.[171]

So when a group of twenty-one Colorado newspaper editors and publishers was asked to attend a luncheon with President Kennedy at the White House in June 1962, invitees Arthur and Morley weren't

intimidated, and were eager to see old friends. Morley was awarded a seat of honor right next to JFK, and Arthur was seated almost directly across the U-shaped table.

The meeting was described as an exchange of ideas, and it served as an unveiled attempt by Kennedy to get some political will on his side as he tried to improve the economy and tend to brittle world political affairs. Kennedy met with similar groups from several other states around the same time.

The Associated Press reported the meeting was "an informal, light-hearted affair." Morley was quoted in the story, saying the luncheon was "lots of fun – very interesting and provocative." And she was "impressed also by Mrs. Kennedy's refurbishing of the White House." (Earlier that year, First Lady Jacqueline Kennedy gave a widely watched televised tour of her French-inspired White House renovations.)

"The president with patience and good humor spent two and one-half hours answering questions," wrote Jack Foster, editor of the *Rocky Mountain News*. "His youthful face, marked with the inevitable lines of two years in office, did not reveal the disappointment he must have felt in the defeat of his farm bill the day before."[172]

Attendees were served crab crepes and sole grenbloise, along with a California white pinot wine. After the meal Kennedy and others smoked cigars (JFK did not drink the wine – he was working), and the conversation continued.[173] Morley was charmed, but emphasized in an editorial that she would not change party affiliation. She noted with humility that she'd used the wrong fork for the first course.

"The President in person is even more intelligent, articulate, forceful, knowledgeable, witty, and just plain attractive than he appears to be on television," MCB wrote.[174]

Kennedy had visited Durango while on the campaign trail in 1960, a visit he recalled two years later at the White House luncheon. Their economic views differed, but Morley realized she was talking to a fellow social progressive.

"Mr. Kennedy said he remembered Durango well and that a benefit of conducting a national campaign was the opportunity it provided to visit all parts of the country," MCB wrote. "We discussed the progress being made on the Navajo and Ute reservations, the need for more education facilities everywhere – he is particularly concerned about the problem of 'drop-outs,' equality in employment, and a host of other topics."

Kennedy knew well that Morley's father and uncle were powerful newspaper and magazine publishers with political influence in the Midwest and East. Mike Cowles's *LOOK* Magazine, in particular, printed regular features on the White House and its operations.

For Arthur, it was the third president he'd visited in the White House. "Seeing the White House under the Kennedys was especially interesting to me as I had been there in my teens when my father was in the Hoover administration and again in my twenties when I worked for Nelson Rockefeller during the Roosevelt era," Arthur wrote in a *Herald* editorial.[175]

He, too, was impressed by Kennedy, who would die from an assassin's bullet seventeen months to the day after the luncheon.

"The young President is a man of unusual and distinctive abilities," Arthur wrote. "He is better informed on a wider variety of subjects than his predecessors for he spends many hours of study on state papers. ... His toughness is a needed quality. Today's problems are so big that even his opponents should feel relief an able man is in the White House."

Four months later, in mid-October 1962, the Cuban Missile Crisis would frighten the world, and JFK would need that toughness. Although the crisis nearly precipitated a nuclear showdown, his administration's actions led Russia to remove nuclear missiles from Cuba.[176] The *Herald* supported Kennedy's actions.[177]

Morley and Arthur's party affiliation was not about to change. But in the 1964 presidential race, with the choice between ultra-conservative Republican Barry Goldwater of Arizona and the more moderate Democrat Lyndon Johnson, the *Herald* endorsed Johnson. That Democratic endorsement didn't go far down the ticket. Wrote Arthur for the edition of November 1, 1964:[178]

> The *Herald* this Tuesday is supporting the national ticket of the Democrats and the local La Plata County ticket of the Republicans because we feel that there are many in the local organization who will be genuinely concerned about the future of the party.
>
> Republicans who are concerned about [Goldwater's] approach to foreign policy, his attitude towards the vital issue of race, and many domestic problems find deeply held convictions at stake. … Surely there is a point where what one wants for one's country is more important than party.

In 1968, when Nixon again ran for president, the *Herald* was back in the Republican camp. This was interesting, considering that Morley had both family and regional ties to Nixon's opponent, Minnesotan Hubert Humphrey. But Humphrey was seen as a bit too liberal by the Cowleses and Ballantines. Both Morley and Arthur were in Minneapolis when Humphrey was mayor and was elected US senator. Humphrey and the Cowles family knew each other well. Arthur had covered Humphrey briefly during his reporting gig with the *Minneapolis Tribune*.[179]

The unsigned *Herald* endorsement just before the November election read:[180]

> The Republican and Democratic candidates for president

are abler men than many in their own parties concede. The *Herald* publishers will vote for the Nixon-Agnew ticket. The country needs a president, free from the [Lyndon] Johnson heritage and able to make fresh approaches.

The endorsement concluded with this prescient thought about a person's capacity to change, but not prescient in the way the writer wanted to believe: "The Presidency does remarkable things to a man and Nixon could be that man."

Nixon, of course, grew paranoid in the White House, recorded his conversations, had aides who arranged to spy on the Democrats, and resigned in disgrace during his second term, in August 1974. Family lore says that Morley and Arthur wrote vying endorsements in 1968, with Morley supporting Humphrey and Arthur supporting Nixon. A search of newspapers within two weeks of the election turned up only the Nixon endorsement.

In later years when Morley was publisher, she occasionally would write about a national figure she'd known. Humphrey (1911-1978) began his political career in Minneapolis, and served as US senator before becoming vice president under Lyndon Johnson from 1965-1969. He battled racism throughout his career – an aspect that endeared him to the Cowles family – and was a lead author of the Civil Rights Act of 1964. Morley wrote in 1978:[181]

> When the war ended, one of my late husband's [Arthur's] first reporting assignments for the *Minneapolis Tribune* was to cover Mayor Hubert Humphrey. Then in 1948, at the Democratic national convention, he burst upon the national scene with his demand for a strong civil rights plank in the party platform. "The time has arrived," he said, "for the Democratic party to get out of the shadow of states' rights and walk forthrightly into the bright sunshine of human rights."
>
> Hubert Humphrey loved people, all kinds of people, big people and little people, black, brown, and white people. He loved life, and all during his, he worked to improve the lives

of others. He embodied compassion and understanding. And although he never achieved the presidency, future history books will rank him ahead of some who did.

Morley's father, John Cowles, followed his children's lives closely, and even more so after he retired. He subscribed to *The Durango Herald* by mail. "That was an excellent article you wrote for the January 23rd *Durango Herald* about Hubert Humphrey," John Cowles wrote to Morley, "and I am sending it to all my children."[182] He reminded Morley that the foreword to *Sunlight on Your Doorstep*, a book about the history of the *Minneapolis Tribune*, was written by Humphrey in 1967.

Morley wrote a year later about Nelson Rockefeller (1908-1979), whom Arthur had worked for at the State Department in the early 1940s and who had remained a family friend. "After the Nixon debacle, when [President] Ford desperately needed a man of integrity, respected by the citizenry ... Rockefeller again did his duty to his country and accepted the post [of vice president]."[183]

Lending Support

While Morley and Arthur extended readers' views beyond Durango, they also paid considerable attention to matters and organizations on a local and regional level. That included Fort Lewis College and the railroad.

As the name indicates, Fort Lewis was originally a military post. It was constructed in 1878 in Pagosa Springs and moved in 1880 to a rural spot seventeen miles from Durango, south of Hesperus. The fort was decommissioned in 1891 and converted into a federal boarding school for Native Americans, mostly local Utes. In 1911 the school was ceded to the State of Colorado and turned into an agricultural and mechanical arts high school for all, including Native Americans. Then in the 1930s it became a two-year college, which was eventually controlled by the State Board of Agriculture.

Soon after the Ballantines' arrival in Durango, it was suggested, in 1953, that Fort Lewis use the $300,000 in its building fund to construct a branch in Durango. Morley and Arthur jumped on board.[186] Their embrace of the college would be unswerving and impactful.

State legislators were losing interest in Fort Lewis, funneling money to other institutions the majority considered more worthy. The formation of a Durango branch was considered by many – including the Ballantines – as a way to save the institution from closure.[185] Only 150 students attended the school in 1953-54. Without state legislators' help, to continue to exist, Fort Lewis would have to become a locally supported junior college, a prospect deemed not viable by locals. With state support, moving to Durango, and expanding to a four-year institution, Fort Lewis could thrive, Arthur wrote in an editorial in February 1954.

It had taken the Ballantines no time at all to see that moving the college campus into town – from the boondocks so far from the population center – was imperative for the town's future growth. The economic effect would be significant. And even more vitality would come from the added cultural dynamic of an institution of higher learning.

The Ballantines pushed the move in any and every way. They joined forces with the president of the then-junior college, Dale Rea, and backed his and others' efforts to move the college, starting with editorials. It seems obvious today, but at that time not everyone wanted Fort Lewis A&M (agriculture and mechanics) to lose its rural roots – specifically the nearby Dryside residents who had jobs there. And some feared the changes that would come to Durango.

"[Rea] was joined by a cross-section of the community, including Dr. [Leo] Lloyd, bankers [A.M.] Camp and Nick Turner, merchants [Fred] Kroeger and Jackson Clark, newspaperman Arthur Ballantine, lawyer William Eakes, and a legion of determined others," Fort Lewis professor Duane Smith wrote in his Durango history, *Rocky Mountain Boom Town.*[186]

Gov. Ed Johnson made it official by signing the legislature's bill in March 1955. The physical move took place over two years. The college opened on the mesa above Durango, then called Reservoir Hill or Airport Hill, in September 1957. Enrollment tripled in the first six years.

"The college transfused fresh blood into the local economy and enriched the cultural life," Smith wrote. "It encouraged Durango in other ways as well and may truthfully be said to have been the most significant development since the turn of the century."[187]

The Ballantines helped Fort Lewis in ways large and small. One of the first concerns of those traveling to the new school above town was an annoyingly rough road. Students called it the "Burma Road," and banded together in 1958 to get it fixed.

"The road to the campus has been full of chuck holes, washboard ruts, and inches of dust that clouded around cars commuting up and down the hill," a student wrote in the school paper.[188]

Arthur Ballantine took up the issue in a *Durango Herald-News* editorial: "The road is a hazard to students. It creates a most unfavorable impression on tourists, visiting legislators, and state officials."[189] In other words, it was an embarrassment to the city. Arthur and members of the local Kiwanis Club collected $9,000 and paid for the city to pave the road in the late summer of 1958.

Once the campus moved to Durango, President Rea advocated another upgrade before his resignation in December 1961. He believed, and others on campus and around town fervently agreed, that Fort Lewis A&M should be established as a four-year college. In March 1961 the state legislature made the college in Pueblo – now called Colorado State University-Pueblo – a four-year-degree school. Durango knew it needed to do the same, not only to compete for students and faculty, but also to raise money for new buildings and improvements.

As the state legislature convened in 1962, the Durango delegation lobbied and finagled and won the day. In February the legislature officially made Fort Lewis A&M a four-year-degree-granting institution, with a slight twist. Local advocates, as a way of selling the plan, had proposed Fort Lewis would use a revolutionary, year-around trimester schedule, allowing students to graduate in three years. In a story that appeared in *The Denver Post*, Arthur noted the turnaround the college had made since he and Morley had arrived in town. And he couldn't help sounding like a proud papa:[190]

> On the verge of closing down ten years ago, Fort Lewis today is the state's newest senior college about to experiment with converting the usual four-year liberal arts curriculum into three years of year-round study. In 1952 Fort Lewis, the only state-supported junior college, had an enrollment of less than 150, many recruited for the football season.
>
> There was little zest for putting money into the deteriorating campus sixteen miles from Durango. There was no excuse

for its existence. Colorado had taken over the old US Army post on condition that Indians would always receive a free education. ...

Fort Lewis, already over 700 students, has thrived the last six years. The community is proud. The quality of teaching is improving. The campus has keen interest in new ideas.

... Southwest Colorado has a personality and uniqueness which will appeal to many interesting types of students.

The Ballantines extended their support of Fort Lewis College far beyond advocacy in the newspaper. In 1964 they began what would be a decades-long financial devotion to the college. They were energized by the growing need to preserve the history of Southwest Colorado and the Four Corners area.[191] The worry was that irreplaceable papers and cultural artifacts would be scattered or lost. An institution dedicated to the collection and study of these items was necessary, Professor Robert Delaney told all who would listen.

Morley and Arthur listened intently. They wanted Fort Lewis College to be known for something unique, for some area of expertise and academic distinction. The subject that could draw national and international scholars to the school, they realized, was the unique history, landscape, people, and art of the Southwest. The vision was shared by others, including Fort Lewis President John Reed, and of course Delaney, chairman of the Humanities Department.

The Ballantine Family Charitable Fund stepped up and made a generous donation to launch the Center of Southwest Studies. "Until Arthur and Morley Ballantine, *The Durango Herald* publishers, provided a $10,000 gift for the establishment of the Center, the College had neither the funds, the manpower, nor the organization to make possible a systematic collection of documents, records, letters, and interviews that will help to tell the story of the development of the Southwest," President Reed said.[192]

"The Center wouldn't have existed without Morley and Arthur," Smith, professor of History and Southwest Studies at Fort Lewis beginning in 1964, said simply. "It was their idea and they made it happen."[193]

Delaney was named director of the new Center. He, his wife Ria (a Fort Lewis instructor of German and Latin), and the Ballantines had become fast friends and shared many adventures together around the Southwest. Originally the Center's collection was housed in a small library in a tiny room in the Academic Building (now called Berndt Hall). The Center greatly expanded in 1967, moving to the top floor of Reed Library and taking over several rooms and two offices. It was destined to move and expand again, but not for another three decades.

In 1968 the Ballantines helped form a Cultural Committee at Fort Lewis. This committee focused on programs in the arts and sciences "that will enrich the liberal arts program of Fort Lewis College and add to the intellectual and cultural environment of the San Juan Basin."[194] A gift from Arthur and Morley had already established a Visiting Scholar Program with a similar goal.

Two years later the Fort Lewis College Foundation was formed "as a vehicle for receiving, managing, and allocating private gifts to the

The Ballantines supported the Center of Southwest Studies from its inception at Fort Lewis College. Pictured here at the dedication of the Arthur Ballantine Jr. Room in May 1980, are, from left, FLC President Rexer Berndt, Morley, Richard, Dr. Robert Delaney, Elizabeth, Helen, and Bill.

college" and utilizing those gifts to the fullest, according to then-president of the school, Rexer Berndt. Arthur Ballantine was elected in 1970 as first president of the foundation's seventeen-member board of directors.[195] The foundation continues today as a vital source of financing and support for improvements at the college.

Many people contributed to Fort Lewis's survival during this period. But without the Ballantines' whole-hearted support – and financial generosity – the college would not have become the successful institution and the arts and cultural hub of the area that it is today.

Long before the college and influx of tourists arrived, Durango was a center for mining operations. It was surveyed and platted in 1880 to serve as a smelter town, a gathering spot for all the ore and coal that came from the surrounding mountains. Its location along the Animas River provided a relatively flat area where those who supported the mining industry could live.[196]

Several railroads served the area during Durango's infancy in the nineteenth century, carrying ore and cargo among the small towns and mines of the San Juan Mountains. But the most important was the one that operated between Durango and Silverton, forty-six miles to the north. It began operations in 1882, a line of the Denver and Rio Grande Railroad.

By the time the Ballantines arrived in 1952, seventy years later, the narrow gauge steam-powered line between Durango and Silverton was starting to figuratively derail. The original purpose of the link – the delivery of ore and supplies – was in question.[197] The economy was changing, and along with it the means of transport. Trucks could now deliver some of these loads, and the mining industry was losing steam.

Railroad owners, the Denver and Rio Grande Western, were adamant that it needed to move freight, not passengers, to survive. Although tourists had discovered its charms – rugged scenery and a feel for the Old West – by the early 1950s, passenger revenue was a distant second priority to the D&RGW. The situation seemed bleak. The railroad petitioned the federal government to close the line.

"The narrow-gauge train was just beginning to be discovered in the 1950s and the railroad was resisting it," Arthur Ballantine said in a

1974 interview.[198] "We did a great many things [to save the train]. The editorials really weren't so important as the politics – getting to our senators and representatives."

By the late 1950s the train was attracting 35,000 passengers a year and was becoming known nationwide. It received a huge boost from its presence in the 1956 Best Picture-winning *Around the World in 80 Days*, based on the Jules Verne book and starring David Niven and a very young Shirley MacLaine.

"The narrow gauge has come to stand throughout the United States for the glamorous, colorful mining days," Arthur wrote in 1959.[199] "It appeared in full-page color in *LIFE* magazine last summer. It has been seen all over the world wherever *Around the World in 80 Days* has been shown."

Since the D&RGW wanted nothing to do with a tourist operation, city leaders under the ebullient William M. White Sr., president of the First National Bank of Durango, formed a group in 1959 to buy the railroad and turn it into a nonprofit tourist train. The Pueblo-based White family had purchased the seventy-five-year-old Durango bank in 1954. They were public-spirited, eager boosters for Durango as well as for the other Colorado towns where they had banking interests. William, known more informally as "Bill," went around town with his booming voice and charm and ginned up support for purchasing the railroad.

By then the Whites and the Ballantines had become friends, and Arthur became one of nine trustees of the Helen Thatcher White Foundation – formed to buy the train and named in honor of William's wife. Arthur was named the foundation's secretary.

The group signed a $250,000 deal with the railroad on December 4, 1959. Arthur was there for the ceremony, done with pomp and circumstance in the private rail car Nomad, built for nineteenth-century railroad president, Gen. William Jackson Palmer.[200] In the Nomad, Palmer had entertained such guests as President Ulysses Grant.[201]

The deal was still subject to approval from the Interstate Commerce Commission. "Approval by the ICC would mean year-after-year passenger hauling by the doughty little train for tourists, vacationists, and

railroad fans," *The Denver Post* wrote in a front-page story the next day.[202] "Only the train's awakening of tourist interest in latter years has saved it from abandonment."

Alas, the ICC hurdle could not be cleared and the deal fell through. Arthur himself pointed out the sticking point – nonprofits aren't taxed – in an editorial following the signing ceremony. Unfortunately, those opposed to the deal didn't buy into his counterpoints:

Arthur, right, co-signed an agreement to purchase the railroad for $250,000 in December 1959, aboard the Nomad car. Also present are D&RGW President Gus Aydelotte, left, and Bill White, middle.

"The only drawback to the proposal is the loss of tax revenue to governmental units in La Plata and San Juan counties – a total loss of $76,000. … While the San Juan loss is smaller, it is an even bigger problem for San Juan since it represents a sixth of tax revenues."[203]

Arthur went on to point out that total abandonment of the line would be worse for Silverton (the San Juan County seat), and that an expected influx of tourists would likely increase the town's revenues in the long run. But Silverton residents were not convinced. They objected to the foundation's deal, and thus, the federal commission voted it down.[204]

The D&RGW did not stop trying to abandon the line, but others, including the Ballantines, resisted and the issue festered at the local and federal levels. Finally, in 1962 the D&RGW was required by the ICC to continue operating between Durango and Silverton. Forced into this position, the railroad reconsidered how tourists, as well as ancillary businesses, might make the line sustainable. It was now attracting 40,000 passengers per year. With an influx of tourists in mind, train owners spent $1 million in the mid-1960s developing the area near the Durango train depot with a Western theme.[205] (The D&RGW struggled to sustain the line for two more decades until Charles Bradshaw, a Florida citrus titan, fertilizer plant owner, and train enthusiast, purchased it in March 1981.[206] He renamed it the more tourist-friendly Durango & Silverton Narrow Gauge Railroad.)

Arthur became a director of the Colorado Visitors Bureau in the 1960s. He and Morley fully understood the charms of the Southwest and the still-untapped potential for tourism. In a story that appeared in *The Denver Post* in March 1963, Arthur discussed the future.[207] As well as the train, he listed Mesa Verde National Park, the surrounding mountains and rivers, and Navajo lands as attractions. A new paved highway – US Highway 160 from Towaoc to Tuba City, dubbed the "Navajo Trail" – had just been completed through the Navajo reservation in fall 1962. The road provided a shortcut to the Four Corners for many coming from the West, including highly populated California.

From the 1963 *Post* story: "Ballantine forecast that new attractions added to the vacation dreamland aspects of the area like the San Juan, San Miguel, and La Plata ranges, Mesa Verde National Park, and the gorges of rivers like the San Juan, Animas, and La Plata will combine to bring an eventual five million visitors annually into the Four Corners and San Juan Basin."

Arthur's quote in the story: "We just now are beginning to realize and develop the full potential in this area. … Only since [World War II] have we begun to make our natural assets accessible, with new highways and air transportation, and to make them more attractive by providing our visitors with new facilities."

By 2019, the Durango Area Tourism Office estimated that 1.7 million visitors came just to Durango annually.[208] Arthur's five million for the Four Corners and San Juan Basin was close, and illustrates what a visionary he was.

The Ballantine Way

Arthur and Morley gladly took up the mantle of representing Southwest Colorado's interests. Simultaneously, they relished the chance to fight for the benefit of humanity. These dual, or more accurately multiple, interests, combined with their growing reputation as regional and statewide leaders, assured they would never have a dull moment.

During the Colorado governor's race in 1956, while endorsing the Republican, Donald Brotzman, *The Durango Herald* was careful to say that the Democrat, Steve McNichols, was a fine man as well. Morley and Arthur had spent time with both candidates at a Colorado Press Association meeting. McNichols narrowly won the election. And he didn't hold any grudges.

In July 1957, McNichols named Morley Ballantine to the executive committee of the governor's commission to study legislative reapportionment. Changing the boundaries of legislative districts to more accurately represent the population was then – and is now – a touchy subject, particularly in rural areas that often feel underrepresented. Morley was the only San Juan Basin representative and the only woman on the eleven-person executive committee, which traveled around the state to listen and gather information at fourteen meetings.

Arthur wrote in an editorial, "I think [Gov. McNichols] has made a pretty good choice. Once my wife sets out to learn about something

Arthur receives his lifetime membership from an unidentified NAACP representative. It was a gift from his mother-in-law, Betty Bates Cowles.

she usually accomplishes her objective."

Civil rights were nothing new to Morley or Arthur, who continued to champion the cause in Durango. Morley's mother had been aligned with black causes in Des Moines and Minneapolis. Both John and Betty Cowles were involved in civil rights and enrolled their four children as lifetime members of the NAACP, the National Association for the Advancement of Colored People. Arthur was sympathetic to the causes of Hispanics and Native Americans.

The Civil Rights Act of 1957, signed into law by President Dwight Eisenhower, established the US Commission on Civil Rights. The task of this commission, headed by John A. Hannah, the president of Michigan State University, was to investigate, report on, and make recommendations regarding civil rights issues.

Many state commissions were then established to report to the US commission, and in September 1958 Hannah announced the appointment of Arthur A. Ballantine Jr. as chairman of a five-person Colorado advisory commission on civil rights.[209] The Colorado group went right to work, and by February 1959 had issued a preliminary report on housing in Colorado, based on conditions in urban areas, specifically Denver. Durango had and still has few African-American families, although Hispanic and Native American families suffered from discrimination here.

"[Minority groups] are forced to live in crowded conditions, in substandard housing and are often victimized as to prices, sometimes even by members of their own groups," said the Colorado group in a report co-authored by Arthur.[210]

The Colorado committee publicly endorsed a 1959 state legislative bill on fair housing. The bill passed, directly attacking "what the committee found early this winter to be the biggest unsolved civil rights problem in Colorado," the committee stated in its official report to the federal commission in early September 1959.[211] In a report that sounds as if it could have come directly from Arthur's typewriter, optimism for continued progress was muted with a warning:

> However, should mistakes be made, the Jews could find themselves the objects of hatred. The Ku Klux Klan, active in the '20s, could return. It would still be fairly easy to stir up emotions against citizens of Mexican, Oriental, and Indian descent. Such potential dangers emphasize the importance of making our children accept and treat all Americans as Americans.

Arthur, in a September 1959 *Durango Herald-News* editorial on the commission's findings, seemed well ahead of his time in his observations. Laws, he noted, only solved part of the problem.[212]

> The commission found that legislation is practical on such subjects, provided the majority can be persuaded to accept the laws. ... No matter what statutes are on the books, people who do not believe in them will find ways to avoid them.
> Did you know that the restaurant sign, "We reserve the right to refuse service to anyone," is an automatic sign to minority groups that they are not wanted? It is important not only to have civil rights legislation but to persuade the people to accept it.

As the years went by, both Morley and Arthur continued to join numerous commissions and boards. They had a hard time turning down anything they believed would help their community or the communities that had influenced them.

Arthur joined Durango's Fine Arts Council and served as president. He served as chairman of the Durango Public Library trustees. He was named to the First National Bank of Durango board of directors, one of the most influential and community-building boards in town.

One of Arthur's deepest concerns was education; while in Minnesota he had served on the governor's fact-finding commission on public schools, and this became a life-long focus.

In the late 1960s Arthur began a six-year stint on the Colorado Advisory Council on Title III, a national program that fostered innovative and exemplary projects in public education. Three of those years he headed the council. President Nixon appointed him to the twelve-member National Advisory Committee on Title III in 1973, and he served eighteen months as chairman.

Arthur wrestled with perennial issues: How much local control should there be? Why is there growing dissatisfaction with public schools? How should drug use and sex education be handled? And a continuing and loud refrain: Are schools being asked to do too much?

"Schools today are assigned duties which are only indirectly connected with the acquisition of knowledge in the academic sense," he wrote in a six-part series titled "A Layman's View of Public Education," which appeared in the *Herald* in January 1972.[213] "Are the schools solely responsible for developing good physical and health habits or do they share the responsibility with parents?"

Overall, he came away impressed with the hard work being done by educators, noting that public schools' problems were more broad in scope and complex than most people outside education realized. People needed time to fully absorb the picture.

"A dominant impression is the number of dedicated and intelligent people that are working on education at all three levels," he wrote. "If progress has been slow, it's due at least in part to the size of the task as indicated by this series."

He concluded by saying, "Coloradans can count themselves lucky, because we do live in a state which puts a premium on good public education and keeps education comparatively free from political pressures."

Southwest Colorado was lucky to have both Morley and Arthur representing it at the state level. It's often difficult for the region to find qualified and willing participants for that duty because it almost always means multiple trips annually to Denver – at best six to seven hours by car, three or more by plane when you figure in airport transportation. It's a huge, financially taxing commitment that generally means multi-day trips. Morley and Arthur had the means to do this, while also bringing a wealth of expertise and clout to whatever committee or cause they served.

Morley's role with the League of Women Voters grew. She served on the local board from 1955-1965 and the state board from 1960-1965. Other state commissions and committees included Anti-Discrimination (1959-1961), Educational Endeavor (1959-1963), and Higher Education (1966-1967). In the mid-1960s Morley served as president of the Southwest Colorado Mental Health Center.[214] In 1968 she was named chair of the Colorado Associated Press board, the first woman to serve in that capacity.

Of course, MCB kept readers informed of her doings. She wrote in a March 1960 editorial:[215]

> The suggestions for improvement in public education that were made by several elementary and secondary teachers who appeared recently before our committee on education endeavor at the state capitol have often been equally vociferously voiced by local teachers. We returned again and again to the question: "Why are administrators paid more than good classroom teachers? Isn't it more important that young people be taught by the best persons available rather than 'promoting' such teachers with an increase in pay to doing office work?"

Morley's varied interests included women's and reproductive issues. In the 1970s she served on two new state commissions, the Population Advisory Council and the Commission on the Status of Women. Gov. John Love appointed her to the population group in 1972.

In 1975, Morley, still and always a Republican, was appointed by Gov. Richard Lamm, a Democrat, to serve on the Colorado Land Use Commission. Interestingly, the news broke while Morley was in Antigua, and Lamm was awaiting her return to make it official.[216] Lamm had worked with Morley on the population council and found her to

Morley's brother-in-law John Cross joins her and his nieces Helen (left) and Elizabeth in Antigua.

be "a woman of competence."[217] Ironically, she replaced Fort Lewis College President Rexer Berndt, an ally of the Ballantines, on the land commission. Berndt had irked Lamm when he'd voted for development of the proposed Beaver Creek ski resort near Vail.

Morley and Arthur believed in the importance of the arts and supported them wholeheartedly with time and money, both locally and statewide. In 1971, in conjunction with the Colorado Council on the Arts and Humanities and by invitation of their Aspen friends Courtlandt and Triny Barnes, they had the honor of co-chairing the Festival of the Arts, which brought around 1,000 people to Aspen.[218]

The Ballantines had established several connections in Aspen, the most prominent being the Barneses. Like Arthur, Courtlandt hailed from New York; he was a graduate of Yale, where Arthur had received his law degree. After establishing a second home in Aspen, Courtlandt was named chairman of the board in 1952 of the newly formed Music Association of Aspen. He remained on the board for a quarter century.

Another good Aspen friend was Bil Dunaway, a 10th Mountain Division soldier during World War II who ended up as owner of the *Aspen Times* in 1956. Like the Ballantines, Dunaway was a believer in freedom of the press and made sure his readers knew what their government was up to. His editorials won countless awards during his ownership from 1956-1994.[219] He also championed and promoted his town, becoming a founding member of a bank and investor in broadcasting stations and a raceway.

Although they put energy into issues beyond their community,

Morley and Arthur never lost sight of Southwest Colorado. They supported anything they believed would improve Durango. Don Mapel has observed this for two generations of Ballantines.

After a stint in the Navy, Mapel arrived in Durango in 1970 with his wife, Sandra, and infant daughter, Meredith. (Meredith, incidentally, later attended Morley's boarding school, Rosemary Choate, with her encouragement.) Don Mapel joined the family business, the regional Coca-Cola distribution company. He also became involved in community issues, one of which was a downtown viability group called Heritage for Tomorrow. Mapel, Fred Kroeger, and others developed an idea for a boulevard along the river to move traffic. The Ballantines helped promote that idea, which never came to fruition. They also got behind the plans for Purgatory ski area and Bodo Industrial Park, which did come about.

The Ballantine way is to push for things on the editorial page, but to work even harder behind the scenes. "I think that's to their credit," Mapel said.[220] "They believe in what they believe in, and then they go after it. I think the Ballantine influence – not only philanthropic but just the general well-being and development of Durango – they were significant, significant contributors."

Both Morley and Arthur grew up in families with a tradition of philanthropy. They continued this practice in Durango, believing it part of their mission. In 1957 Morley and Arthur established the Ballantine Family Fund to give financial assistance to worthy charitable, educational, literary, or scientific nonprofits.[221] The seed money came from Morley, who converted 150 shares of her Minneapolis Star and Tribune Company stock into $5,625.[222]

Original trustees were Morley and Arthur; and family friends James M. Noland, the judge; and Frederic B. Emigh, the attorney who had helped the Ballantines settle in on their arrival in town. The fund's founding papers were signed December 23, 1957, in Emigh's office in Durango.

Through the fund, they planted seeds that would grow. Morley and Arthur knew that small gifts to a wide variety of causes would encourage the development of local nonprofits. But they also focused their support on a few areas such as Fort Lewis College, women's issues, and the arts. Contributions centered on La Plata and Montezuma counties, and some to San Juan County (Silverton), but schools with Ballantine connections such as Harvard, Yale, Rosemary Hall, Concord, and Fountain Valley were beneficiaries as well. In the 1970s, perennial favorites included Planned Parenthood, the Durango Fine Arts Council, and the Fort Lewis College Foundation.

By the late 1980s the fund was helping both the La Plata and San Juan county historical societies, as well as other cherished causes such as the Women's Resource Center in Durango and Crow Canyon Archaeological Center near Cortez. Former *Durango Herald* managing editor Ian "Sandy" Thompson took over as Crow Canyon director in 1986. Thompson was also a Ballantine Family Fund trustee.

In 1987 the trustees were Richard Ballantine, Morley Ballantine, Helen Healy, Elizabeth Ballantine, William Ballantine, Ian Thompson, Don Schlichting, and Jackson Clark Sr.

Through the years, donations tilted toward Southwest Colorado: Native American causes through Fort Lewis, Four Corners Opera, and Music in the Mountains; and several organizations that supported children, women's causes, and education for the underprivileged: the Adult Literacy Center, the Women's Resource Center, the Rape Intervention Team, The Mothers Center of Durango, and the Southwest Safehouse, to name several.

The Ballantine Family Fund received huge financial boosts in 1994 from Morley, and in 1997 from her, Richard, and his wife Mary Lyn. By the 2000s the fund was granting ten times what it had in the late 1980s. In 1999 the fund established its first paid position, naming Nancy Whitson as executive director. Whitson, who for a period was the *Herald's* director of human resources and the fund's director, added a touch of professionalism, creating a website and moving much of the operation online.

The list of beneficiaries continued to grow, and those named here simply scratch the surface. The Ballantines gave in other ways, too, serving on boards, providing advertising space to nonprofits, and sponsoring events privately and through *The Durango Herald*.

The fund envisioned by Morley and Arthur back in 1957 continues, as strong as ever.[223] Its assets are around $5 million. As of 2022, trustees were Richard Ballantine, Elizabeth Ballantine, Mary Jane Clark, Helen Healy, Richard and Mary Lyn's sons Christopher and David, and Karen Sheek. The grant manager was Briggen Wrinkle, who was also director of the Community Foundation Serving Southwest Colorado. Wrinkle took the place of Whitson.

Family and Friends

One of Morley's favorite people was her mother's younger sister, Sarah "Sally" Bates (1903-1985), whom she called Aunt Sal. When Aunt Sal's daughter, Morley's cousin Matilda "Tilly" Lorentz, talked about coming to Durango, the Ballantines gladly obliged. After her freshman year at Carleton College in Minnesota, at age eighteen, Tilly spent the summer of 1957 in Durango. She lived with the Ballantines, who put her to work.

Tilly would spend the next three summers coming to Durango and working at the newspaper. Arthur at one point offered her a permanent job at the *Herald-News*, which ultimately she turned down. Tilly came to love Durango. She molded into the Ballantine family lifestyle, and Morley and Arthur became role models.

Morley's cousin Matilda "Tilly" Lorentz worked at the *Durango Herald-News* in the late 1950s.

Her childhood had been structured, much of it spent in a classroom of some sort, with little time to herself. Morley and Arthur, unlike Tilly's parents, went places with their children. Frequent family outings included many drives (too many, for Elizabeth's way of thinking) up the Junction Creek canyon west of town.

"I came to very quickly realize that the way Arthur and Morley were with their family was the way I wanted to be with my family one day," Tilly said.[224]

In the summer of 1957 Tilly filled in at the *Herald-News* wherever needed – circulation, advertising, and in the back shop. Tilly would constantly pester Arthur with questions as they walked to the paper in the mornings, across the Animas River on a wooden, swinging bridge.

She returned in 1958 and lived with *Herald-News* reporter Nancy Elliott and her son Mike. One of her plum writing assignments that summer was to cover a *LOOK* magazine crew which had come to Durango to put together a piece on Judge James Noland. *LOOK*, owned by Mike Cowles, was doing a series on people who were prime examples of a certain profession. (Noland and his wife, Helen, were Ballantine family friends.) Arthur assigned Tilly to follow the LOOK crew around and write about it.

When she came to Durango in 1959, she drove out in her Jeep with her boyfriend, Don Hoagland, a newspaper reporter in New Jersey. Don returned east, but later in the summer flew back and asked Tilly to marry him. The engagement announcement first appeared in the *Durango Herald-News*. The wedding was set for October in Orangetown, just north of New York City, because that's when the Ballantines would be back East for a publisher's conference. It didn't give Aunt Sal much time to prepare. "Mother was furious," Tilly laughed.

Meanwhile, Elizabeth spent nearly a year in 1958-59 living with Aunt Sal and attending school in Rome, Italy. So when the Ballantine family headed for its somewhat-annual European vacation in the summer of 1959, their daughter was waiting to join them.

Tilly was not the only family relative to work at the newspaper in that period. Arthur's sister Barbara's daughter, Joan Cross, came to work at the *Herald-News* in the 1950s. Morley's brother John's son, John "Jay" Cowles, spent a summer with the Ballantines, working as a news assistant.

The tradition would later continue with Helen Ballantine Healy's daughters, Morley, Katherine, and Sarah Healy; Elizabeth's son, Will; and Sarah Friedman, a granddaughter of Morley's sister Sally. They all worked at the *Herald* from the 1990s to the 2010s.

A nonfamily pipeline extended to Harvard and Yale. Jim Rousmaniere, whose father knew Arthur Ballantine Jr. through Harvard and Oyster Bay connections, contacted *The Durango Herald* during his sophomore year at Harvard. He was given an internship in the summer of 1965.

Rousmaniere drove west, bravely leaving the big-city life he had known in New York and Boston. Still a disheveled teenager, along the way he lost his shoes, likely while camping out. He arrived at the Ballantine home and met Morley.

"I showed up at the door shoeless, explained that I looked forward to a summer in Durango and then asked if perhaps Mr. Ballantine might have some spare shoes for just my first day of work."[225]

For Rousmaniere, everything about this compact environment was new. "A definable, self-contained community with all the operating parts and functions: the government offices, Main Street shops, the train depot, the school. In that setting I began to get a sense of community," he wrote in 2021. "This appreciation was generally enhanced by [Morley Ballantine]. I viewed her as being very much part of the community as both an observer and as a participant."

His time at the *Herald* stoked a passion for journalism. After college and a Peace Corps tour, in 1970 he began a four-decade career in the newspaper business, starting as a reporter in Keene, N.H., and spending time in Baltimore and Washington, D.C. Later, he was editor and publisher of the *Keene Sentinel* in New Hampshire.

More recently, Chase Olivarius-McAllister, the daughter of a Yale classmate of Elizabeth Ballantine's, came to work at the *Herald* in 2011 and stayed as a reporter until 2015.

Morley and Arthur could have invested in a summer getaway cabin at private Electra Lake just north of Durango, as many of their friends did. But they traveled often, and they had their own lake getaway. They

brought their children nearly every summer to Glendalough, the western Minnesota retreat and game
farm the Cowles family had gained when it purchased the *Minneapolis Tribune* in 1941.

At Glendalough, about three hours' drive from
Minneapolis, children could explore, adults could
converse, and family could gather. The main lodge
and several guest cottages were located near the northwest shore of
Annie Battle Lake. There were tennis and croquet courts, and a bowl-
ing alley. Outdoor activities included bass fishing, water skiing, bike
riding, and hiking through the woods.

Nature abounded, making it a special treat away from the city, particularly during the hot summers. Waterfowl populated the lakes and
marsh; Canada geese came through on fall migrations. White-tailed
deer inhabited the forest.

For Richard, Elizabeth, Bill, and Helen, it was a place to meet and
bond with their many cousins; there were sixteen grandchildren in
total. Each of John and Betty Cowles's four children symmetrically had
four children of their own.

"Glendalough was really a haven for me," said Bill Ballantine. "I have good memories of seeing my cousins at those younger ages."[226] He remains grateful to his grandparents for the opportunity to go there, and to work on the farm. Bill came by himself around age thirteen and worked on the farm for several weeks, doing whatever the gamekeeper needed. Chores included feeding and watering the animals, cutting pheasants' wings, looking after the turkeys, and more. He received a small wage.

Richard developed a bond with his Uncle Russell, who was closer to his nephew's age than he was to his sister (Richard's mother) Morley. Both shared a love for mechanical devices, which ultimately meant sports cars. But at Glendalough in the early 1950s, Richard remembers Russell show-

The Cowles grandchildren have many fond memories of their times at Glendalough, ca. 1964. Back row, Richard, Bill, Elizabeth, Tessa Cowles, and Helen; middle, Jay Cowles, Jane Sage Cowles, Margaret Bullitt; front, Fuller Cowles.

ing him how to build locks on the lakeshore, using a fascinating system of wood pieces and tin.[227]

Grandmother Betty Cowles stayed at Glendalough for several weeks each summer, and John would generally show up Friday afternoon and stay through the weekend. Betty assigned rooms to guests in the lodge or cabins. "It was absolutely wonderful to get to know our grandmother and our grandfather, and then particularly our cousins," Richard said. "It was just an idyllic extended family environment."

And there were indoor activities. A jigsaw puzzle was always in process, and card playing often dominated evening action. The adults might play bridge, but the children would play a more active game called "pounce," in which several contestants aggressively raced to stack cards in numerical order. Arthur was one of the few adults who got down on the floor with the children to play.

Newspapers were plentiful, many coming from Minneapolis of course, and were perused in the morning by nearly everyone. Those finding an item of interest would read it aloud, making breakfast a social event. When there was discussion, it was often about politics, the state of the country or world affairs, or stories from John Cowles Sr. about whomever he'd been hobnobbing with.

Helen recalled annual two-week family summer trips to Glendalough. As the youngest of the Ballantine children, she spent time with younger cousins in the designated "children's room."[228] There was a certain decorum to be observed at the adult dining table, and Helen's cousin Jay Cowles, John Jr.'s son, recalled that children weren't permitted at the adult table until age twelve.[229] One time, Helen was sent from the table with her other cousins for laughing too much. At the large, adult dinner table, the older cousins were quizzed by John Cowles Sr. on current events and played more word games.

"Granny" Cowles, perhaps trying to lure her granddaughter Elizabeth for a visit, described the Glendalough scene in a July 1968 letter:[230]

> This place has never been lovelier, so green and lush and peaceful. The weather has been fine, sweaters in the morning, warm, hot sun during the day, water is pleasant. Temp chilly

in the evening and superb for sleeping. The loons call … and the food is good. The record player goes, loads of books and magazines. This weekend probably there will be action on the tennis court with Russell and Gretchen and John and Sage here.

Glendalough would remain in the family until 1990. The death of Morley's mother Betty in 1976 had brought to a close the frequent family get-togethers at Glendalough. When a gathering was planned in 1989, there was no "Granny" Cowles with whom to make arrangements. Morley and her family, consisting of her four children, their spouses, and her eight grandchildren ages one to seven, had to arrange to rent it.

"We're renting it to see if reality measures up to memory, for we spent happy times there while my parents were alive," Morley wrote to family members on June 30, 1989.[231]

After forty-nine years of Cowles Media Company ownership, in 1990 Glendalough was donated to the Nature Conservancy, which in turn passed it on to Minnesota's Department of Natural Resources to become a state park. For the children of John and Betty Cowles, and for the children of Arthur and Morley Ballantine, it was the bittersweet end of an era. No longer could there be private family gatherings, or hunting trips attended by luminaries of business and politics.

The announcement by David Kruidenier, chairman of Cowles Media (and Morley's cousin), came on Earth Day, April 22, 1990. "Glendalough, associated with the company and the Cowles family for almost fifty years, has been dedicated to the enjoyment of wildlife," Kruidenier said. "We're confident that under the Conservancy's stewardship, that objective will continue and this valuable environmental resource will be preserved for future generations."[232]

Said the Nature Conservancy's state director, Margaret Kohring, in 1990: "This is the single most important gift made to the Nature Conservancy in Minnesota."

John Cowles' special hunting grounds, where Dwight Eisenhower visited just before announcing his presidential candidacy in 1952, was converted into the non-motorized Glendalough State Park in 1992. It remains that way today. Interpretive displays and a video at the rebuilt lodge on the north side of Annie Battle Lake detail the history of *Minneapolis Tribune* ownership.

The 1,924-acre state park in Otter Tail County includes 30,000 feet of undeveloped shoreline on five lakes. The woods north and east of Annie Battle Lake were reserved almost entirely for wildlife and the northern hardwoods that dominate. Farm fields were returned to prairie grasses.[233]

Minnesota may be renowned for its lakes, but nearly all their shorelines feature development. Glendalough's are not developed, making this gift particularly special. Visitors can camp, ride a paved bicycle loop, picnic, fish for sunfish and walleye, swim, hike several trails, and look for wildlife – deer, fox, eagles, loons – from numerous observation decks.

Life at Home

When the Ballantines moved to Durango in 1952, most streets were unpaved and very dusty when dry, which was often. Passing cars left trails of dust that would slowly settle. The children enjoyed the bucolic scene when sheep shuffled along the gravel road, kicking up large dust clouds during drives to and from the high country.

"We loved it and so did the children, because the sheep came through in the spring and in the fall, going to and from winter pasture, and it was fun to hear them in town," Morley recalled.[234]

It was a low-tech existence, both because of the times and because of Durango's remoteness. Television signals didn't yet reach Durango because of the surrounding mountains. It took several years before Durango got a signal from Albuquerque, Elizabeth Ballantine recalled.[235]

The family shared one heavy telephone in the hall outside the kitchen; an operator answered when they picked it up. The conversion to dial telephones occurred in 1956.[236] Morley was active politically and socially, while Arthur became, among other things, chairman of the San Juan Basin Boy Scouts in 1956 and 1957.

In September 1956, Hollywood again used the Durango area as a movie backdrop, this time to film *Night Passage* starring Jimmy Stewart and Audie Murphy, two of the biggest names in show business. The Boy Scouts persuaded the two to speak at a function at Smiley Junior High, and Arthur introduced them.

Actor Hugh Beaumont, who played a minor role in *Night Passage*, a year later would create his most famous role as Ward Cleaver on the television show *Leave It to Beaver*. This show, which ran from 1957 to 1963, came to personify the white American suburban experience of the era. It featured a loving and thoughtful stay-at-home mother, an equally loving father who could lay down the law when necessary, and two sons who sometimes found trouble but were never mean and always did what was right in the end. The show continued its popularity in reruns for decades.

Arthur introduces Jimmy Stewart at a Boy Scouts function in 1956. Stewart and Audie Murphy, who also attended the event at Smiley Junior High School, were in town to film *Night Passage*.

Yet, *Leave It to Beaver* did not reflect everyone's reality, and whatever reality existed in that era was changing. In the West, for example, women tended to be more resourceful and independent. It wasn't a total shock for someone such as Morley to express her views or report about her world travels. In the newspaper business, reporters and editors are immersed in controversy, and a thick skin is a job requirement. Morley developed a thick skin and a stiff backbone.

Morley and Arthur shared decisions. He ran the business and dealt with finances; she ran the household and looked after the children, always with household help. The opportunities and journalism in Durango, with abundant chances for public service, appealed to both. They made the most of those opportunities.

Wherever they were, Morley and Arthur knew how to navigate social circles, and they made friends quickly and easily upon arrival in Durango. Among their first good friends were the Clarks – Jackson Sr. and Mary Jane, their son, Jackson II, and their daughter, Antonia. The

Clarks owned Jackson Hardware when the Ballantines arrived.

Jackson Sr.'s mother, Marguerite Jackson Clark, enjoyed hosting large parties in the legendary "Big Room" of her home at the top of Farmington Hill. That might be where the Ballantines and Clarks met. "I'm sure my mother-in-law had a party for them," Mary Jane recalled.[237] On that or another occasion, Morley and Arthur both wrote their names in lipstick on the kitchen wall and ceiling – a practice encouraged by Marguerite. The names and the kitchen wall still exist, nearly seventy years later. Many a highball, martini, and Manhattan was consumed in the Big Room.

"People were well-dressed and respectable," Elizabeth Ballantine said, "but with a wild side."

Mary Jane, who gave birth to daughter Antonia in April 1953, borrowed maternity clothes from Morley. Mary Jane and Morley played bridge together on Wednesday nights when their husbands were at meetings. Arthur and Jackson Sr. became comrades for several causes, including Fort Lewis College improvements.

Newspaper publishers know better than to expect everyone to like them. Among Arthur's good friends was Bob Duthie, a local attorney who'd moved to Durango in 1950 after law school.

Duthie found the locals to be provincial and had some difficulty attracting clients. It helped Duthie to marry a local woman, Mary Connors, in 1951. The perceived snubbing from locals gave him some affinity for the Ballantines' role as newcomers.[238]

Duthie became a member of the Elks Lodge, a popular club on East Second Avenue where locals would congregate for a couple of post-work drinks in the late afternoon before heading home for dinner. Duthie and a couple of other Elks nominated Arthur for membership. The anonymous vote was cast, with each member dropping a small white (for inclusion) or black (for rejection) ball into a container. Whether it was from jealousy, or maybe something the *Herald* printed, two or three members dropped in black balls, and that's all it took. Arthur was rejected.

Their social web reached far and wide, and they could find family or friends from coast-to-coast, and continent-to-continent (mostly Europe). This network included lawyers, politicians, academicians, artists, and even one Hollywood writer-turned-Wyoming rancher.

Like Arthur, Otis Carney (1922-2006) was an East Coast scion, an Ivy League (Princeton) graduate, and a World War II veteran. Both ended up as reporters at the Minneapolis papers around 1947, Arthur at the *Tribune* and Carney at the *Star*. Carney didn't last long in newspapers, but he and Arthur, and their families, remained friends wherever they settled. Like many of their peers, Arthur and Otis both ended up in the West.

For Carney, his wife Teddy, and their three boys, it was Beverly Hills, Calif., for several years. Carney was a well-known television screenwriter and novelist. In the early 1960s, Arthur and Morley apparently pitched to him the concept of a TV show based on a Colorado newspaper. And apparently, he took it seriously. Carney wrote to Arthur and Morley in March 1961.[239]

We often think of you both and hope that we will have a chance to come Durango-way again. It was such fun catching a glimpse of you here. ... I'd like to be able to tell you that we could do a series about the Durango newspaper on television, but after much development in arriving at a very workable format, with interesting people, we're told by the networks that it doesn't have enough adventure or what they call "situation comedy." Next year we are only going to be seeing adventure and situation comedy out of the idiot box, I'm afraid.

In 1963 the Carneys purchased a cattle ranch in the outback of Wyoming, and eventually moved away from the bustle of Beverly Hills. Arthur and Morley went to visit once in Wyoming, but it was a little too far afield and rugged for their tastes.

The 1950s and 1960s were an era of profligate drinking and smoking of cigarettes. Perhaps the modern reader not old enough to have experienced the 1960s has watched the popular television show *Mad Men* (which aired from 2007-2015) and thus has some reference point to the subject.

Ashtrays were ubiquitous, from homes to offices to automobiles to airplanes. Cigarette smoking, seen frequently in Hollywood movies and on TV, was, to borrow a word from the times, "cool." Alcohol bottles weren't uncommon in private offices. At a lunch or dinner business meeting, a drink or more was almost an understood necessity.

Newspapermen and women were no exception. The stereotypical, gritty news reporter smoked and drank to kill the pain of digging up the truth and allowing a career to consume his or her private life. That was the stereotype, but there was truth in it.

Smoking and drinking prevailed in the lives of Morley and Arthur Ballantine. They both smoked up to three packs of unfiltered Camel cigarettes during a typical day. Perhaps they, like others of their era, were influenced by the use of Camels by news broadcaster Edward R. Murrow. "I'd walk a mile for a Camel," the brand's slogan professed.

"I remember the smell of tobacco in the car and on trains when we traveled," Elizabeth Ballantine said. "It was okay to smoke on airplanes

and everyone did."[240]

Morley never took herself too seriously and shared her defeats, Elizabeth said.[241] Her attempts to quit smoking were among those defeats. She revealed her transgressions repeatedly in editorials. On June 22, 1962, for example, she announced that she had once again smoked her last cigarette and was girding to face the battle against weight gain. But then, two years later, on June 30, 1964, she identified herself, along with several other *Herald* employees, as "ex-non-smoking" writers. She complained that tar guard filters used to lessen nicotine intake had not been helpful.

Later, in the 1990s, Morley again tried to quit and announced to readers that she had. When she picked up the habit again, she was too embarrassed to buy cigarettes in La Plata County. So she asked son-in-law Paul Leavitt to send cigarette packs to her.

Late afternoon meetings to discuss work issues were a good time for a drink. Sometimes this would be at a bar, but often this was over at the Ballantine home, where Scotch or bourbon was the base. Some referred to Arthur's strong concoctions as "Ballantine Bombs."

The children were allowed to drink – in moderation – and learned to hold their own in adult conversations.[242] A drink meant that it was time to discuss news or politics, tell stories, share humor and fun. "We knew to recognize the telling signs of inebriation when voices grew shrill and insistent," Elizabeth Ballantine said. "And of course among our relatives were alcoholics who joined self-help groups. So we understood the consequences of indulgence."

On their travels, Arthur and Morley made sure to take along a bottle of Scotch or vodka – just in case they arrived somewhere late. The hotel bar might be closed, or the liquor store too far away.

The Ballantines made it a habit to have visitors at their house after work, any time after about 5:00 p.m. These occasions would begin with a round of Arthur's strong drinks. He had a sense of humor and an engaging personality that drew out people's thoughts and beliefs. He always had a good story to share and enjoyed listening to others.

Arthur wouldn't pay attention as his filterless cigarettes burned down. He'd scratch the top of his head and ashes would drop all over him, oblivious to it all. His hair was often unkempt. He cared little about his outward appearance.

Bev Neal, the wife of Tommy Neal, who worked as a *Herald* sportswriter before serving as state representative from 1965-1970, predated Arthur and Morley in Durango. She wrote in 2009:[243]

> Arthur and Morley came to Durango when Tommy and I were no longer newbies. I was always in awe of their intellect, but Morley [and Arthur] had the ability to make me feel like I had things to say that were right and true. At Ballantine parties, Arthur would make a point of coming to sit on the floor next to the person who looked lost and maybe had no one to talk to. Morley made time and attention not just for the [Gov.] John Loves and [Rep.] Wayne Aspinalls of the world (dates me, doesn't it?) but also for the rest of us. She made us feel wiser and worth hearing out.

Morley and Arthur were frequent party-goers on weekends, often to promote some local cause, and their circle increased. They began hosting parties as well, and the children recall many instances where they'd be introduced to their parents' friends. "They loved to give parties," Helen said. "We would always be trotted out to shake hands and say hello to everybody at the start of the evening – and then go disappear. And we were fine with that."

The Ballantines' influence in the community continued to grow. Access to the media was important, and that brought politicians, business people, and others to the house.

In 1957 the Clarks sold the hardware store and bought into the Pepsi-Cola business, creating the Jackson David Bottling plant. At the same time, they created Toh-Atin Gallery to sell Native American handicrafts that Jackson Sr. was given in payment for Pepsi on the Navajo Reservation.[244]

The Ballantines and Clarks skied and took frequent trips together around the Southwest. In 1961 they traveled through the Navajo Reservation to Window Rock and Page, Ariz., over Thanksgiving. They stopped for a picnic along the way, then took a walk along the nearly completed Glen Canyon Dam.

At a small restaurant on Thanksgiving evening, the sometimes-frugal Arthur told the stunned children: "You guys all have to order hamburgers." Out of earshot of Arthur, Jackson II complained: "Who ever heard of a hamburger for Thanksgiving?" Antonia said her brother whined about it all the way home, until Mary Jane finally relented: "If you quit complaining, I'll make you a turkey dinner when we get home."

Jackson Clark II and Bill Ballantine were just a few months apart in age and became friends. For Bill's birthday, the party would start at the swimming pool in the basement of the old high school on East Twelfth Street, which became the district administration building. It would continue at the Ballantines' house on West Third Avenue for cake and games.

In the spring of 1960, the Ballantines purchased a house at 175 West Park, just a couple blocks away from their West Third Avenue home. After several months of remodeling, which included a major addition of a garage topped by a recreation room, they moved into the West Park house in the fall of 1960.

With that move, they decided to donate their old house at 1689 West Third Avenue, valued at $15,000, to St. Mark's Episcopal Church as a rectory. It was named the Morley Cowles Ballantine Rectory. The Ballantines added $10,000 to the gift, bringing the total donation to $25,000. St. Mark's then sold its old rectory and used those funds to reduce debt on the parish hall it had constructed in 1957 under Rev. Philip Hawley, priest from 1945 to 1967. Arthur was confirmed as a church member on May 3, 1962, during a ceremony at St. Mark's.[245] The parish hall was renovated in 2004 to add modern heating, cooling, and electrical equipment. Morley continued as a member of St. Mark's until her death in 2009.

An outdoor pool at 175 West Park was ready for play in the summer of 1961. The pool was the focus of many a gathering, but also provided midday recreation. Arthur and Morley often left the *Herald* at lunch and crossed the swinging bridge spanning the Animas River to reach home. It was about a five-minute trek. Then they'd don swim gear, do a few laps in the pool, fit in a quick meal, and return to work.[246]

The Ballantines used the pool as a social gathering spot, and after a dip, talk would often turn to politics or issues of the day. The Clarks were frequent guests. Jackson Sr. was more conservative than Arthur; for example, he was a national delegate for Arizonan Barry Goldwater at the 1964 Republican National Convention. While Goldwater represented the more conservative wing of the party, Arthur and Morley were both progressive Republicans, considered the Eastern liberals. Goldwater was later given credit for reforming the party and paving the way for Ronald Reagan's 1980 presidential victory. But in 1964, Goldwater was crushed by Lyndon Johnson, whom the *Herald* had endorsed despite his being a Democrat.

"There was a lot of discussion. And it was all friendly, too," Mary Jane Clark recalled. "It was easy to disagree and talk about it. It was very civilized. That was such a contrast to what it's like today."

Even the children got involved, whether they wanted to or not. "Morley always talked to children like they were adults," Jackson II said. "She would ask them serious questions and allow them to participate in the conversation, which I thought was good."

Jackson earned a journalism degree from the University of Colorado in 1973. He was an "unemployed ski instructor" not long after that and accepted a temporary role as *Durango Herald* sports editor. Jackson recalled Arthur as a kind man who was constantly pushing his glasses up his nose; he never attacked people with malice, either in print or in person.

"You'd think you got reprimanded, but you weren't sure," Jackson joked.

The Ballantine family never hesitated to help the less fortunate, the Clarks said. They remembered how Bill Ballantine discovered that a boy about his age was living on the hill above them, so Bill befriended him and began taking food to him. Arthur and Morley investigated a little further and discovered the mother of the boy, Ray, had eleven children and was working as a prostitute. They lived in a ramshackle house in Santa Rita, a cluster of such homes south of town that has since disappeared. Bill was ten or eleven at the time; he remained friends with Ray until his friend's premature death in his twenties.[247]

Arthur helped the woman and her son as much as he could. "That was Arthur," Mary Jane said.

Antonia graduated from Durango High School in 1970 and headed to Utah for college. During her freshman year she volunteered at the Planned Parenthood clinic in Salt Lake City. Morley was very supportive of Antonia and would ask her questions about her experiences. "She really fostered that in women," Antonia said. "I think that became apparent through the decades in Durango, but back in the 1960s that was certainly the influence she had on me."[248]

Salons

As The Enlightenment era gathered momentum in 18th century France, the concept of the "salon" flourished. The idea was to gather both men and women in an exchange of ideas. A host would invite people, set the agenda, and run the meeting. Up to that point women had been mostly excluded from philosophical and political discussion because it generally occurred in places – cafés and parliament, for example – where women were not allowed. For women, it was a chance – finally – to speak their minds.

Overarching concepts of The Enlightenment were religious tolerance, personal liberty, and improvement of human nature. These salons gave birth to ideas that spurred the Declaration of Independence and the French Revolution.[249] Later, writer Gertrude Stein's salons in 1920s Paris became renowned.

Arthur and Morley took the salon concept and brought it to Durango. They knew it was important to stay in touch with the pulse of the community, to talk to leaders in their fields on a regular basis. To understand how people were feeling, what issues they cared about. And they also realized that they could play an important role by cultivating relationships, by gathering important and thoughtful experts and having them bandy about ideas.

Several times a year Morley and Arthur invited various locals, often those of influence or experts in a certain field, to their home and had

Morley and Arthur relished wide-ranging discussions with fellow Durangoans.

them talk on a subject for perhaps three to five minutes. A general discussion would follow. Hors d'oeuvres and cocktails were provided for guests – to stimulate conversation, of course. Somewhere around a dozen people usually attended.

Topics ranged widely, everything from the effect of a spike in gas prices, to investment in China, to the local college, to tourism. Subjects could be timely or eternal, straightforward or philosophical.

"Those were really, truly salons, and an opportunity to learn and meet people across different parts of the community," said Andrew Gulliford, a Fort Lewis College professor. "You learned from each other very much in a kind of classroom/seminar setting."

Guests ranged from the highly influential, such as Air Force four-star Gen. Ronald Fogleman in later years, to an investment banker or just someone who seemed to have something interesting to offer.

These salons served as a thought-provoking influence around the community that wouldn't have happened with the newspaper in the hands of someone else, said Pam Patton, a long-time friend. They provided a valuable give-and-take in an atmosphere that didn't allow someone to be boorish or to dominate the discussion.

"You look around the room and there's all these people that you don't know, but (the Ballantines) know them all," Patton said. "Or you sort of know them … but they're not on your social schedule."

Growing Up a Ballantine

Morley and Arthur spent many days side-by-side in the office, their desks facing away at a right angle. Morley focused a bit more on writing, Arthur on the business side, but their spheres intermingled constantly. "Our life has continued to center happily around *The Durango Herald*," Arthur wrote in 1971. "Our mutuality of interest both at home and professionally has been rewarding."[250]

Bill, Helen, Elizabeth, and Richard Ballantine with their parents in 1965.

When they arrived home from work their attention usually turned to the four children, each with different interests and needs and issues. Around town, there was little separation between the Ballantines and the community. The children learned to ski at the small Third Avenue Ski Hill, greatly improved in 1955 by Colton Chapman, Dolph Kuss, and Arvo and Wilho Matis.[251] The four Ballantine siblings attended elementary and junior high schools in town.

There is disagreement among Arthur and Morley's children as to how much animosity the family endured from townsfolk who may have been jealous of their wealth and position. Richard does not recall any such animosity, but both Elizabeth and Helen do.

One neighborhood boy would hurl rocks and taunts of "communist" at Elizabeth, who was known to her family and friends as Betty, as she rode her bicycle to school. The Ballantines were perceived as being too left wing by some conservative Durangoans, particularly the active and vocal John Birch element. Helen had a similar experience with a classmate. At times, Elizabeth felt like her family was in an alien spaceship in Durango, yet all four children had plenty of friends and cliques to hang out with.

The children of Morley and Arthur all recall their house as an active place, with people in and out, and frequent dinner gatherings. Their parents were often out of town, tending to the state and even national committees they joined, and traveling for fun and visits. Elizabeth, by then a twenty-year-old college student, was working for US Sen. Peter Dominick in D.C. in the summer of 1968. Morley's nephew John "Jay" Cowles, just fourteen, was living at the Ballantines' Durango home and working as an intern at the *Herald*. An August 9 letter from Morley to Elizabeth gives a hint of this bustle:[252]

> We're going to Santa Fe next week for two nights but only on one can we go to the opera, unfortunately. ... When we return [Washington, D.C., journalist] Helene Monberg will be here and we plan to spend a day with her and Fred Kroeger and Sam Maynes touring area water projects. ... We still plan to go to Glendalough on Saturday, August 24, returning on August 27. ... Hope it works out that you will join us. ... Fiesta [Days] parade is in the morning and today is Jay's last day on the job. We have a box for the rodeo tomorrow afternoon and whether we will have guests is as yet an uncertainty. ... Fight the good fight and have fun, dear girl.

Having children provided plenty of both opportunities and excuses for getting outdoors in the San Juan Mountains. Wrote Morley in 1957, "The advantages of small-town life in the Rockies have been many for we enjoy skiing, riding, going on pack trips, etc., together."[253]

Ski outings included trips to the top of Coal Bank Pass, where families would unload, ski down along the power line poles to Mill Creek Lodge, and then head back up for the next run. Sometimes the Ballantines would spend Saturday night at the lodge when it was owned by the Scobies, Art and Rose, the latter of whom entertained on the piano. The children could also ski in town at Chapman Hill, then called Third Avenue Ski Hill. Before Purgatory ski area opened in 1965, the Ballantines also took trips to Stoner, a long-since-defunct ski area northeast of Dolores.

Elizabeth recalled plenty of family summer picnics along Junction Creek just northeast of town, and family photos show her and Richard having fun wading in the creek on sunny days. "Daddy would give us five cents if we would get wet in the stream, dunking our bodies and heads," she said.[254]

Each Christmas season the Ballantines would join several other families – the Elliotts, Schobers, Clarks, and others – and head up Junction Creek to chop down yuletide trees. Following the tree cutting, the families would gather at someone's home for lunch.

Athletics were not an emphasis or forte, but the family did play tennis together at the elementary school courts, the children taking lessons from private instructor Mary Ruth Bowman (1927-2020). Bowman moved to Durango from North Carolina in 1959 with her husband, Frank, and strove to give girls and women equality in sports. "I've been a women's libber since I opened my mouth," she once said.[255] Mary Ruth Bowman was a family friend, and partner in several causes with Morley, including the League of Women Voters.

The Ballantine pool was one of only two in town at private homes. The other was indoors. So it was a big deal for the Ballantine friends, and for the children's playmates, to get a chance to come swimming.

Barb Eggleston Conn, a classmate of Elizabeth's in kindergarten, remembers several aspects that were different about the Ballantines and their home, which she always found to be a welcoming place. When she showed up the first time to swim, Arthur and Morley were at work. It was still a bit unusual in the early 1960s for married women to be working. The Ballantine housekeeper was there, and that was another first for young Barb.[256]

"The majority of women were homemakers," Conn said. "Their house had a whole different dynamic."

Most Durangoans perceived that the Ballantines came "with wealth" from "back East," even though Morley grew up in the Midwest and Arthur had spent six years in the Midwest before Durango. That was fair to some degree, as Arthur was a native Easterner and Ivy Leaguer, and Morley had spent several school years in the East. But it discounted Morley's solid Midwestern roots and mores.

Conn, a native of Durango, remembered standing in the Ballantine dining room, looking up at the wall, and being shocked to see a nude picture. "That is not what our typical homes had in them!" Several girls would have a slumber party in the rec room upstairs, and Conn recalled a sock-footed Arthur checking in to wish them goodnight.

Her friend Elizabeth would disappear for a week or two on travel vacations, even for a year the time she went to live in Italy with her great-aunt. But when Elizabeth returned she would "just fit right back in," Conn said. "She didn't boast about what she was doing." Different groups of girls would hang out, go to movies, ride bikes, play tennis, get a nickel Coke at Parson's Drug, and Elizabeth was often in the mix. "When she was around she did stuff with us."

Later, after eighth grade at Smiley Junior High, when Elizabeth went to boarding school "back East," that was different, too. Conn didn't recall other classmates doing anything similar, other than a few boys heading to military school. They'd still see Elizabeth in the summer. They may have had expanded worldviews from travel and political connections, but, "The whole family was down to earth," Conn said.

Outdoor activities, for one, kept the children down to earth. During summers the children would often spend a week or two at Ah! Wilderness, a guest ranch along the train tracks in the Animas River canyon. Elizabeth and Helen loved the horses.

As Morley and Arthur joined committees and boards both near and far, their time at home decreased. Nannies looked after the children when they were gone, either at work or meetings or traveling. Both Morley and Arthur kept their children on edge by including any and all family triumphs, tribulations, and traumas in their editorials.

Middle school years can be among the most stressful as one strives for social acceptance. Elizabeth, referred to as "our seventh-grade daughter," prepared to host her first party in fall 1960 at age twelve.[257] Arthur was stunned, MCB wrote, when he noticed Elizabeth's two best friends weren't on the proposed guest list. Imagine having this conversation in the public domain:

Helen was especially fond of riding horses.

"Daddy," she wailed, "They aren't in the seventh grade. I can't have them. They know all about it. They didn't have me to their parties. And these others I just have to have."

"You mean you don't ask your best friends because they're in the eighth grade and you're not?" the head of the family queried, sensing his first strange sociological phenomenon in teenage party-giving. "Why do you 'have to have' some of the others?"

She mumbled something.

"Oh," he said, brightening. "You mean you want to have them so that in case they give a party, they 'have to have' you. It's kind of insurance for your future social life. Why didn't you tell me?"

"Oh Daddy," she wailed again. "That sounds so crude.

What would Anne's mother say if she heard you?"

It went on, with Elizabeth requesting her younger siblings be removed from the house during the party, which would include dancing.

> "Not to have your brother and sister? They ask you to their parties!" Father sounded stunned with horror at her point of view. "Besides, I want to dance with Helen as well as with you."
>
> "Dance with me?" [Elizabeth's] voice rose to alarming heights. "You're not going to come, are you? Please Daddy."
>
> "Not come to a party in my own home? Of course, I'm coming. I want to meet all your friends whom I don't know and your mother wants to dance with Bill."
>
> "The party's off," [Elizabeth] told him coldly. "You forget that times have changed since you were thirteen. We're not in the Middle Ages now."

Ultimately the party was back on, and Bill and Helen were allowed to come and would help clean up. The problem of not having enough chairs was left to Elizabeth to figure out. MCB concluded, "And there now the matter rests. We do the cooking tomorrow. But I wish some experienced, wise parent had written a small handbook on teenage party giving. When you've been brought up yourself in the Middle Ages, as you're told repeatedly, it's difficult to know where to begin."

Helen addressed these many unwelcome insights into the children's lives at Morley's memorial service:[258]

> We frequently rebelled about my mother's penchant for writing about our lives in her columns. How would you like to grow up knowing that every trauma about boyfriends, dates for dances, and sibling arguments was going to appear in the paper, the names changed, supposedly to protect the innocent? … We have often wondered how many young men learned they were not the love of Elizabeth's life from reading the newspaper.

We could never convince my mother (and father) to stop writing about us. They loved to bring others into their lives, through the newspaper, through frequent parties, endless volunteer causes and campaigns.

The children wandered freely around town, and sometimes played for hours on boulders behind the house. A trail up the hillside off Seventeenth Street took them to the Crestview neighborhood, where construction of houses was just starting. In the mornings Elizabeth rode a blue girl's bicycle up West Third Avenue to Needham Elementary. She rode it home and back for lunch. "The uneven cracks in the sidewalk, some quite deep, around trees and driveways had to be carefully navigated."[259]

Work always followed Morley and Arthur home, and it wove itself into the fabric of family life. Arthur periodically received calls from an irate reader or advertiser. Sometimes callers would complain their afternoon paper had not yet arrived, and if the subscriber wasn't too far away, one of the children would be dispatched on a bike to deliver it.

When the parents came home each evening at around 5:30, their days were just different enough that they'd compare notes, Richard Ballantine recalled. Arthur might have been working on an issue involving business matters, for instance, while Morley was meeting with someone and writing a story. They'd sit in the living room with a cocktail and talk shop, encouraging the children to contribute. More discussion over newspaper stories and issues bubbling in the community might ensue at the dinner table, where no one was allowed to take a phone call.

"That's how the four of us gained an appreciation for small-town journalism and an idea of the role of its owners," Richard said. "The two of them were really partners."

The children often walked to the *Herald* office, then at 1022 Main Avenue. Today's Durangoans know this as the location of Carver Brewing Co. They'd walk inside, past Don Schlichting's boxer Penny, who slept under Don's desk, toward their parents' adjacent desks. Another few steps took them into the darkroom and to the linotype machines,

past where hot melting lead was made into type, on to the counters for advertising layout, and finally the big, black press. Don had an important role as assistant to the publishers.

Sometimes the children would attend Saturday evening movies at the Kiva Theater, then end up at the *Herald* as the Sunday paper was coming off the press. They'd help the Johnston family, which ran the mailroom, by stuffing inside sections and advertising into the main section. The Johnstons had several duties, including janitorial, and lived in an apartment above the *Herald*. But instead of returning home, the Ballantine children would fall into the Johnstons' station wagon and sleep as they drove south to New Mexico or Arizona to camp on the Navajo Reservation. They'd return home Sunday afternoon, sometimes about when Morley and Arthur were returning from a weekend away.

Usually, each holiday season the Ballantines would go as a family to some party. The children were encouraged to circulate and find out news bits from conversations or what they overheard. "We loved finding out snippets of gossip to bring back to them," Elizabeth said.

The children contributed to the *Herald* in myriad ways. Among their school-era newspaper jobs: Richard and Bill had paper routes, Elizabeth wrote for the *Herald*, including "Junior High Jottings" in 1962, and Helen delivered missing papers.

Richard's paper route, which took him three miles out of town on Junction Creek Road, was his most memorable *Herald* job. Maybe not for the work itself, but for the opportunity it presented. In that era, when you turned fourteen you could operate, on public roads, a motorized two-wheeler with an engine up to eight horsepower. Richard wanted a Cushman scooter, the hot ride of the day. So he arranged a deal with Arthur, where they each paid for half; Arthur would foot the bill up front, and Richard would take a paper route to pay for his half. Arthur arranged for a bank loan for Richard, who paid back the loan from newspaper subscription proceeds he earned, taking $13 every two weeks to the bank teller.

"Every boy wanted to have wheels," Richard said.[260] "And to be able to get wheels – even if it was just two wheels – at age fourteen was very appealing."

Prior to the conversion to

Richard Ballantine used earnings from his newspaper route to buy his first set of wheels.

offset presses, Richard also worked a summer in the newspaper's casting room, where used lead type was melted down and molded into heavy cylinders – called "pigs" – before being recycled into the next lines of type. With the heavy lead fumes this procedure produced, it was a toxic work environment that wouldn't be allowed to exist today.

Bill, often with Helen, on Saturday evenings stuffed comics and other inserts in the Sunday papers. He later took a bicycle delivery route. At around age fourteen he was allowed to operate the drill press in the pressroom, another task someone that young wouldn't be allowed to do today.

Morley and particularly Arthur were eager to push their children from the comforts of their childhood home. It was maybe okay for them to return later, but they needed to see and experience the world beyond Durango. Arthur even told Tilly, Morley's cousin, that it was time for her to move on when she suggested she liked Durango so much she could live there forever.

"Tilly's observation about Arthur pushing his children out of the nest of Durango is true," Elizabeth Ballantine said. "He did not think we should work at the paper (except episodically) and encouraged us to seek careers and direction elsewhere. Durango was too small a pond."

The four children all left for boarding schools when they reached ninth grade. Whether this was negotiable or not, none ever tried to argue. They all went along with the plan. Arthur explained this parenting philosophy in a 1966 column acknowledging Richard's twenty-first birthday as a coming of age.[261]

> A theme in our household has been, "You must do what we, rather than you, think best, at least until you graduate from high school. You don't know enough yet to be sure you enjoy history and hate math, whether early marriage is preferable to playing the field." Despite many compromises in a household where children are treated as individuals from the day they are born, this point of view has had a fair number of victories.

Travel

As focused on Durango as they became, Morley and Arthur – and their children – had plenty of opportunities to expand their worldview. They loved to travel, and they'd get away from Durango several times a year. Sometimes it was to visit family, frequently at Glendalough or in New York, but often it was for pleasure. Europe was a common destination, and sometimes they hit multiple continents on a single trip. And for simple relaxation, Antigua was always a welcome getaway.

Morley and Arthur enjoying a gondola ride in Venice, in 1959.

In spring 1955, with nine-year-old fourth-grader Richard and six-year-old first-grader Elizabeth in tow, they boarded the *M.S. Saturnia* in New York City and sailed across the Atlantic.[262] In Paris they visited relatives, including the Fergusons, John and Helen (Arthur Jr.'s sister, also called Peggy). John, a lawyer, was working for the US State Department. In Florence they met the Bullitts, John and Sally (Morley's

Morley and Arthur enjoyed traveling with friends, seen here in Acapulco with Lee and Virginia Myers and Bob and Carolyn Haas in February 1965.

sister). While the children stayed with relatives, Morley and Arthur continued on to the Middle East. One stop was at the Great Pyramids of Egypt, where Morley, with Arthur at her side, started a three-generation-long tradition to be photographed on a camel in front of a pyramid.

In February-March 1956, Morley and Arthur flew to Antigua, the Caribbean island where John and Betty Cowles had established a vacation home several years before. After some rest and relaxation, the rest of the trip was more of a look at social conditions.

"On the way back, we are going to stop at the Dominican Republic, an independent country under a dictator," Arthur wrote in a *Herald-News* editorial.[263] "We are also going to Haiti to which we are lured by jazz and voodoo. Then we are going to stop in Havana, Cuba, a city which has always fired our imagination."

They didn't keep their travels a secret, and it might have rubbed some Durangoans the wrong way that they were gallivanting around the globe. But the Ballantines enjoyed writing about foreign lands, and the travel vignettes served another, perhaps greater purpose: introducing a fairly isolated community to cultural and political differences in the bigger world. The globe was shrinking, intercontinental trade becoming a greater economic factor, and what happened in a small country in Asia (oh, say Vietnam?) might one day affect them.

Despite a few bumps in the road, within ten years after arriving in Durango, Arthur and Morley seemed fairly content in their corner of the world. In an editorial about a 1961 trip, Arthur talked about the great things New York City had to offer. But he also explained that many New Yorkers didn't have time or inclination to enjoy these cultural events.

"When a Durangoan makes a trip, he can get just as much pleasure from the big city as the natives, with the added knowledge he can get away from the bustle and tensions," Arthur wrote in November 1961.[264]

Family travels were almost always documented in the *Herald* pages, sometimes simply with descriptions of places they enjoyed, and other times with a Durango or state angle of some sort. March 1960 found the family in Central America. Morley wrote this somewhat tongue-in-cheek "Note to the Governor," who was Democrat Steve McNichols at the time, from San Jose, Costa Rica:[265]

> There's a message for all of us in how Costa Rica finances its governmental operations for some two million people, Steve, and on the unlikely chance that you aren't familiar with its program, we thought we'd raise it with you. … Listen to this! Schools are maintained by the profits of the government distillery. It makes excellent rum, we've discovered, so it's not surprising the school program is moving ahead by leaps and bounds.

Four children were difficult to travel with, particularly abroad, so often they took just two. Bill was about eleven or twelve and Helen nine or ten when Morley and Arthur took them on a far-flung journey to three continents. The three-month trip took the children out of school during the early 1960s.

Morley and Arthur joined friends on a horseback trip through Chicago Basin in 1967.

They started in South America, took a ship to Africa, and then toured Europe before heading home, as Helen recalled. She and Bill, to keep up with their studies, constantly kept journals and did schoolwork. Richard and Elizabeth had gone to boarding school, so for Bill and Helen, "that was our big trip," Helen said.

In the summer of 1966, the entire family did travel to Europe – Helen was already there after her ninth-grade year in Switzerland – and stayed together in a farmhouse in Vaucluse, a farming region surrounded by mountains in southeastern France. The "entire" family included not only Morley and Arthur and the four children, but also a niece and nephew, plus Fort Lewis senior Pat Anesi, family friend Ria Delaney, Morley's mother Betty Cowles, and Morley's Aunt Sally. ABJr. wrote of the toil of keeping house.[266]

> Spellbinding as the attractions are, the supporting of from nine to twelve American citizens demands daily attention. The Safeways, City Markets, and Shur-Valus providing household shopping in an hour are non-existent. … A summer abroad in a rented house is a marvelous experience but let no one fool you. One half the waking hours [are] spent in keeping the operation going.

They explored the Southwest Colorado mountains as well. One highlight was an early September 1967 horseback trip through Chicago Basin, into the heart of what would be designated the Weminuche

Wilderness in 1975. That was before throngs of backpackers populated this spectacular high country. Their five-day loop began at the train tracks along the Animas River at Elk Park, headed up Elk Creek to the Continental Divide, then wound south and back through Chicago Basin to Needleton, and along the Animas River back to Cascade Creek.

The large group included Morley and Arthur; Elizabeth, Bill, and Helen; several of the Barker family (owners of the Strater Hotel); Dr. Dean Furry and his wife Nancy; and well-known cattle rancher and outdoorsman from Mancos, Bill Crader, in the lead.[267] Morley described the trip over Columbine Pass:[268]

> It was perfectly beautiful, lunching just below the summit of the pass, and then words become inadequate to describe the first glimpse of the high peaks in Chicago Basin and the mountain tops stretching into the distance, as far as the eye can see, from the narrow and steep Columbine pass. The beauty is breathtaking and then when awareness of exactly how steep and narrow the trail is down the side comes, all breath is gone.

Those who venture into this oft-tracked area in modern times will read this MCB observation with envy: "We ... were passed by a solitary backpacker. He was the only individual outside of our party we saw during the five days."

Her final thought: "This country in which we live is incredibly grand and everybody who can, should see it."

Later in September 1967, Morley and Arthur, this time with Richard as part of the group, explored Canyonlands National Park, established just three years previously. Morley wrote about their trip into the Needles District, featuring headlines such as, "New Canyonlands Park Indescribably Handsome, Unpopulated." We can laugh ironically at such headlines now, but don't think that MCB was unaware of the future. In fact, a "sub" headline read: "Time To See It Is Now, Before Paving And People Come."[269]

At the time, the area featured one Cold War-related danger unknown to the modern visitor. Guided Athena missiles fired from Green River, Utah, and heading to White Sands, N.M., would drop their first-stage booster rockets into the area of Indian Creek State Park, adjacent to Canyonlands. A sign warned visitors to vacate during the launch dates.

A College Degree

Morley's determination to gain a college degree, sidelined by an early marriage, frequent moves, and then family responsibilities and a busy career, was not fulfilled until her children had left the household or were on the verge of doing so.[270]

After the children had all reached their teens, or close, Morley tried again. Now approximately a junior, she started in 1963 by taking two summer classes at Fort Lewis, which a year previously had been deemed a four-year institution (and might explain the timing). MCB wrote in a *Herald* editorial in July 1963:[271]

> Oh, this back-to-school business! It's hard work. When you go to college when you should, right after high school, it's easy to become totally engrossed in your work. … Your parents fuss if they think you're spending even a little time thinking about your social life, say, or what to wear next weekend.

With family responsibilities, the house to look after, and a newspaper to run, Morley's challenge was immense. Time was not her friend, nor were the children, who, she wrote, didn't seem to want to discuss the flooding of the Euphrates in 4000 B.C. or ancestral Puebloan culture. Her lively description would resonate today with any woman trying to juggle a job, family, and college:

"But when are you going to the grocery store?" one of the children interrupts. "What are we having for dinner tonight?"

"Did you remember to phone about the heating system checkup?" my husband interjects. "And you say there's another sprinkler in the garage. Where?"

And so the life of the mind becomes concerned once again with the more mundane questions of immediate living.

The low point of my current quest for additional knowledge arose over transportation. Transportation – the question of how to get seven people where they want to be at the time they're due – has occupied much of my husband's time this summer. One recent morning he thought he had every detail of the day's activities covered. He would be in Cortez for the day. Our eldest would drive the possessors of jobs at the times scheduled. The younger ones had dates that made walking possible.

"But how am I going to get to Fort Lewis?" I wailed. "I can walk to the library in town but how am I going to get up the hill?"

"What's the matter, Mother? Aren't you strongly enough motivated about your schooling to walk? You're always telling us how everybody walked to school in your day, blizzards or not. Here's your chance to show it," our eldest told me sternly. "Motivate!"

I realized that the dates of Juan de Oñate's colonization expeditions into New Mexico were dimming. I realized that I no longer could remember the names of the three varying accounts that have been pulled together into the Book of Genesis.

"Don't forget," (the youngest) said, "Get straight A's now, just the way you tell us to do every day all winter long."

Well, I shan't, but it's a lot of fun and I'm certainly learning a lot that I didn't know before. But let no one tell you it isn't hard work to pick up the threads of an interrupted formal education.

Morley continued her studies into the 1970s, reaching her mid-for-ties and beyond. Her fellow students, of course, stayed the same age – mostly late teens to early twenties. Morley was older than many of her professors. But that didn't dissuade her.

Elizabeth, Bill, and his first wife, Connie McLeod, celebrate Morley's graduation from Fort Lewis College.

Pam Patton, then a twenty-year-old senior from Bayfield, met Morley in the summer of 1970 in a Spanish II class. Pam's first thought when she saw this middle-aged woman taking notes and asking questions was she was taking it too seriously: "Oh great, just what we need. We just want to get the credits and get out of here."[272]

Then she sat next to Morley, who didn't acknowledge the age barrier and talked to Pam, who was approximately the age of Morley's daughters. Morley was taking the class not just to gain more credits, but also to improve her Spanish, which she used not only for trips to Central and South America, but around town. Morley had a goal to read Spanish books in the author's language.

"Here was this woman who was so competent and capable, and she was taking this class to learn. I was just trying to graduate," said Pam, who served on the Fort Lewis student council. "I just liked her."

On one occasion, Morley invited Pam to the West Park house for an after-class drink. Pam got to meet Arthur, who sternly counseled her to start reading newspapers, or she'd never be a literate person. "Whoa, I'd better get on it," Pam told herself.

It took Morley a dozen years after starting, but she received a bachelor's degree in Southwest Studies from Fort Lewis College on Saturday, April 26, 1975. She invited her brother, John Cowles Jr., chairman of the Minneapolis Star and Tribune Company, to come and give the commencement address.

With her college degree in hand (actually, she placed it prominently in a frame on the fireplace mantle), and after turning fifty in May, Morley joined Arthur for a month-long trip to the East Coast and Europe in September/October. The ship *Queen Elizabeth 2* took them from New York City to Cherbourg, France. They spent time in Paris, London, and Italy, where Arthur's brother John was living with his Italian-born wife, Rosina, in Florence.[273]

A Well-Lived Life

When he was interviewed in June 1974, Arthur discussed many Durango issues, such as Native Americans, land use, Front Range dominance, tourism, and more. The world had changed, with improved travel making it possible for Arthur to influence both his local community and national affairs. He was enamored of the small-town life where one could enjoy neighbors and influence events, as well as affect the national scene, as he did with his work on Title III.

His view from Durango had grown keen. Of the dominance of the Front Range, which includes most of Colorado's population, including the Denver area, he said:[274]

> I think the smaller parts of the state are practically ignored by the big city. ... Of course, the small guys are always watchful of the big guy, and it's obvious that the whole metropolitan area – Boulder down to Pueblo – is going to grow at such a greater rate that it makes some people in this area somewhat nervous.

On the economy:[275]

> Durango has always depended on its natural resources one way or another. ... If you go through the history of Durango,

they built the railroad to bring the ore up from the mines. At one time there were three smelters in Durango. Timbering has been an important activity. Agriculture has been an important activity, although we faced that problem which is happening everywhere now – not only are there fewer and larger farms, but the developers are buying up farmland which a lot of us are not too happy about. [But] it's awfully unfair to tell the farmer – when [he gets] these enormous prices for his land, when he's faced with a small margin of profit – that he can't sell his property.

Then the oil people came here … in the '50s and a lot of oil exploration offices. … Tourism has become a very important factor in the Durango economy, and the narrow gauge train has been more important than the numbers. … Mesa Verde now attracts about a half-million visitors a year.

On their decision to settle in Durango:[276]

We've grown steadily more content with our decision to move west ever since we've moved here. We made such a big move and there are a few moments when you wonder whether you've done the right thing. Such questions have not occurred to Morley and myself during the last several years. We like our lives and intend to stay here.

We like to travel very much. We enjoy going back to see our relatives in places like Minneapolis and New York. We have a good time when we do it, but we're always glad that we've got Durango to look forward to.

Arthur lived twenty-three years in Durango. One might ask: Did he and Morley truly believe in 1952 they would stay that long? Likely that's academic, as they weren't planning that far ahead. The early years were focused on day-to-day scrambling to produce a newspaper and raise a family. They took a chance on Durango, gained some close friends, made some enemies, and became part of the fabric of a close-knit community. By 1975 it was hard for them to imagine leaving.

Arthur Ballantine Jr., in 1975.

Close family relative Matilda "Tilly" Lorentz Grey said that Morley once told her Arthur pined for a US Cabinet position such as Secretary of Transportation. His father served as Undersecretary of Treasury, so for a Ballantine, this wasn't far-fetched.[277] Also, his connections with Harvard and Yale classmates kept him in the loop among people who might actually get him such a job.[278] But he found value in being a big fish in what he and Morley must have sometimes felt was a very small pond. Their involvement on state and national committees quelled or satisfied those big-pond yearnings.

Grey talked with Arthur extensively during internships at the *Durango Herald-News* in the summers of 1957, 1958, and 1959. "He was quietly ambitious."

By the summer of 1975 the four children had launched their careers far from Durango. Arthur and Morley were fine with that and had encouraged it. Richard, thirty, was living on a farm in Longmont, thirty miles north of Denver; Elizabeth, twenty-seven, was working on her PhD at Columbia University's Russian Institute in New York City;[279] Bill, twenty-six, was a university student in Seattle; and Helen, twenty-three, was married and about to start on a master's in business in Lawrence, Kans.

Whether Morley and Arthur just decided it was time, or if perhaps Arthur had a conscious or subconscious premonition of his ill health,

it's interesting that in June 1975, the four children were appointed to *The Durango Herald* board of directors. The children returned to Durango for a board meeting at the first of November. Helen recalled staying a day extra to work out some financial issues she had agreed to take on, since that was now her field.

The next weekend, November 8-9, Arthur attended a Rocky Mountain Conference on "media and the law" in Aspen. As a newspaperman with a law degree, Arthur especially enjoyed these two subjects. The meeting included publishers, journalists, district attorneys, and lawyers.

Participants were lauded for their congeniality as well as their progress on touchy issues – two qualities also dear to Arthur's heart.

"The participants learned a great deal from each other at the conference," Arthur wrote in a *Herald* column that appeared November

12.[280] (He now used the initials AB, not ABJr. He'd made the change in 1965.[281]) "Some of the points will be reflected in the writing of future editorials."

A few days later Morley traveled to Denver for a meeting of the Colorado Land Use Commission. After the meetings concluded on Friday, November 14, Morley flew back to Durango, and was greeted by family friends, the Vandegrifts, who drove her back home. It was early evening.[282]

That same Friday, Arthur had spent a fairly typical day at the *Herald*. He attended a lunch meeting of the Fine Arts Council, regretfully missing out on a simultaneous meeting of the Chamber of Commerce at which Fort Lewis President Rexer Berndt spoke. He wrote a column that day (to run Sunday) about how the local teacher's union, the Durango Education Association, had gone too far in its beefs with the school district, had damaged the public image of teachers, and had created bad blood unnecessarily.[283] It was an issue that would continue to fester.

After leaving work he shared a drink and conversation with two key *Herald* employees, Don Schlichting, associate publisher, and Stan Usinowicz, managing editor.[284] He then returned to 175 West Park.

Morley arrived home, and as they did nearly every evening with a cocktail, she and Arthur caught up on events.

"I knew exactly what we'd do after I reached home and we did: have an affectionate chat about the day's events, sharing our experiences as we have for more than [twenty-eight] years, make a few plans for the weekend, and go to bed," Morley recalled.

So that's what they did. When Morley woke up a bit later, she quickly realized that Arthur was unresponsive. She called for emergency help, but it was too late. He'd had a massive heart attack.

It was November 14, 1975. At age sixty-one, Arthur Ballantine was dead.

Part III

ON HER
OWN

The Shock

Morley was no stranger to sudden loss. But this was different. This was her husband of twenty-eight years, a man she'd closely shared every aspect of life with – work, home, play, love.

A rescue net awaited her, and it included a tight web of friends she had developed in the community. Durangoans were terribly upset by Arthur's death, and this feeling poured and trickled out all over the country. And, of course, the children and other immediate family members rushed to comfort her and share her suffering. If Morley hadn't fallen completely in love with Durango by now, this moment sealed that sentiment. She wrote in an editorial that appeared Tuesday afternoon, hours after the morning memorial service for Arthur at St. Mark's Episcopal Church:

Morley and Arthur were avid world travelers and enjoyed writing about their experiences in the *Herald*

What has impressed this family since [Arthur's death] has been the overwhelming outpouring of love and of help, of tangible and intangible support. People who shouldn't be, flying here to share grief, residents interrupting busy schedules to come by and give a tight hug, the wonderful generosity about food – all kinds of living incidents have made the almost unbearable blow just a bit easier to bear.

John Cowles Sr. wrote in a letter to family: "The Durango City Library and the First National Bank were closed for the funeral service, and the church had to install a loudspeaker in the parish house so that the overflow crowd, who could not get in the church, could hear."[285]

About 175 people dropped by the house after the funeral. Neighbors brought food.

To get her away from the attention, however briefly, Morley's brother John and sister Sally drove her "out in the country to some supposedly out-of-the-way restaurant for a meal, and when they went in the waitress embraced Morley and broke out in tears so that she could hardly serve the meal."[286]

The public attention was appreciated, but in some ways added another burden. "It was just terrible," close friend Mary Jane Clark recalled of Arthur's passing.[287] "But she handled it really well. And her family was there for her. I think everyone tried to be as helpful as they could."

The Clarks were heading to Mexico for a long-planned vacation, but Mary Jane went over to visit with her "heartbroken" friend before leaving. "She was just amazing," Mary Jane said. "She was a very strong woman. I think she could handle about anything."

Arthur's final *Herald* editorial, the one he'd written Friday about the Durango Education Association damaging the public image of teachers, ran as planned on the Sunday after his death. It appeared as always on page two, and if you clipped out his obituary on page one that day, you'd find the final paragraphs of his editorial on the back.

Tributes began streaming in from friends, strangers, politicians, and fellow journalists.

Arthur "set an example of excellence we all would do well to follow," wrote Colorado Gov. Richard Lamm. "He combined that mosaic of traits that made him a full human being. He was industrious, compassionate, fair – a total person. His death is a great loss to Colorado."[288]

Wrote long-time friend George Franklin, a classmate at both Harvard and Yale Law School:[289]

> To anyone in Durango on the day of the funeral it was very evident he had earned their respect and love. He hated sham; he did not like things to be prettified. He loved people for what they were and he did not need to gloss over their defects in order to care for them. ... He loved life and lived it with zest. I remember his telling me a few years ago that he had found each age of life different and fascinating, though often difficult, and that he wanted so very much to grow old and to have a chance to experience every single part of it.

Arthur's death forced many to take stock of their own existence, to look deep and judge the quality of their own lives. Wrote Charlie Langdon, a *Herald* reporter and editor:[290]

> Each of us is given the opportunity to make peace with himself, and to give love and understanding to his family, and to contribute to his community. It is, I suppose, part of our human condition that we are not always up to the job. Arthur was. He was a giver and not a taker. He literally poured his time and energies into the town and college and library. He encouraged the arts and was a positive force in civic and commercial affairs.
>
> ... He left Durango a much better community than when he and you found it. The quality of life here is largely his monument, and you know better than I do that it is a treasure.

Arthur's younger brother, John "Jack" Ballantine, emotionally moved by the week he and his wife, Rose, spent in Durango for

Arthur's memorial, wrote a letter "To the Ballantines and Those Who Put Up With Them." An excerpt:[291]

> Arthur's way was so full of understatement (often down-right awkwardness) that most of us had not realized how much he cared, and we cared. ... While none of us will ever think of Arthur with anything but delight, his untimely death leaves a great gap. The most monstrous thing about it is the number of things we now will have to do for ourselves – mind our own consciences and money and gossip.

Arthur's four children wrote a touching editorial that appeared in the *Herald* a week later.[292] And it definitely wasn't "prettified." It began:

> Daddy always said that however we were brought up, we would consider our upbringing wrong. ... [This position] al-lowed Daddy a great deal of autonomy and distance which might have been disastrous for us. At the same time, we were given responsibility for our own behavior. We were fortunate that he set such a compelling example to follow.
> ...Superficially, he was an embarrassment while we were in our teens. His disheveled appearance, his absent-mindedness, his humor at our expense caused many painful moments. At the same time his love and affection, determination, and in-tense pleasure at other human beings communicated them-selves to us.
> He always hoped to stretch our minds and emotions as far as possible, a process of which we were not always aware nor fully appreciative. Luckily, he lived long enough for us to per-ceive the wisdom in his approach. He hoped we would never stop growing.
> Thanks to him, we won't.

Morley took in these heartfelt emotions, steadied herself, and began to look ahead. She had to have faith that her training and abilities could

overcome the loss of her constant partner, her nightly foil with whom to bounce off ideas, one-half of the newspaper operating team. In front of her was the great, wide open. She certainly wasn't looking at Arthur's death as an opportunity, but ultimately, it was.

Days after the service, Morley opened Arthur's safe deposit box and found it in "apple-pie order." She wrote, "I thought once again of his all-encompassing thoughtfulness for others, for he believed it inconsiderate for a spouse not to have his affairs in order as life can come to an end for anybody, any place, any time."[293]

Carrying On

With her world shaken to the core, it was time for Morley to make some decisions. Twenty-three years prior, she and Arthur had made the bold move to Durango from Morley's native Midwest. Her parents still lived in Minneapolis. She could return to the Midwest with her two-plus decades of newspaper experience, and possibly take some type of position with the Cowles papers in either Minneapolis, where her brother John Cowles Jr. was running things, or in Des Moines, where her cousin David Kruidenier was in charge.

"When Arthur died," she told an interviewer in 2005, "I thought about moving back home, back to the Midwest. I had family there. But I finally decided that [Durango] is where my life is. So I stayed."[294]

That decision, however trying it was, didn't take long. On Monday, just three days after Arthur's death, Morley led her children to the *Herald* and addressed the uncertain staff. Were big changes coming? Were their jobs safe? To the extent she could, Morley soothed them. She announced that the *Herald* would not be sold, and she would continue to live in Durango and run the paper.[295]

Morley was now sole publisher, but her children were helpful with various tasks and as members of *The Durango Herald* board of directors.

To help her mother and the newspaper, Elizabeth Ballantine, now twenty-seven, immediately left the Columbia University Russian Institute in New York City and returned to Durango. She began work as

a reporter and remained for almost a year before taking a reporting job at the *Des Moines Register* in 1976. Helen Ballantine Healy, in the process of getting a master's in business and accounting certification, looked over company finances from Kansas. Five years later, in 1980, Richard would leave the Longmont farm with his recent bride, Mary Lyn Allen, a paralegal assistant he met at a Denver law firm, and returned to Durango, where Richard would become assistant to the publisher.

Morley remained fully in charge. She was up to the challenge of carrying on by herself what she and Arthur had begun. She had the tools and wherewithal – an intelligence and commanding presence – learned and honed over her now fifty years, to handle the job with grace. In an era where it was common for demure women to be bullied by louder, brasher men, Morley was neither demure nor bullied.

"When you talked business with Morley there was no gender consciousness," said family friend Jim Foster, who compared her with former British Prime Minister Margaret Thatcher.[296] "You never had this feeling, 'I've got to be careful what I say, I'm talking to a woman.' ...

She was composed, she was strong, she had a clear mind, and could express it clearly – all kinds of leadership qualities where gender wasn't important."

Morley had always bristled at being stuck with only the women, as on social occasions when men might stereotypically gather in one room to smoke cigars and discuss politics, while women would gather in another to gossip. "She liked to mix it up with the men," said her son Richard. "She didn't like being sequestered with the women. She had opinions, she was informed."[297]

Of course, it was impossible to let go of Arthur instantly. The *Herald* ran a series of his old columns, running into January 1976, in commemoration of his life. Morley endured several months of soul-searching. She wrote a heartfelt and hard-hitting column that same month about what to do with the Antigua house. Her parents weren't up for the travel anymore, and she wasn't certain if her children wanted to keep it up.

"Did the Caribbean have a place in our future as it had in our past?" she pondered in an editorial she started in Antigua.[298] The column focused on conversations with Antigua friends also suffering from loss.

> I had a long discussion about the pain of death with a friend of my parents, widowed a year ago. Earlier the two of them had lost two of their adult children in an automobile accident in Denver, innocent victims of a high-speed police chase. She said that, after much thought, she had concluded that the pain of losing grown children was greater than losing a mate. I wondered how anything would be greater than the latter but inwardly prayed that I'd never be in a position to make the comparison.

Her flights back home took her through Miami, where she got more tough news.

> When I checked in that night from Miami with my parents, I learnt my mother was in the hospital undergoing tests. On

the way home I stopped in Minneapolis to see her. She looked miserable. Friday my brother phoned to say the tests were positive. No, nothing becomes any easier.

Elizabeth Bates Cowles died December 17, 1976.

The Cowles family at their Minnesota retreat, Glendalough, in 1954. Back, from left, Morley's brothers John Jr. and Russell; front, Morley, her parents Betty and John Cowles, and her sister Sally Cowles Bullitt.

As the 1970s became the 1980s, running a newspaper in the black became a more and more difficult proposition. Around the country business costs rose, while advertising sales and circulation remained flat. An economic downturn in this same period – a recession lasting from approximately 1980-1983 – made the financial issue more acute.

But Morley and the Ballantine family refused to do what many like-sized newspapers did: cut staff to save costs, or sell to a chain that would do exactly that. Always at *The Durango Herald*, reporting the news, keeping the community informed and engaged, was the top concern. If it wasn't making money, that was tolerable. But if the *Herald* wasn't winning awards for excellence, that was cause for worry. Morley took seriously what she believed was an obligation to provide complete and accurate information; the public needed that to make intelligent decisions. Meanwhile, however, the paper's profit margin fell to nearly nothing.

The *Herald*, like many other newspapers, performed job printing – small commercial jobs such as printing letterhead or circulars. It was an adjunct business that could be profitable, but only with a large volume of work. In the early 1970s the *Herald* job shop did about $60,000 worth of business annually, which was not enough to make it profitable. That total did not increase, and in 1981-82, the *Herald* phased out the job shop.[299] Soon, however, something much bigger took its place.

As Richard Ballantine came on board in 1980 as assistant publisher, he watched for opportunities that might help the business as a whole remain strong. One day in the fall of 1982, a Mountain Bell sales manager named Hugh Riddle came to the *Herald* to sell an idea.

Mountain Bell was then the telephone service provider for several Rocky Mountain states.

Riddle's job was to sell advertising for the Yellow Pages – the Mountain Bell phone book – but he had tired of the traveling involved.

He put his grand plan to Richard: Hugh and his wife Diane knew how to sell advertising for a phone book. The *Herald* had credibility in the community and knew how to design and publish things. They could combine their talents, Riddle proposed, and put together a Southwest Colorado phone book superior to Mountain Bell's. Richard was intrigued, but this was a new animal, far from the usual daily publication.

"An annual product seemed very, very strange, and somewhat difficult," Richard said in a 2021 interview.[300] He and Morley discussed the opportunity and decided it was worth the risk.

"A powerhouse from Bell Yellow Pages has volunteered to lead us into the thicket," Morley wrote to her family in October 1982.[301] "I [and Richard] like it because there's no need for front-end money."

Their first phone book, with a red and white cover and a color photo of the train, designed by Nancy Leach, came out in 1983. It covered five counties in Southwest Colorado and was called the *Red Book*, a name that inadvertently got them into hot water.

The name *Red Book* was already taken, an impressive letter from a team of Chicago lawyers informed them, threatening legal action. Richard and Riddle were chagrined, and decided it was best to change the name. In 1984 it came out as *Directory Plus* (still red, Richard noted with satisfaction), and in addition to a Southwest Colorado edition, a book was published for Farmington, Durango's neighbor in northern New Mexico.

As they cannibalized their competitor's advertising, the Ballantines and Riddles expected a reaction from Mountain Bell. They were stunned when none came. "Mountain Bell was uninterested in our success," Richard said. "They thought on a higher plane." Mountain Bell would let the "little guy" reap his rewards.

The *Herald* bought out the Riddles' share of the business in the late 1980s. As years went by and newspaper advertising became harder to come by as media habits changed, *Directory Plus* became by far the company's largest revenue source. The business expanded into southern New Mexico in 2000, forming a sister company, Rio Grande Publishing. Together the two *Directory Plus* companies produced nine phone books.

Directory Plus's success allowed the *Herald* to continue supporting comprehensive news coverage commensurate with a newspaper many times its circulation. Community members still complained about *Herald* coverage, as they are wont to do, but those with an inkling of perspective understood that the Ballantines' product was exceptional, particularly for a town the size of Durango.

A New Partnership

Morley's editorials had evolved over twenty-three years, from 1952 when she was raising four high-spirited children, to 1975. They evolved again when she instantly had total responsibility for a thriving newspaper. She still wrote about travels, but her topics became even more widely varied, and often took on a more serious tone.

Whatever she was writing about, MCB connected with her readers at a basic level. She understood the concerns of business leaders, single mothers, homeowners, educators, and people just trying to complete mundane tasks like using a computer or navigating their vehicle around town. And it helped her credibility that as the years passed, she transformed from newcomer to community icon.

But Morley's travels to Des Moines and Minneapolis in her roles as director of the Des Moines Register and Tribune Company and Cowles Media Company (Minneapolis) were taking a huge hunk of her time and energy. A possible merger, the dissolving of merger talks, and questionable management decisions were giving board members a headache. With a growing list of civic responsibilities also demanding her attention, it was time for a change.

By mid-1983 Morley was ready to take something off her plate. She decided to cede day-to-day control of the newspaper to her son Richard. The big announcement came just after Memorial Day, in a rare above-the-nameplate story on June 1, 1983:[302]

Richard Ballantine, thirty-seven, has been named *Durango Herald* publisher by the *Herald's* board of directors effective October 1. Morley C. Ballantine, publisher since her husband, Arthur Ballantine, died in 1975, will become chairman of the board effective immediately.

The Durango Herald editorial board in 1991: from left, Dan Partridge (managing editor), Bill Roberts (opinion page editor), and Richard Ballantine (publisher); Morley, in front, was chairman of the board and retained the title of editor.

Morley was quoted in the story: "In this swiftly changing time when we're in transition between the age of technocracy and the coming information age that prophets predict ... it's important to have vigorous leadership. Richard's grown up in the newspaper business and he's seen how it has changed in the past decade."

She had concluded that putting day-to-day decisions "on hold" had been unfair. "This way," she noted, "people can know right away what the answer is."

It wouldn't be quite right to say she gave complete control to her son, as Richard is first to point out. Morley maintained the title of editor. "She was very candid with me," Richard said. "She said, 'Richard you frequently split infinitives and mishandle apostrophes.' And she was absolutely right."[303]

Luckily there remained qualified and dedicated editors to fix grammatical errors. Under Richard's leadership the standard of journalism that had garnered a long list of awards never wavered. To all who followed, "the Ballantines" came to mean Morley and her son Richard.

After Richard took over as publisher in 1983, MCB continued writing editorials periodically, and began a weekly column called "Editor at Large." That gave her freedom to write about what caught her attention, what she thought was important or amusing. That included symphony, book, and film reviews; news of the local arts scene; women's rights and opportunities; community projects; and memories of Durango's past. She had plenty of past to share, but she blended that with a look forward. One week was a movie review of *Saving Private Ryan*, the next a shout-out to Music in the Mountains for a successful season.

When something around town was out of order, she chimed in vociferously, as in this 1992 column:[304]

> What in the world is going on with the drive-up mailboxes outside of the post office? They're on the side of the front *passenger* seat. … In this day of the bucket seat and floor gear shift, sliding over isn't easy.
>
> Flip a coin, gents. The city can reverse the flow of traffic or postal employees can walk across the alley to empty the boxes. After all they're the ones undeterred by "neither snow, nor rain, nor heat, nor gloom of night … from the swift completion of their appointed rounds." The situation at the moment looks like the creation of second-graders, or perhaps a committee. Some say it's the work of city planners. Oh come on!

She didn't shy from mentioning two of her favorite nonprofits: "The Durango Arts Center has a September membership drive, and if you are not a member now, you should be. It is a wonderful umbrella organization, representing something for everyone. The Women's Resource Center is another powerhouse, eager to make that goal with almost 500 members."

The inquisitiveness learned from her father never waned. She had always asked questions until she got answers. That style allowed her to broach the touchiest subjects, including death and dying. In a September 2000 column she talked about her belief in the Hemlock Society, an assisted suicide advocacy group then based in Denver. Its director was about to visit Durango, a visit that Morley had played a major role in arranging.[305]

Mark on your calendars Saturday, September 16 at 2 p.m. in the Smiley Auditorium for an all-encompassing discussion. Any suggestions for additional participants including yourself? Phone any of [the organizers]. We haven't finished our own phoning about this most important subject.

Books were among her favorite subjects. She would constantly ask friends what they were reading, and often these books would become part of a column. This was also another method of connecting with her community. MCB marveled that the first three J.K. Rowling *Harry Potter* novels led the national fiction best-seller list in October 1999:[306]

Pam Patton is about finished with *The Sorcerer's Stone*; my son Bill has read the second volume; and retired financier Allan Hamilton goes to the head of the class as having read all three!

One of her favorite annual December columns continued to be simply rehashing the book reports done by students in friend Sandra Mapel's Miller Middle School language arts class. It was Morley's method not only to promote reading by youths, but to draw them toward the newspaper – and give readers some Christmas present ideas.

Nathan McGrath likes *Winterdance* ... by [Gary] Paulsen, about running the Iditarod, the Alaskan dog sled race. He describes it as "a great story about men, dogs, and their souls conjoining."

Hannah Harter recommends *The First Two Lives of Lukas-Kasha*, by Lloyd Alexander. Her review begins, "Have you ever found yourself feeling you were in a whole different world? Well, for the mischievous Lukas-Kasha, that's exactly what happened."

Morley concluded her December 1998 column:[307]

All of these reports this year were neatly done on what I take to be computers. When they were all hand-written, most were practically illegible, and it was extremely difficult to translate them. Now they're fun to read. At the same time, I trust handwriting has improved.

As years passed Morley found herself attending more and more funeral services. When you reach your seventies and you enjoy being surrounded by people, *and* you've lived in one place a long time, this is just what happens. Many of her columns in the 1990s and 2000s were odes to Durangoans, big and small. MCB wrote as Editor at Large in November 1999:[308]

> Joe B. "Kinky" Peters, who died late last month at eighty-six, was a kind and gentle person, blessed with a good sense of humor. He was active in Rotary and a dedicated member of United Way in the early days when it was just being established and the going was tough. I remember serving with him on an early-day mental health board when that too was just being formed. ... Peters will be remembered warmly by all who knew him.

And as one tends to do with age, Morley rued the seemingly loose morals of the next generation:[309]

> It's high time that President Clinton Saturday devoted his radio speech to the nation to the subject of violence distributed by the entertainment industry. ... "Every one of us has a role to play in giving our children a safe future, and those with greater influence have greater responsibility," he said. ... We wish his list had included a specific reference to language. The obscenity, the vulgarity, the brutality that serve as conversation in many a late-night movie or on a talk show are dreadful. Too many children must grow up considering this normal, human dialogue. Awful!

Morley remained proud of the tradition that she and Arthur –
bringing the benefit of their own vast media experience – established
in Durango beginning in 1952. Of the media's role and responsibility,
she said in 1992:[310]

> For democracy to function successfully, its citizens need to
> have information about the wide variety of topics important
> to their government. They need complete information and
> they need accurate information. It's a newspaper's responsibil-
> ity to provide this information. … As long-term editors of the
> *Herald*, we've thought of ourselves as socially liberal and fiscally
> conservative. We believe that there is an important role for
> government to play in our lives but, at the same time, the best
> government is that which governs least.

Her deep knowledge base can be attributed to the family trait of
being inquisitive. But Morley took that to new levels, being willing to
explore various cultures, religions, spirituality, and walks of life, particularly those she didn't understand or were new to her.

Katherine Barr moved to Durango in 1974 with a group that lived
in what they referred to as an "intentional community." They took
pains to avoid the label "hippies" that some wanted to stick on them.
As an example, Heartwood Cohousing, developed in the early 2000s
just west of Bayfield, is considered an intentional community. Heartwood emphasizes strong community relationships, low stress, being
outdoors, and eating organic food.

Morley and Arthur were intrigued by Barr's community and wanted
to know more about it. Along with other community members, she
met the *Herald* publishers in the summer of 1975. Barr, a rare woman
carpenter, renewed her friendship with Morley in the late 1990s
through a mutual acquaintance and became a frequent visitor to 175
West Park Avenue. She put succinctly what is a leitmotif among friends
who describe Morley.[311]

"How inquisitive she was about everything," Barr said. "She would engage in any sort of conversation and wanted to know all sides of a story. She was just very curious about so much."

During a discussion, Barr said, Morley often answered a query with the phrase, yes, no, and maybe. "In other words, she was saying, there's nuance here. Let's keep digging. She would have an opinion underneath that, but it was her way of continuing the conversation. I loved that about her too."

Barr noticed quickly how Morley helped and supported women in leadership and in getting ahead in nontraditional jobs – such as Barr's trade as carpenter, or even Morley's own position as newspaper publisher. "She was just so adamant about that," Barr said. "Her position was so clear that women can not only do anything, [but] that being a woman … adds something that's of benefit in leadership. … She just lived it."

As a lifelong progressive, Morley continued to roll with the times and changing social mores. When Barr began dating Linda Barnes, Barr discussed that new relationship with Morley just like they'd discussed other personal and family matters. If Morley was uncomfortable with this relationship, she put those feelings aside and took the opportunity to ask probing questions and learn. It probably did stretch her ways of thinking, Barr said. "I think that was a real testament to her openness."

Barr and Barnes held a "commitment ceremony" in June 2002. Their families came to Durango, and on the night before the big occasion, Morley threw a large rehearsal dinner – a picnic, really – in the backyard of her West Park home. About 200 people attended the dinner catered by Cyprus Café owner Allison Dance, with the Jeff Solon Band entertaining.

Morley didn't always tell her story subjects they would appear in the paper – just ask her children – and that was the case with Barr and Barnes' ceremony. MCB used the occasion to share her thoughts and to educate her readers about a same-sex relationship. An excerpt from her column about the ceremony:[312]

> The ending was a blessing from the Apache Indian tradition:
> "For while you are two persons, there is but one life before

you, go now to your dwelling place to enter into the days of your togetherness, and may your days be good and long upon the earth."

Nice, isn't it? And good for any pair wishing to make a commitment. … Most of us had not been to a commitment ceremony before. We were impressed.

Starting from 1990, Morley's closest working partner – other than her son Richard – was Bill Roberts, the editorial page editor from 1990 to 2017. The editorial board consisted then of Morley, Richard, Roberts, and managing editor Dan Partridge. Roberts is still amazed that the *Herald* took a chance on a "forty-year-old, washed-up bartender," and he remains very appreciative. The Ballantines did not regret their decision.

"I was always honored that my thoughts and opinions were taken into account," Roberts said.[313] "At the very least they were given a polite hearing." He described the Ballantines as "unfailingly polite," but ultimately, there was no question who the boss was. One incident sticks out for him in illustrating this point.

The editorial team took turns writing the day's editorial. But often, particularly as Morley aged and wasn't involved in day-to-day operations, the duty fell to Roberts. After discussion among the board one day, Roberts returned to his computer to write up the opinion. He spent several hours, researched diligently, rewrote several times, and spell-checked to craft what he thought was a fine piece. It explained whom readers should believe on a certain issue, and why. (He doesn't recall the exact subject.) He polished it off, and for the final step came up with a headline: "Who Do You Trust?" channeling the great Bo Diddley song "Who Do You Love?" Unfortunately for Roberts, the singer was no grammarian.

The next morning when Roberts arrived at his work desk, a newspaper lay on his keyboard, open to his editorial. A red grease pencil had been used to circle the "Who" in the headline, and on the side the editor – obviously Morley – had written in "WHOM."

"That's all I saw or heard," Roberts recalled. "That was it. Not a word, ever. Just that big, red circle." Roberts took the message to be, "At my newspaper we're going to use proper grammar."

It stuck with him: "I'll be damned if I'm ever going to say 'who do you trust,' or anything like that. I almost want to hum along to the song saying, 'Whom do you love.' I will never forget that lesson."

Countless times, Roberts experienced the depth and breadth of the Ballantines' experience and connections. Some was their upbringing, some their wealth, and some the fact that, as the only daily paper, the *Herald* had huge importance to a large swath of the state. Governors, congressmen, state representatives – all would stop by to visit with the editorial staff. Many had served with Morley or Richard, or even Arthur, on various state commissions.

One reporter was out covering a nationwide story in 1998 in southeast Utah when Colorado Gov. Roy Romer arrived in a helicopter. Romer gave a short briefing to a small group of assembled media. A policeman had been shot and killed in Cortez, and a large manhunt involving local, state, and federal agents had ensued. Upon hearing a reporter was from *The Durango Herald*, Romer immediately brightened.

To the reporter, the governor's response seemed incongruous to the location in the middle of the desert, and to the seriousness of the briefing: "Ah, the *Herald*. Say hi to Morley Ballantine for me!"

What the reporter came to understand only later was the long and deep connection. Romer, as a state senator from the Denver area, had attended the *Herald's* new plant dedication in 1965, and had undoubtedly crossed paths with both Morley and Arthur many times before and after.[314]

Dick Grossman, who began writing a column on overpopulation issues for *The Durango Herald* in 1995, attended the International Conference on Population and Development in September 1994 in Cairo, Egypt. Grossman, an obstetrician, was there with his son, and John Byrd, a professor of finance. They were excited to bump into Tim Wirth of Colorado, a former US senator who had been appointed by President Clinton as Undersecretary for Global Affairs. Wirth was chair of the US delegation to the Egypt conference and had a lot on his plate.

The three Durangoans identified themselves as representatives of the *Herald*. Wirth – the lead US conference attendee, halfway around the world from Southwest Colorado – paused just a moment before addressing them: "And how is Morley Ballantine?"

In 1995, after hearing *The Population Bomb* author Paul Ehrlich speak, Grossman became motivated to write a book, *50 Simple Things,* about what people could do to slow population growth, modeled after a popular book of the period. He visited Morley to see if she could help him connect with a publisher. Instead, she invited him to write a twice-a-month column for the *Herald*. As far as Grossman can tell, he has the only regular newspaper column on the subject. He calls it "Population Matters."

Grossman was one of the few local doctors who would perform abortions, and he received support from many of the same people who supported Planned Parenthood, including Morley.

It is true that politicians who knew Morley realized she was a key to their popularity in Southwest Colorado. But many showed her an undeniable love and respect that went beyond politics.

Morley may not have gotten back to the White House for an intimate luncheon with the sitting president, but she did attend President Clinton's State of the Union address on January 20, 1999. Clinton was undergoing impeachment proceedings at the time. Congressman Scott McInnis, a Republican from Grand Junction, arranged the occasion. Morley wrote:[315]

> I had the good fortune to be among the more than 650 (by my count) in the visitor's gallery [balcony] of the fine old House chamber. … The diplomatic corps was seated above the podium, Hillary Clinton's party was on its left from the speaker's position, and I opposite in a splendid seat, on the aisle in the second row.

After Clinton's speech finally ended – "too long," Morley commented – she found herself waiting for an elevator with Jesse Jackson and Rosa Parks.[316] Parks had just received a long, standing ovation when Clinton referred to her historic civil rights deeds during his speech. Jackson, also a renowned civil rights leader, and Parks had no way of knowing that Morley and her family had a lengthy history supporting the civil rights movement, but Morley made sure they knew she was on their side.

> I congratulated each of them for having made a secure place in history and asked Jackson what he was doing these days (I felt that was about as explicit as a stranger could be). "Trying to make America an even better place," he replied with a smile, and I realized he's even handsomer than his photographs.
>
> That's the impression of the evening I came away with: A vast majority of our fellow citizens who care about our country, not the bitter minority, motivated largely by hatred, who are determined to, at all cost, "get" the president.

The rate of politician visits grew as election time neared. The *Herald* editorial board welcomed the chance to meet and interview candidates, or those who were campaigning for a certain amendment or tax. The *Herald* didn't purposely foment animosity among election foes, but it is true that the more contentious a local race became, the more advertising money candidates would spend with the paper.

Don Schlichting, who worked thirty-six years at the newspaper, said, "Election years were always big at the *Herald* – a lot of activity, a lot of work, a lot of fun."[317]

The Ballantines couldn't resist a good opportunity to bring people together, so election night became a big party at the *Herald*, with catered food, beer, and wine available beginning around 6 p.m. People filled the main floor, friends reunited, connections were made, and the buzz was palpable and exciting. This was a night for the *Herald* to shine, to demonstrate its ability to serve and unite the community.

As results came in, and as people loosened up from the alcohol and camaraderie, the intensity in the building rose. For reporters – if they could stand the noise – it was also a thrill. And it was handy when local candidates showed up and they were right there for reporters to interview.

The news staff didn't have a great deal of interaction with Morley by the 1990s, but welcomed the personal contacts that presented themselves. Election nights were one opportunity; the annual company picnics and Christmas parties were others. Certain story assignments obviously came from "above," namely Morley, by way of the managing editor.

On occasion a *Herald* newsroom member would give Morley a ride to an event – a play, a talk, even a family gathering. Bill Roberts was asked to pick up Morley on his way to a 1993 Thanksgiving dinner hosted by Richard and Mary Lyn at their home on Florida Mesa. He said sure, wondering how it would go. During his restaurant days he'd modified his 1979 Volkswagen Scirocco into a courier vehicle for boxes of lettuce, tomatoes, and other such produce. The back seat was long gone, as well as other car parts. From the driver's seat, if you looked between your knees you saw the pavement speeding past.

To Roberts' relief and admiration, she never said a thing about the state of the vehicle. "If Morley was riding in it, it was the princess's carriage," Roberts said. "And that was that."

Morley supported women in various roles, particularly in business, and that included *The Durango Herald*. By the 1990s, no department was without several women, and there was even a woman in the male-dominated pressroom.

Women in the newsroom, as editors and reporters, were of course nothing new under Ballantine ownership. That went back to the 1950s, when Nancy Elliott served as a reporter on the small news staff and handled the women's pages. Morley's Señora San Juan begat other women's columns and what newspapers refer to as a "society" column. The *Herald's* "society" news, it should be emphasized, was much less snooty than most papers', including events from county fairs to art gallery walks to family gatherings to couples' anniversaries.

Sally Morrissey took over Señora San Juan when Elliott went on vacation in 1964, and continued on as a columnist and news reporter until 1982. After a break, during which she volunteered with the Peace Corps, Morrissey returned to the *Herald* and began her "Sally Says" column about happenings around town. She finally retired at age eighty in 2000. Ann Butler took over, and Morley came up with the new column title "Neighbors," which Durango native Butler wrote from 2000 until 2017. Butler, who became one of the most recognizable women in town, soon added full-time reporting to her "Neighbors" duties.

With Morley's full blessing, Richard hired the newspaper's first female managing editor in late 2004. Alice Klement, a former journalism professor at the University of Northern Colorado, ran the newsroom from 2005-06. (Electa Draper had served as co-interim managing editor in the mid-1990s.)

As much as Morley supported women, sometimes differing interests clash. Nancy Whitson recalled an instance where harassment of women vied with the freedom of art. "The only conflict we had," Whitson recalled, "was about a picture on the wall in the main conference room. It was a photo of a naked woman sliding down the banister with a huge grin!"[318]

An employee had brought up the issue at a sexual harassment training when Whitson, human resources director from 1995-2010, was talking about subtle forms of harassment. "When I talked to Richard (Ballantine) about it he said, 'You'd better talk to my mother.' I brought it to Morley's attention that someone might find it offensive. She basically said, 'tough,' and that if someone found *art* offensive they shouldn't be working there."

By 2002 the Ballantine family had easily set the record for longest ownership of a Durango newspaper. June 1, 2002, marked the fifty-year anniversary of Morley and Arthur Ballantine's purchase of both the *Durango News* and *Durango Herald-Democrat.*

The Ballantines decided to celebrate, and Elizabeth Ballantine encouraged and organized, inviting family and friends to Durango for four days of sightseeing, adventure, meals, and – since it was board of directors time – even a serious meeting or two. The gathering was held August 8-11, 2002, a Thursday through Sunday.

Among the attendees, many of whom stayed downtown at the historic Strater Hotel: Morley's four children – Richard, Elizabeth, Bill, and Helen – with their families; Morley's three siblings – John Cowles

Jr., Russell Cowles, and his wife Marguerite (Margey), and Sally (Sarah) Doering; Arthur's nephew – John Ballantine with his wife Ann; Morley's cousin Tilly Grey; Morley's nephew Jay Cowles (John Jr.'s son); Morley's nephew, by her first marriage, Ed Gale; Morley's cousin Mary LeCron Foster's son Jeremy Foster and his wife Angela; and Morley and Arthur's friend Ria Delaney.

For the Ballantines, it was a chance to celebrate and share with family and friends the improvements they'd made at the newspaper and the changes they'd helped create elsewhere, specifically at Fort Lewis College.

The first gathering was Thursday evening at the Center of Southwest Studies, with a few short speeches commemorating the fifty years. The celebration returned to the Center the next morning for a tour of both Fort Lewis and the Center of Southwest Studies, led by Andrew Gulliford, the center director. The next stop was Cortez, for a dedication of the new building with state-of-the-art printing plant. The Ballantines had purchased the Cortez paper in 1999. The tour continued west of Cortez to Crow Canyon Archaeological Center, long a beneficiary of the Ballantines.

The highlight was a Saturday afternoon chartered-train ride to a catered dinner at the Cascade Wye. More than thirty relatives and friends rode the train, along with a contingent of current and former *Herald* and *Directory Plus* employees.

The recent Missionary Ridge and Valley fires had left scars easily visible as the train cruised through the Animas Valley north of town. As devastating as the fires were, the *Herald's* news coverage perhaps never shone brighter than that summer of 2002. The tireless newsroom staff kept the public informed both with the daily paper and its increasingly important online presence. Keeping its website up to date was a new challenge to the *Herald* and other newspapers – one that was obviously going to shape the future of media.

Following the fire, the Durango Herald Small Press published a popular commemorative book about the destruction and the heroic efforts of firefighters to save hundreds of homes east of Durango. *Fire in the Sky: Colorado's Missionary Ridge Fire* was 117 pages.

The gathering concluded Sunday, for those still in town, with a 10 a.m. brunch at Morley's West Park home.

Minding the Family Business

As brothers John Sr. and Gardner "Mike" Cowles aged, they had turned operations of their newspaper and media companies over to others, including the next generation. John Sr. retired from the Minneapolis board of directors in May 1976, at age seventy-seven. Over the years John's and Mike's offspring, and other family members, had gained shares in these large and valuable companies. So the question arose as to who among Gardner Cowles Sr.'s grandchildren might take charge.

In Minneapolis, it had ended up being Morley's brother, John Cowles Jr., in the lead role, and in Des Moines it was her cousin David Kruidenier.

Morley entered the thick of battles in Des Moines and Minneapolis as both companies struggled to survive. These battles complicated an already busy life after Arthur's death. She was appointed a Des Moines Register and Tribune Company board director in 1977, and a Minneapolis Star and Tribune Company director in 1982. She found herself frequently in airports, traveling to meetings. She also found herself in the middle of delicate family politics, and making decisions against their wishes, even against her own brother's interests.

A major contributing factor to these internecine battles was a recession in the early 1980s that hit the Midwest particularly hard. Profits in both companies declined. Both took on debt to finance acquisitions

May '68

Morley saw her family often while helping oversee the family-owned businesses in Minnesota and Iowa. Here, they mark John Cowles Jr.'s new leadership role with the Minneapolis Star and Tribune Company in May 1968. Front, from left, Morley, her parents John Sr. and Betty, and her sister, Sally (Sarah); back, John Jr. and his wife Sage, Arthur, Russell's wife Gretchen, and Russell.

such as newspapers and radio stations, and this made their financial situations more vulnerable.

The Des Moines and Minneapolis companies worked out a merger proposal in September 1981, and depending on the source, this was either to thrive or just survive. In February 1982, however, the Des Moines side called off the impending merger. Later that year to cut costs, the Des Moines company sold two radio stations and ended publication of the afternoon *Tribune*, merging it with the *Register*.[319]

Morley's appointment as a Minneapolis director in 1982 coincided with the company changing its name to Cowles Media. The new name better reflected its diverse assets that included television and publishing. That same year, directors, who included several family members, lost confidence in John Cowles Jr. as company CEO. First he shut down the *Buffalo Courier-Express* that September without consulting the board. His firing of Donald Dwight as publisher in Minneapolis drew further antagonism.

"[Directors] were troubled by what they saw as a lack of communication and were concerned about Cowles' abilities as an operator and manager," according to the book, *A History of Cowles Media Company*.[320] "By the time of the January 1983 board meeting, the die was cast. Cowles had not regained the confidence of the board," which included his sister Morley.

For Morley Ballantine, for *The Durango Herald*, for the Cowles media empire, 1983 was a watershed year. It elevated the role of some family members, plunged other family relationships into uncertainty, and reflected the changing role of newspapers in general.

Morley wrote to daughter Elizabeth and son-in-law Paul on February 7 from Minneapolis. She had seen them at Christmastime in Moscow, where Elizabeth was studying for a year.

"This has been one hell of a month since we were together and I am delighted it's over," she began.[321] About John Jr.'s resignation she wrote, "I'm not prepared to discuss it yet, if ever, thanks in part to the muddle [Des Moines Register and Tribune Company President Michael] Gartner got us all into during the merger talks."

She'd had her first eye surgery in 1979, and her serious eye troubles had just begun. En route to Chicago for a meeting with the Cowles Media Company board in January 1983, her retina "collapsed," as she put it. She somehow ignored the problem temporarily, suffered through the meeting, and then traveled to Miami to help her Uncle Mike Cowles celebrate his eightieth birthday on January 31.

Then she returned to Minneapolis for right eye surgery. Doctors gave her a fifty-fifty chance of seeing again with that eye. A few days later she was able to see something out of it, and was ready to head south for some much-needed R&R.

"Now I feel free at last and am off to Antigua (with friends)," she wrote February 7. "As I can neither snorkel nor play tennis, that sedate group will be fine. They are all good bridge players."

John Cowles Sr., meanwhile, was cooped up in the bedroom of his Minneapolis home, dying. The news that his son had been deposed didn't exactly cheer him up, Morley reported after a trip to his bedside.

"Father is frail. Took the news about John, who told him, in silence," Morley wrote. "I told Father this trip that I was deeply sorry about it, but that John and I loved each [other] very much and he took that too in silence. I wanted THAT on the record with him. It wouldn't surprise me if one morning Father simply didn't wake up."

John Cowles Sr. died at his Minneapolis home of cardiac arrest on Friday morning, February 25, 1983, at age eighty-four. So just weeks after dealing with the trauma of helping usher her brother out the door in Minneapolis, Morley, along with the entire family, was now in mourning.

She was being pulled in multiple directions, as another letter to Elizabeth and Paul attested in May. She had wanted to join them as they sailed from Hong Kong to San Francisco – their last adventure overseas after their year in Russia.

"I regret very much not accompanying you and drinking with Paul and maybe, even, playing bridge," Morley wrote from Durango on May 3.[322] "But the [Cowles Media Company] annual meeting with [cousin] David [Kruidenier] at the helm for the first time and a meeting of the voting trust and what John [Cowles Jr.] plans to be the last session before [her parents' house] possessions are dispersed tugged at my conscience."

After John Cowles Jr.'s resignation. David Kruidenier was elected to replace him as president and CEO. Kruidenier continued as chairman and CEO of the Des Moines Register and Tribune Company as well. "It's quite unusual to replace a CEO in an ordinary business," Kruidenier told the *Washington Journalism Review*, "but it's infinitely more complex when you add family relationships. It was a very difficult decision."[323]

John Cowles Jr. didn't concur with the decision, but no permanent family rift developed. "While I agree with much of their concern, I disagree with their conclusion," John Jr. also told the *Journalism Review*. "Nevertheless, I have high regard for the outside directors individually: I respect the possibility of their being right, and I shall remain on the board myself."

It was just four months after the turmoil in Minneapolis that Morley stepped down as *Durango Herald* publisher and Richard Ballantine stepped up. By fall of 1983, Elizabeth, thirty-five, had returned from the Soviet Union to Des Moines, where she'd been a reporter from 1976 to 1982, to work on her thesis and teach history at Drake University. She also was pregnant with her and husband Paul Leavitt's first child. Paul worked as a reporter and later city editor at the *Des Moines Register*.

Gardner "Mike" Cowles Jr., now eighty, was based in New York City and had stepped away from all involvement with the Des Moines media company. "I think it's a mistake for one generation that's basically retired to mastermind what another generation shall do," he told *The New York Times* in early 1983.[324]

Because of the business climate and poor decisions, things weren't going well for that next generation, which included Morley. As *Fortune* magazine wrote in an April 1983 story about Gardner Jr., "It [is] the third generation, now in control of the remaining family properties, worth an estimated $350 million, that [is] in trouble."[325]

Kruidenier was in charge of that next generation, but his critics pointed to a poor track record as an aggressive investor in Des Moines. Again, from *Fortune*:

> Kruidenier took over a profitable paper in 1971 with cash reserves of $11 million, went on an acquisition binge that ran up a staggering $40 million debt, and last year, after four years of declining operating earnings, posted the paper's first overall loss since Gardner Cowles Sr. bought it nearly eighty years ago.

The chaos in Des Moines was equal to that in Minneapolis. Several Register and Tribune Company stockholders, including some family, began to push for a sale of the company. Most family members, led by Kruidenier, resisted. The fourth generation's allegiance to the newspaper and media empire was not so great.

Between 1983 and 1985, Morley was busy keeping up with the volatile Des Moines situation. The beginning of the end came in November 1984, when three Register and Tribune Company executives put together a $112 million purchase offer with Dow Jones & Co. to purchase the Des Moines company. To the Cowles family, this seemed like a betrayal. Morley was among those "shocked" by the offer, and board trustees voted to turn it down.[326]

News of the offer, however, prompted other bidders to make a play. The stock value rose, making a sale more enticing. And it became apparent that among Gardner Cowles' grandchildren (the so-called "third generation"), the wish to sell was pervasive. Most of the "fourth generation," which included Morley's children, were even less inclined to save it for the family.[327]

Morley rushed to Des Moines as trustees met to discuss offers. The company was officially put up for sale, with bids due by January 25, 1985.[328] Gannett, publishers of *USA Today*, emerged the winner with a bid of $165 million. On January 31, the *Register* reported the sale:[329]

> The *Des Moines Register* was sold Thursday to Gannett Co., the nation's largest newspaper chain, for a price that made the sellers' jaws drop. Gannett agreed to pay about $200 million cash for the *Register*, the *Jackson* (Tenn.) *Sun* and two twice-weekly Iowa papers. ... The transaction will end eighty-two years of Cowles family ownership of the *Register*.

The actual purchase price exceeded the bid because it included several TV stations and a news syndicate. Directors approved the bid eight-to-zero, but not all family members were happy with the result. Elizabeth Ballantine had tried to stay out of the chaos, but had opposed the sale, calling it "terribly sad," since she had thought of the newspaper as "a family trust."[330]

Elizabeth, like many family members, understood the historical context. They knew the story of how her great-grandfather, Gardner Cowles Sr., purchased a flailing newspaper in 1903, and turned it by skill and dedication into one of the Midwest's most respected news gatherers and policy shapers.

The sale announcement came on Gardner "Mike" Cowles' eighty-second birthday. He was just turning a year old when his father made the purchase and moved the family from Algona to Des Moines. The *Register* reported that Jan Cowles, Mike's wife, said Mike characterized the sale as "marvelous" and had faith in Gannett to continue the family tradition.[331] Mike died five months later, on July 8, 1985, in New York; his lifespan coincided almost perfectly with the family's ownership of the *Register*.

The official handover to Gannett occurred Monday, July 1, after a meeting at the *Register*.

"Monday was a solemn day for a few heirs of Gardner Cowles [Sr.],"

The Register reported.[332] "After the meeting they walked through an exhibit of *Register* and *Tribune* artifacts – pictures of Gardner Cowles and his first editor, Harvey Ingham; cartoons by Frank Miller and Ding Darling; plates from historic front pages. A few said the sale never should have happened…. 'Of course, this is a very sad day,' said Morley Ballantine, a cousin of Kruidenier and a company director. 'Some of us hated to see the family give it up. But I have high hopes that Gannett will do for the *Register* what it deserves.'"

The family carried on and made the best of the situation. Later that year, Elizabeth Ballantine, Paul Leavitt, and their one-year-old son, Will, moved to Virginia so Paul could take a job with Gannett's flagship paper, *USA Today*.

A few years later, it appeared the *Minneapolis Star and Tribune* would go the way of the Des Moines newspaper. John Cowles Jr. turned sixty-one in 1990 and had grown weary of managing his father's estate and other trusts, and was ready to sell. But his eldest son, John III, known as Jay, wasn't yet ready. Neither were his cousins Richard Ballantine, who'd been appointed a board director in 1988, and Elizabeth Ballantine. The three led an effort among cousins to convince John Jr. not to sell, to give the next generation a chance to run it.[333] They were successful.

Morley, John Jr., and David Kruidenier resigned their seats on the voting trust – a select group picked to represent the family stockholders, who owned about sixty percent of the company – in December 1990. Cousins Elizabeth Ballantine and Jay Cowles were among their replacements. This voting trust consisted of about forty third- and fourth-generation family members, mostly on the John Sr. and Gardner Jr. branches, who met twice a year to discuss the business.

Elizabeth noted, and Jay Cowles concurred, that many of their generation shared a common point of view regarding the important role of newspapers and many other values. Conversation at the dinner table during family gatherings at Glendalough, Jay said, had a strong influence on his family's generation.[334]

In 1993, Richard retired from the Cowles Media Company board of directors, and Elizabeth was elected a director along with her cousin doctor Elizabeth Bullitt (the daughter of Sally Cowles Bullitt Doering, Morley's sister).

On top of her affinity for journalism, Elizabeth Ballantine, now forty-five, had established an impressive resume in other realms, including academia and law. It was a resume that dovetailed slightly with her father's. She had earned a Master of Studies at Yale Law School four decades after Arthur Jr. had received his Yale law degree. She had taught history at a university, received a J.D. degree in law in the midst of raising two children, and begun a lifetime commitment to board work in media and education.

Elizabeth Ballantine and Jay Cowles spent several long years – much of the 1990s – constantly flying around the country, attending meetings, trying to figure out how to make it work to keep Cowles Media Company in the family. It was a labor of love, but they were fighting a difficult battle. As the '90s progressed, the attitude of the voting trust changed. As it turned out, only Jay Cowles was playing a key role in operating the company. Economic conditions changed too, making a sale more attractive. Elizabeth and Jay eventually came around to this view, willing to consider a sale if the buyer shared the Cowles family's journalistic and civic values.[335]

In September 1997, Cowles Media Company revealed it was looking into operating options with other companies. Elizabeth Ballantine, as managing trustee of the Cowles Family Voting Trust, and Jay Cowles, as chairman of the board of directors, said that they and other family members had together reached the decision to sell. The family believed that if it was going to operate such a large business, more than just one family member should be involved in a substantive way in shaping its direction. Jay Cowles agreed on this point.[336]

On November 13, 1997, came the announcement that McClatchy Newspapers was acquiring Cowles Media for approximately $1.4 billion. Elizabeth called it "very exciting," and was confident that McClatchy would continue the tradition of strong journalism in the Twin Cities. She became a member of the McClatchy board of directors.[337]

Advocating for Women

Without designing a grand plan, Morley began to make an even larger impact on the world around her. This was the standard her family had set, and she had set for herself. Her resume now showed two-plus decades as a publisher, and her credibility as a business leader, journalist, and Durangoan was firmly established. Opportunities presented themselves, and she took advantage of those as she lived life to the fullest.

Morley backed issues that she believed supported women's rights, which could be unpopular and political. This included the intertwined causes of abortion funding and population control.

Morley, ca. 1991

Women's organizations were gaining strength in Colorado and nationally. This was the era of debate over the Equal Rights Amendment, championed by the National Organization of Women, or NOW, a group considered radical by some, but which Morley joined in the mid-1970s.[338] The ERA was passed by Congress in 1972 but never ratified. With the influence of her recently deceased mother strong in her heart, these were natural issues for Morley. She put energy into both editorials and action.

In 1976, as part of a nationwide effort to commemorate the upcoming International Women's Year, Morley was one of fifty-two women appointed to the Consultant Council for the Colorado Women's Conference. She was the only Durango representative. Fifty-six state meetings were held in 1977 on "the rights and responsibilities of women." A national committee then made "recommendations to eliminate the barriers that prevent women from participating fully and equally in all aspects of national life."[339]

At the same time, in late 1976 and early 1977, Morley became a charter member of the Women's Forum of Colorado, the third oldest such forum in the country. The Forum held its first meeting in January 1977. Membership is by invitation-only and limited to 160.[340] It was incorporated to gather "women of significant and diverse accomplishments," to exchange ideas, develop bonds, and exert influence in state matters. It included Colorado's women leaders in business, government, education, the arts, and journalism.

American women were, and still are to a great extent, taught that beauty will take them a long way. Morley had both beauty and brains, and while she didn't disdain the former, she focused on and encouraged in others the latter. In a June 1977 editorial, MCB compared an event she attended in Boulder, the Colorado Women's Conference, with an event held that same weekend in Sterling, the Miss Colorado pageant. "It was enough to make almost any woman, liberated or not, either weep or guffaw, depending," she wrote.[341]

Morley described the underhanded shenanigans involved in the pageants, including mothers sponsoring lightly attended pageants merely for their daughters to win scholarships and perhaps further their acting or public relations careers.

She wrote that the board chairman of the Miss America pageant called the swimsuit lineup "the acid test of poise," by exposing "any gross physical deformities." Her editorial juxtaposed that shallow attitude with "Lean on me, I'm your sister" as the theme at the Boulder Women's Conference. MCB concluded: "It doesn't take a great deal of imagination to suspect that just the opposite was the unspoken thread through the Sterling affair.

In the 1980s her belief in equal rights for women led her away from the Reagan Republicans, who were more conservative than the Eisenhower and even the Nixon Republicans before them. For example, in 1984 she joined Colorado Taxpayers for Choice, and was listed as an "advisor" on the organization's stationery. The group opposed an amendment to the Colorado Constitution that would cut off public funds for abortion.

"We will need every resource to defeat this cruel and discriminatory proposed [constitutional] amendment. Please continue to use your extensive influence to help us do so," Mary Hoagland, treasurer of Colorado Taxpayers for Choice ("NO on #3") wrote to Morley, while thanking her for a generous $500 contribution.[342] To Morley's and the group's dismay, this amendment passed.

Morley had also joined Republicans for Choice, a national Planned Parenthood project. In the 1980s the Reagan administration, because of its opposition to abortion, proposed ending $100 million in US support to international family planning programs.[343] The Reagan administration unveiled its new position paper prior to an August 1984 UN International Conference on Population in Mexico City.

Morley became such a proponent of world population control that the director of the Population Action Council, Werner Fornos, honored *The Durango Herald* with an "Award for Media Excellence" in January 1981 in Washington, D.C.[344] The award was for "fostering support to solve the world population crisis through a demonstrated commitment to share ideas, knowledge, and experience towards the ultimate objective of reducing population growth and creating a better life for all the world's people."

Morley's support for Planned Parenthood in Durango, as well as annual donations from the Ballantine Family Fund, were extremely welcome by those in the thick of the pro-choice battle. Durangoan Pat Rustad, a self-professed "feminist," worked at Planned Parenthood for thirty-two years as a health care assistant. She recalled that *The Durango Herald* prominently displayed a story about the large March 1986 "March for Women's Lives" pro-choice rally in Washington, D.C.[345]

"She was an inspiration for many of us older women when we were fighting feminist battles," Rustad said.[346] "For those of us early feminists in town, she was always there for us, always supportive. That was a very good thing when we weren't so popular."

Morley kept an eye on national and local Planned Parenthood happenings. In July 1982 an MCB *Herald* editorial called a local United Way board of directors decision to eliminate funding for Planned Parenthood "unfortunate."[347] Morley was upset, but didn't anticipate the even more indignant reaction of a relatively new employee.

Deborah Uroda, a *Herald* reporter from 1981-86, became furious with letter after letter to the *Herald* demonizing women who had abortions. Age twenty-seven at the time, Uroda typed out a revealing story about having gone through an abortion. It was about, "how I was such a young girl, and how I was so frightened at the age of nineteen to have a child, and so poor. It really felt like the only option I had."[348]

Morley read the as-yet-unpublished story, and called the author into her office. Uroda was apprehensive, not knowing why she was being summoned. To Uroda, Morley, still the publisher at the time, was "an imperial figure," "the big boss woman." She was "damn smart," well-read, connected, intimidating. "Of course my heart [was] beating hard," she recalled of this watershed moment in her life.

"My dear girl," Morley asked Uroda, "do you really want to have this published?"

"Yes I do," Uroda responded. "People need to know that women who have abortions don't do it lightly. They have to have a choice."

"I'm very proud of you, young woman."

Said Uroda, nearly four decades later: "She cared enough to make sure I knew what I was in for. But she was also very proud of me and supportive for speaking my piece."

In her Editor at Large column the next year, Morley celebrated the occasion of Planned Parenthood of Mid-Iowa naming a new building after her mother, Elizabeth Bates Cowles.[349]

In 1986, Morley became a founding member of the Women's Foundation of Colorado. The foundation was created to accelerate economic opportunities for women, mostly through lobbying efforts and grants. Key issues are education, child-care costs, equal pay, and equal opportunity in the workforce. The philosophy is that equitable opportunities for women will create "stronger families, communities, and economies."[350]

Morley parlayed her involvement in the Women's Foundation of Colorado into a more local effort. The foundation, only a year after its creation, and with Morley's backing, sponsored a meeting in Durango to discuss women's issues. Forty-five women attended the Saturday, May 16, 1987, gathering at Fort Lewis College.[351] It was the first of five such meetings the Women's Foundation sponsored around the state, and this one brought women from as far as Alamosa. The attendees broke into small groups to discuss jobs, domestic violence, health, child care, housing, and education. MCB wrote a column that appeared two days before her sixty-second birthday:

> There was a great deal of vitality, of energy, brains, and commitment represented. I was fascinated to meet a number of the younger women I had known only through name recognition. In the general session that followed, where somebody from each group reported the gist of the discussion, it was made clear that the overwhelmingly desired object was a women's center.

A meeting was set for June 25 at the Durango Mothers Center for further talk about a women's, or resource, center. And later that year, with Morley as a founder and board member, the Durango Women's Resource Center became a reality.

The Center was viewed as a one-stop shop, especially for single and recently divorced women with limited job skills and education. Buzzwords were "self-sufficiency" and "personal empowerment." It was designed not only for women in crisis, but for small-business owners, and to provide resources and tools for girls in La Plata County. The Center also served as a facilitator of sorts, working with other social service and community organizations. It assisted 200 women in its first year, and as of 2022 assists about 1,400 a year.

Much of the Center's growth came under the directorship of Susan Lander, who held the reins from 1994-2001. By then Morley was no longer on the board, but remained very involved. Susan leaned on her, and vice versa.

"Morley would call me and had this funny way with her voice. She'd go, 'Su-SAN??'" Lander said.[352] "And I knew I had to do something." While not exactly demanding, Morley had a way of getting done what she wanted done. "She was a great mentor," Lander said. "She was very open and approachable – of course, she was intimidating because she was who she was. I respected her and honored her, but I felt comfortable talking to her and going to see her."

The Women's Resource Center initiated events that Morley championed such as Womenfest, and programs such as Ready>Set>Go. Womenfest drew 300 or more attendees for an annual fall event featuring talks and workshops.

"Womenfest '98 takes place Saturday, and for women it's clearly the place to be," MCB wrote in a 1998 Editor at Large piece.[353] "When the first one took place just three years ago, it was evident from the start that making possible a number of workshops on a variety of topics was clearly an idea whose time had come. Equally interesting was the number of experienced women around who could lead discussions of sophisticated subjects."

Ready>Set>Go, or RSG, began in 1998, emphasizing economic self-sufficiency. Trained, volunteer mentors worked with women weekly for three or more months. Morley wrote in December 1998:[354]

> RSG takes into account the fact that women struggling to get ahead financially usually face other problems such as difficulty in balancing the demands of family and job or domestic violence or the threat of it. There is the need for competent, affordable daycare; often financial planning advice is sought. In short, all kinds of help is needed and RSG has women trained in a variety of specialties who can help.

For Lander, Morley was always a steady, valuable resource who would take her calls and welcome her visits. "I just hadn't had such an influential, strong, giving woman for a long time that mentored me and would help me if I had a question, and direct me," Lander said. "Say, 'do it this way,' or 'do it that way.'"

After more than thirty years, and with some new programs and events, the Women's Resource Center is going strong.

Around 1990 a group of career media women in Southwest Colorado established a local branch of a national organization, Women in Communications Inc., or WICI. They met once a month, and scheduled presentations from either locals or out-of-town experts.

It was a great day, members realized, when Morley Ballantine became engaged with WICI and became a regular.

"Here she was, the publisher of *The Durango Herald*. ... The matriarch of communications was there with us," said Uroda, who by then was director of college relations at Fort Lewis College. "It was important to have someone of her caliber encouraging us in our pursuit of professional development."

Joanne Spina, then a public information officer with the La Plata County Sheriff's Office, was among those who spearheaded the group.[355] "She was so charming and entertaining and knowledgeable about everything," Spina said of Morley. "It was like sitting at the knee of the master and you just wanted to hear every story she could tell."

With her ability to encapsulate an issue and her droll sense of humor, "She knew how to bring things to a head very quickly," Spina said. "She put the point on things."

Perhaps most important, Morley gave an aura that it was nothing unusual for women to take roles that traditionally had been men's.

"She normalized it for us," Spina said. "She didn't see it as anything extraordinary. She just felt that that was her place all along. That was the feeling she gave you as well. She had such self-confidence in her abilities, that this is where she belonged. That she was the most competent person in the room."

Spina knew from private conversations with Morley and from what others told her, that Morley continued to closely follow Spina's career. In 2017, Spina became the first woman to take the role of La Plata County manager. It was an occasion that Spina wished Morley could have seen.

Promoting Education

As a newspaper publisher with a growing reputation and impressive resume, Morley's ideas and presence were valued. Her deep appreciation for education made volunteer work in that field a natural fit.

In 1976 Morley became one of the first female board trustees at Fountain Valley School, the boarding school in Colorado Springs from which both Richard (1964) and Bill (1968) had graduated. She served as trustee for nearly twenty years. A major gift from the Ballantine family helped the school, in 1999, complete a living area for both students and faculty, called the Ballantine House.

Morley also was trustee at Choate Rosemary Hall, the boarding school in Connecticut from which she'd graduated back in 1943. (Rosemary Hall for girls merged with Choate School for boys in 1971.)

More and more, she was called upon to deliver talks. This was not her natural milieu. She preferred smaller gatherings where her soft voice could be heard. She worked to improve her public speeches, and toiled overtime to write them.

Often her talks revolved around journalism, but sometimes around education, or philanthropy, or women's issues. A couple of times she gave commencement addresses – in 1978 at Colorado Women's College in Denver and in 1980 at Simpson College in Indianola, Iowa.[356] Simpson simultaneously awarded her an honorary degree, Doctor of Humane Letters.

To begin her address to Simpson graduates, she pointed out that her grandfather, Gardner Cowles, had been born just fifty miles east in Oskaloosa, Iowa, and his first job after graduating college was as school superintendent in Algona.[357]

> Obviously education has long been of interest within my family and so it is that I am honored to be here today. ... After sixteen years of formal schooling, one would be entitled to think that the learning process was coming to an end. Paradoxically, this is not true. What you have been doing is putting building blocks in place, and you have really just begun.

Morley, who had turned fifty-five a few days prior to the address, shared many of her life's lessons with the 150 or so graduates. Change, adaptability, and finding happiness were among the main themes.

> I have lived my adult life thus far in the time of the greatest change that mankind has yet seen. ... Change, of course, is unsettling and threatening, and rapid change just that much more so. But surely one of the most important items I have learned is that the unexpected should be expected. This fact shouldn't produce fear or paranoia; rather, it should evoke in us a sense of wonder, of excitement. Truly, what next?
>
> Something else I've learned about life: logic, reason, fairness, loyalty often do not apply nor do they always win over reality. It is fair to say ... that life is not fair. If you expect it to be, you will be disappointed.
>
> Happiness: there's another adult consideration. ... To strive to be happy is an important effort. Our forefathers, in the dedication of this land, put it third in importance, after life and liberty. ... A trouble is that some people (men and women alike) go looking for happiness in the most curious places. It does not come from the beauty parlor or Wall Street or a singles bar or your local sports car dealer. Rather it comes from giving love and receiving it and, more paradox, sometimes the

latter is more difficult than the former. It comes from something you are pleased with and proud of. It comes from children, from friends, from a hike in the mountains, from shared laughter.

Rather, feel guilty if you are not happy, for it is your nature to be so.

At age thirty-four, Sherry Manning became one of the youngest college presidents ever in America. This was the fall of 1977, and the Maryland-raised woman – and mother of two – was excited to take the top post at Colorado Women's College in Denver. But she was disappointed that among the school's trustees was just one woman, Katie Stapleton, who shared Manning's chagrin and wanted to do something about it. Most boards at that time, whether colleges or charities or businesses, consisted of mostly or all men.

Manning, in reflecting on this era, pointed out that it was the time that women in America began to rapidly redefine their roles. "The mission of a women's college was barely a notch above a finishing school, but things were changing," Manning said.[358] "Betty Friedan, Gloria Steinem, and others had stirred the pot of unrest for women to do and be more."

A landmark and well-publicized study by Elizabeth Tidball, published in 1973, showed that the success rates for graduates of women's colleges were well above those of women graduates of coed schools. They were more successful in professional life and even had lower divorce rates.

"CWC, which had struggled financially … offered an incredible opportunity to build on that research and turn around an institution that had a tradition of sound academics with the ruggedness of the West," Manning said.

Stapleton had met Morley through their joint philanthropic efforts. She knew that Morley was still finding her way after Arthur's death, still setting a path for a life without her constant companion. Stapleton was adamant that the CWC board needed more women, and, rightly or wrongly, she believed Morley needed "something to do." She suggested that Morley be invited to give CWC's spring commencement address, and this would give Manning a chance to evaluate her as a potential trustee.

Manning was so busy during graduation in spring 1978, that she barely had time to meet Morley. Her first impressions were favorable, although she saw Morley as "fragile." What Manning didn't know was how bad Morley's eyes were, which contributed to her impression.

In October 1978, Manning flew to Durango to court Morley for the board. When she arrived at the *Herald*, there was a snag: Morley was unavailable. Something unexpected had come up. As she walked around Durango to kill time, Manning felt the disappointment of wasting so much effort and money – a plane ticket between Denver and Durango was not, and is still not, cheap. But that evening she took a chance and called Morley at the *Herald*.

"I apologized for bothering her, but said as long as I was in town, I'd love to take her to dinner – she had to eat dinner somewhere – and she said, 'yes.' I learned later that night that her longtime editor [Louis Newell] had just unceremoniously walked off the job, and her challenge that morning was getting the paper out. When I heard that, I knew Morley was my new trustee!" From then on, the women were on a first-name basis.[359]

Morley approached her new role with gusto. Colorado Women's College recruited students from around the state, and in Durango, Morley created a model for doing this. She arranged for Manning to meet with the local paper (not hard), talk on the radio, speak with local high school students, and call on alumnae and potential donors. All in a whirlwind day-plus on Manning's "whistle-stop" tour of Western Colorado. CWC trustees in other towns on the tour saw what Morley had done and followed the model. For a few years this was an annual event.

"After a long day of interviews and speeches, I'd stay with Morley, perhaps take her to dinner, then we'd talk late into the evening, about the *Herald*, about Arthur, about her children," Manning said. "She became more than a trusted and effective trustee; she became a dear friend, a mentor and model for me."

At that time there weren't many women who were role models as leaders. Just being able to discuss things, to talk about what Morley was doing – which was a lot – helped the CWC president immensely. Manning later became a notable and successful business entrepreneur in the educational field.

"I'd never met anybody who had such a rich life," Manning said of Morley.

Manning was trying to figure out how to balance a career, a husband, and two children – along with the challenge of directing a large enterprise. Some women told Manning that working so much was ruining her children's lives. Morley was a sounding board with experience in all these areas. "Hello Dear Girl," Morley would say each time in greeting, and instantly with that welcome, Manning felt the intimacy of their friendship.

Morley would spend hours talking about her four children, now all entering or in their thirties, and what she expected and worried about for each. Manning's children were still very young. "I guess I just didn't know that you could have children that you loved with your entire heart, with no reservation, and still be looking at them with a critical perspective."

Manning visited Durango and Morley several times a year. Often in the summer she'd bring her husband, Charles, and their two children. Morley introduced the Mannings to Colvig Silver Camps, an outdoor adventure camp a few miles east of Durango, and the children spent several summers there. With Morley's coaxing, their daughter Kelly enrolled at Fountain Valley School, where Morley was a trustee and Sherry was later a trustee.

Charles was Colorado's deputy executive director of higher education, and Morley enjoyed talking to him about Fort Lewis College and aspects of higher education. Charles would water the grass for Morley, and hose off the deck of the pool.

It wasn't long before Morley and Sherry had to redefine their relationship. CWC, despite increasing enrollment, could not overcome its financial hole. In 1982 it merged with the University of Denver, and Manning's tenure was over. She lost track of most of the trustees, but not of Morley.

When Colorado Women's College merged with the University of Denver in 1982, Morley became a DU trustee. And that's when she met Dan Ritchie, named a DU trustee at the same time. It didn't take long for the two to become friends as they found themselves with "fights in common," Ritchie recalled.[360]

Ritchie was finishing a stint as chief executive officer of New York-based Westinghouse Broadcasting, so he and Morley related successes and tribulations of the media business. "She was a great fighter," Ritchie said, "a very strong, smart, principled lady you could trust with your life. She would do what she said she would do. She told the truth, and her judgment was terrific."

Morley was generous in contributing to the university, and was interested in music, the arts, and women's matters. They both supported a program to help deserving disadvantaged students get free tuition. Like Ritchie, she was interested in making DU not just a good university, but a great one. So when Ritchie was named the school's chancellor in 1989, he leaned on Morley. She was very supportive as the school went against many trustees' wishes and established a study abroad program.

"We really believed the whole world needs to work together and get to know one another," Ritchie said, and it's not hard to imagine Morley saying something similar. Most University of Denver students now take advantage of the program. Ritchie remained chancellor until 2005. Whenever he needed a confidant, Morley was there for him.

"While I was chancellor and as long as she was able to receive anyone, I would drive to Durango to see her," Ritchie said. They'd spend a couple of hours together in the morning and then have lunch before Ritchie returned to Denver. "She was so much fun, and so smart, and such a good person, I just missed her."

Morley left the DU board of trustees in 2002. At the university's June 2002 commencement ceremonies, she received an honorary degree, the so-called Doctor of Humane Letters, for her contributions and dedication to the school. "Which," Ritchie said, "we don't do very often for retiring board members."

Organizations

Morley was an early member of the esteemed Colorado Forum, an invitation-only, nonpartisan group of men and women leaders in various fields around the state who delve into key and tricky issues. It is one of the state's most powerful lobbying groups. The seventy-seven members, several of whom live in Durango will publicly support a policy only if there is 100 percent agreement.[361]

The Colorado Forum supported the Animas-La Plata water project, for example, and sent members to Washington, D.C., to speak on its behalf. A-LP was a plan to provide domestic and irrigation water to Native American tribes as well as the "dry side" of La Plata County. Morley was an important part of that effort.[362]

"Morley was one of my all-time favorites," said Gail Klapper, a leading voice among Colorado women since the 1970s. Klapper lost a close race for state attorney general in 1982, and has been Colorado Forum president since 1989. Her board work is extensive, and she finds time to raise show horses on a ranch in Elbert, northeast of Colorado Springs.

Klapper described Morley as a rare women's voice in the publishing world, particularly in the 1980s. As a bonus, Morley made Klapper laugh. Most of all, it was her demeanor, and her encouraging people of differing views to speak up, that made her stand out. And when it was her turn, because people knew how much thought she'd put into what she had to say, "Morley spoke volumes," Klapper said. "She always knew what she was talking about. She did her research."

Detailed minutes were kept during meetings and sent to members. It was in the newspaper publisher's blood to edit thoroughly. "I would always receive red-lined copies back [from Morley]," Klapper said. "That's just how Morley operated. I consider myself the red-liner but she was a much better editor than I. … It was symbolic of Morley, because she wanted everything to be in perfect shape, and she made it happen in Durango and she helped us make it happen in Colorado."

Morley continued serving on a statewide level until it became difficult for her to travel.

From 1988 to 1992 she served on a Colorado Association of Commerce and Industry steering committee – Blueprint for Colorado. The association, known at CACI, serves as the statewide chamber of commerce and promotes business-friendly laws. The Blueprint was basically a five-year economic master plan for the state that addressed economic stability, workforce development, taxation, infrastructure, and growth.

At the time Morley served on Blueprint for Colorado the state was trying to bounce back from an economic downturn that occurred in the late 1980s. Sherry Manning, who was also on the board, said Morley would never draw attention to herself, but would eventually say her piece in her matter-of-fact, reasoned, non-demonstrative way. Particularly when it came to long debates over water issues.

"She was very quiet," Manning said.[363] "Very thoughtful, very powerful. … She would wait until everybody had exhausted themselves. And then she would say, 'from the Western Colorado perspective …' And the day was over. It was just so obvious that [what she said] was what you needed to do."

Through her columns, her connections, and her funding, Morley brought a spotlight to multiple nonprofits. Philanthropy and community support were ingrained in her, practically from birth, and she fully believed in them. Morley's brother Russell Cowles, eleven years younger than his big sister, saw how these beliefs were passed down.

"A lot of the concepts, and the moral and ethical values that my mother and father had, rubbed off on all of us," Russell said.[364] "And to a large extent Morley, because Morley was in the same business as my father, and she was the oldest."

The four children of John and Elizabeth Cowles picked up their parents' philosophies directly and indirectly, at dinner table discussions and from seeing their actions. The children saw the kinds of organizations their parents supported most heartily and the kinds of people they associated with – particularly those who were working toward improvement of quality of life both locally and around the world.

Once she had established credibility within the community, Morley's goals became easier to accomplish. And she helped others with worthy goals. If you had a fledgling organization or event in Southwest Colorado, you wanted Morley Ballantine on your side.

As her brother Russell Cowles explained, "It's hard when you are starting an organization to get people to give to you because you have no track record. You have the vision, but you don't have the credibility. So how do you get credibility? Well, you have to get people on board who have standing in the community, who have credibility themselves."

And if you firmly believe in the cause you are supporting, then your gift is its own reward.

"When I have been asked to give money to an organization I believe in," Russell Cowles said, "they ask, 'Do you want your name to be used? Do you want acknowledgment?' And my answer is, 'Only if it will help your mission. It's not because I want my name on the building. Do you see a way that it's going to be a benefit to you, to have my name associated with it?'"

Morley deeply understood philanthropy, and she knew when it was successful and when it wasn't. Her philosophy, from a December 2000 column:[365]

> We believe that the best way to "help mankind" is to make it possible for "mankind" to help itself. When Dottie Lamm was aiding in the founding of the Women's Foundation of Colorado back in 1986 she went around saying that you didn't give a hungry man a fish, you didn't give him six fish either. Instead you taught him how to fish.

Morley's connections helped bring the 1998 Rural Philanthropy Days conference to Durango. It was organized locally by Susan Lander, of the Women's Resource Center, and it was a big success. Rural Philanthropy Days is a three-day conference that rotates among eight regions and is hosted periodically in Durango. It was designed to encourage foundations, which are concentrated along the Front Range, to become familiar with and contribute to rural nonprofits and their communities.

In a September 1998 column following Philanthropy Days, MCB wrote that fifty "funders" got "the feel" for almost 100 Southwest Colorado nonprofits:[366]

> There is increasing evidence that the big state philanthropic organizations are interested in spending more of their funds outside of the Denver metro area. And it's clear that the growing nonprofits – both in size and in number – in Southwest Colorado are better organized, more efficiently run, and meeting genuine needs better than they have ever done before. They're learning how to make their cases. So bringing the two sides together, as was done here for a day and a half last week, is bound to be productive. ... There's a lot going on out there, for sure. Philanthropy Days is helping sort it out.

Morley's participation with the League of Women Voters fluctuated, but her encouragement did not. In 2003 she offered the *Herald's* technical help in hosting a League website. From the time she joined in 1953 she made an impact, introducing ideas – using an agenda, for instance – to streamline meetings that she feared might squander her valuable time. In May 2005, at its fifty-ninth annual meeting, the La Plata County League of Women Voters honored Morley as its first fifty-year member.[367]

"She's always been a faithful advocate and consultant to our LWV," President Marilyn Brown wrote in the local League's newsletter.[368] "Our website ... is the most recent example of Morley's generosity."

When Joanne Spina's mother died of breast cancer in April 1995, Spina decided to coordinate a five-kilometer run/walk to raise money to fight the disease. But she required kickstart funding. Spina applied for a $500 grant from the Ballantine Family Fund, and felt Morley's hand in the rewarding of the money.

The inaugural event was held in October 1995, and it has been an annual affair, raising nearly $150,000 as of 2021 to prevent and treat breast cancer. Event proceeds fund mammograms for women who can't otherwise afford them, and the event itself honors those whose families have been affected by breast cancer.

Morley and Richard have contributed to numerous local causes through both the Ballantine Family Fund and *The Durango Herald*, which supported events – music, sporting events and competitions, and charity fundraisers.

Morley's support of the local arts scene never wavered. She championed finding a home for the arts community for decades. This was a drawn-out process that took an abundance of patience and faith. In the early 1980s local leaders drafted a plan for the arts community to use an old power plant and La Plata Electric Association building along the Animas River.

An MCB editorial in October 1981 touted the plan and encouraged pledges in support of the project.[369]

> The marketing study ... shows the project could generate income of $100,000, when all is in place, against expenses of $40,000. There's no doubt about art, etc., being big business these days. ... With a proper facility here, plus sensible management, a center here would have a positive economic impact.

That plan never came to fruition. But the dream survived. In 1997, the visual and performing arts got a double boost with the opening of both the Community Concert Hall at Fort Lewis and the Durango Arts Center, or DAC, downtown. DAC's home is a 17,000-square-foot remodeled car dealership on the corner of East Second Avenue

and Eighth Street. It hosts exhibits, plays, movies, music, fundraisers, and more.

It took a while for the Durango Arts Center to work out its bugs, and Morley the arts critic made sure to acknowledge a problem in a September 1998 Editor at Large column:[370]

There is something about that stage in what started life as Pat Murphy Motors service garage that swallows words, sentences, whole paragraphs if an actor is not paying attention. From the beginning Saturday night the first [actor] did not project her voice adequately. It faded in and out and unfortunately reminded me of last year's performance of *Lear*, which was so difficult to hear. (A difficult work, at best.)

May 2004, when Fort Lewis College presented Morley a Bachelor's Degree in Humane Letters. Front, Helen Ballantine Healy, Morley, Elizabeth Ballantine; back, Bill Ballantine, John Cowles Jr., and Richard Ballantine.

Morley supported the arts and music in myriad ways. She made sure her newspaper covered local and touring cultural events, and had a strong arts and entertainment section. She served on the Durango Arts Council. She championed Western Opera Theatre, a touring group from San Francisco that performed at the Fort Lewis gym and presented workshops in local grade schools. From 1983-1985, Morley served as president of the Four Corners Opera Association.[371]

She was involved in the creation in 1987 of Music in the Mountains, becoming – along with Bank of Colorado's Steve Parker – one of the initial key sponsors. Morley lent a steady hand and financial support to the continued growth of the festival, which for three decades was held at Purgatory ski area before shifting exclusively to in-town sites in 2019.

History and archaeology went hand-in-hand with arts and culture. She helped the Animas Museum, which showcases history of the area, stay afloat and build a new roof when the time came in the early 2000s.

The study of Native American archaeology was high on Morley's list, and an area of focus in Ballantine Family Fund grants. This started with the Center of Southwest Studies but expanded. Crow Canyon Archaeological Center, now a 170-acre research center and classroom northwest of Cortez, was founded in 1972. Students travel to the area to help with digs and learn about ancestral Puebloan inhabitants. Richard Ballantine has served on Crow Canyon's board of trustees since 1988.

The Ballantine Family Fund has also contributed to the Canyons of the Ancients Visitor Center and Museum (formerly the Anasazi Heritage Center) near Dolores, and to the Mesa Verde Foundation, a nonprofit that supports projects and programs at Mesa Verde National Park. The foundation purchased land and paid for architectural plans for the Visitor and Research Center at the park entrance. The center, opened in 2012, also serves as a needed storehouse of artifacts.

What's Good for the Town

Several months after Arthur died, Morley took his spot as a member of the First National Bank of Durango board of directors. This boardroom was filled with heavy hitters. Meetings among this collection of business moguls and community organizers were the genesis of an outsized proportion of major projects the town achieved.

One of Morley's longtime friends on the board was Robert "Bob" Beers, who owned gas stations and a propane business. As city councilor and Durango mayor in 1961-62, he played a large role in getting the town's streets paved and took a lot of heat for doing it.[372]

Beers also played a big role in the development of Purgatory ski area. He headed the San Juan Development Company, which raised money from interested investors to create the ski area twenty-five miles north of Durango. This effort sparked community buy-in and involvement, something essential for Purgatory to be a success. Morley and Arthur were among eighty contributors who pledged a combined $500,000 to Purgatory developer Ray Duncan.

Beers and Morley (and Arthur) saw eye-to-eye on multiple issues that involved town improvement, and all three were big boosters of Fort Lewis College. Beers served on the bank board from 1959 to 2004, an era that paralleled the time that Arthur and then Morley Ballantine were board members.[373]

Bob Lieb, a businessman who arrived in Durango in 1978 and later served on the bank board, leaned on Beers and Morley when he had questions about important happenings in town.[374] "I figured if I couldn't get a good answer from those two, I wasn't going to get one," Lieb said.

As a woman, Morley was a First National Bank board minority. But her demeanor allowed her to become instantly effective. "I always respected her style," said Steve Short, former First National president.[375] "A lot of times people want to dominate meetings with what they have to say. And their mouth is sometimes getting ahead of their brain. She was so respectful about processing her ideas before she spoke. ... Morley didn't always have a whole lot to say, but when she did talk, it was something you wanted to listen to."

Education being of utmost importance to Morley, she continued to support her now alma mater with zeal. She became a member of the executive committee of the Fort Lewis College Foundation board.

Plans were under way in the early 1990s for a free-standing Center of Southwest Studies, a grand new building that would give the school a unique area of scholastic expertise and focus. But then came 1993 and one of the biggest snowfalls on record. Wet, heavy snow quickly piled high on flat roofs around campus – too quickly to remove before disaster struck. In the early morning darkness of January 19, a Tuesday, the roof of the Fine Arts Building's auditorium collapsed under the weight. It appeared more like a bomb had detonated inside the building than a simple roof collapse. Very fortunately, no one was inside; just two hours later classes were to begin. The 490-seat auditorium – the only formal, large-capacity performance venue in the region, built in 1971 – was destroyed.

A decision was made to reverse course, recalled Sheri Rochford Figgs, who served in the admissions and alumni offices, and took on fundraising chores in coordination with the Fort Lewis College Foundation.[376] The Southwest Studies project would be put on hold, and the college, led by President Joel Jones, would take this opportunity to create a long-sought concert hall. Consultants, however, told Jones that they doubted the foundation could raise the money necessary to rebuild. He and the foundation had faith they could, and enlisted Morley to co-chair their $5 million capital campaign.[377] This was a daunting task.

Sheri Rochford grew up in Durango on West Second Avenue, just a couple of blocks away from the Ballantines. She knew and admired the family, but didn't know them well; Sheri began high school at the time Helen Ballantine was graduating. Now in her thirties, Sheri was excited and nervous to be working with Morley. Quickly she discovered, as she tried to make key connections with potential donors such as the El Pomar Foundation, that having Morley Ballantine on her side was golden.

"We could name-drop her," Rochford Figgs said. "That would be how I could get an appointment."

Don Mapel, president of the regional Coca-Cola distributorship, served alongside Morley on the Colorado Forum, but first on the Fort Lewis College Foundation during her time as board president.

"That's where I came in contact with her influence," Mapel said.[378] "She could get things moving in a rather dramatic fashion. ... If you weren't quite in sync with what she wanted to do, it was uncomfortable. But she was never vindictive. She had what she wanted to get done and was always lobbying for what she thought was important. ... If you had Morley on your side, you were going a long way."

The money was raised, and the 600-seat Fort Lewis College Community Concert Hall opened in May 1997. It gave the area a beautiful, high-quality venue with exceptional acoustics where musicians from rock to jazz to classical are honored to perform.[379] Jones would say that funding and building the hall was the greatest success in his ten-year presidential tenure.

The Center of Southwest Studies had continued to expand its collections under Bob Delaney's leadership.[380] The Ballantines supported him at every step. On May 16, 1980, in a ceremony attended by Morley and all four children, the Arthur Ballantine Southwest Research Room was dedicated on the top floor of Reed library.[381] This room featured exhibits of artifacts and weavings; prominent was a huge ceramic map of the Southwest, designed and created by Delaney and architect James Hunter.[382]

By 1985 the Center had run out of storage space at the library, and the collection was scattered across campus and at five rented storage areas.[383] Delaney retired in 1986. Despite the change of plans due to the 1993 roof collapse, Southwest Studies was not forgotten. Morley wouldn't let this happen.

The chairs were barely bolted in place at the Concert Hall when plans were resurrected for the new Center of Southwest Studies building. Again, a consultant told Fort Lewis that finding money was going to be unlikely; after all, the community had just ponied up big-time for the concert venue. Funding a nearly $8 million project, with a small community chipping in millions, seemed like a longshot. Yet again, Morley, Joel Jones, and the FLC Foundation were not dissuaded.

Beginning in 1997, as campaign chairman, Morley led a three-year drive to raise more than $3 million for construction.[384] The rest would come from state, federal, and matching funds. Sheri Rochford Figgs, tabbed to work alongside Morley in the campaign, was told that Morley was simply a figurehead, and that she, Sheri, would be doing all the real work. That would not be the case at all.

"She was exceptional," Rochford Figgs said. Morley held regular meetings with the committee, either at the Southwest Center at Reed library or at *The Durango Herald*. She planned the agenda, ran the meetings, gave assignments. Deborah Uroda, who knew Morley from her years as a reporter for the *Herald*, by this time was director of college relations at Fort Lewis. In that role, she worked closely with Rochford Figgs on fundraising and understood Morley was not to be trifled with.

"We just knew that if you said you'd have something done, you'd better have it done by the next meeting," Uroda said. "She would brook no fools."

Morley laid down the law in her typical acerbic style when a couple of members were chronically late to meetings. "All the rest of us are on time," she plainly told the group. "We need to agree to all be on time. It's disruptive to those who get here promptly." No one, Rochford Figgs said, was ever late again.

Again, Morley's ability to use her clout and connections came in handy. The possibility of getting federal earmark money (budget funds appropriated by Congress to a specific cause) arose, and Rochford Figgs enlisted Morley to get US Sen. Ben Nighthorse Campbell's help. Campbell lived in Ignacio, southeast of Durango, with his wife, Linda. Morley told Rochford Figgs to schedule a dinner with Linda Campbell and Mary Jane Clark, Morley's close friend. Clark's Toh-Atin Gallery employed the Campbells' daughter, Shanan, and sold the Campbells' jewelry. Apparently Morley made a strong case at the dinner. Sen. Campbell's staff jumped into action.

"The next day … my fax machine was smoking," Rochford Figgs recalled.

Sen. Campbell used his pull to earmark $1 million for the project in the federal budget. Money continued to roll in, and with hard work and perseverance, the $3 million goal was achieved. The Ballantine Family Fund kicked in $500,000. For the remaining $5 million or so, the state of Colorado covered most. To boot, Richard and Mary Lyn donated a $1 million collection of 150 southwestern Native American weavings, and Bill Ballantine, with contributions from his siblings, later donated a large sculpture, "The Intruder" by Ken Bunn, at the joint entrance to the Center and Concert Hall.

After so many years of planning and dreaming, ground was broken May 7, 1999, on a 38,500-square-foot, $7.8 million building to house the Center of Southwest Studies. During a short talk that day during ceremonies at the north end of the Fort Lewis College campus, Morley gave credit to her old friend Bob Delaney for having the original and ongoing vision.[385]

> Bob was always able to convey his enthusiasm for all things Southwest, and he perceived it as stretching all the way through Central America, and that it knew no political boundaries or habit or custom. He went where the digging was. He was infectious. We caught his enthusiasm.

Delaney, unfortunately, had not lived to see the Center's completion. He had died in Albuquerque on November 10, 2000.

For the next twenty months, work progressed on the Center, which includes a museum, library, archival space, classrooms, and a 120-seat lecture hall. It was connected to the new Concert Hall via a stone-pillared arcade in the style of circular stone structures seen in ancestral Puebloan sites around the Four Corners.

The grand opening was set for January 27, 2001. Artifacts, pottery, books, and artwork were hurriedly moved over from the library to the new center in the days prior. Then, the night before, eight inches of puffy snow fell. It was cold; the roads were slick. Despite the storm, "everybody came" the next morning, recalled Andrew Gulliford, director of the Center at the time. "It was a big deal." With typical Durango style, some wore dresses or suits, with Sorels (snow boots) on their feet.

Morley and college President Kendall Blanchard together snipped a raffia ribbon, with Richard, Mary Lyn, and Bill Ballantine looking on. Then hundreds of people streamed into the new center to check it out. Several people gave short talks inside the auditorium, where the packed crowd was standing-room-only.

Morley was a featured speaker. She'd already heard Connie Garcia Blanchard, the president's wife and a native of Spain, talk about the difficulties of getting around in the snow that morning. Connie's car had gotten stuck twice, and during her talk was vociferous in saying that the mystique of living in the Rockies was over for her. Morley couldn't help but deliver a few subtle zingers at times, and on this occasion she sent one Connie's way, pointedly challenging her to adjust to her new surroundings.

You can complain about the snow, Gulliford recalled Morley saying, but *if* you're here long enough, you'll come to appreciate it. Undoubtedly, others in the audience were skeptical of the relative newcomers. Concluded Gulliford, "She could really read a personal, social situation."

This was the culmination of thirty-seven years of effort. From the brainchild of Arthur and Morley, along with Bob Delaney and former FLC President John Reed, the Center of Southwest Studies was now a reality.

"When we had the grand opening, that was quite an accomplishment for the family, and for her to see that beautiful building," Rochford Figgs said.

Since its opening, the Center has functioned as a study center for scholars, a destination for tourists, and a showcase for artists. Gulliford quickly came to understand the Ballantines' influence on Southwest Colorado. Although it is physically isolated, with the nearest interstate about three hours' drive away, Durango isn't socially and mentally isolated. Morley and Arthur fostered that outlook, creating an environment where artists can thrive, and that tourists crave.

They made it the nexus of the Four Corners region. "Yes, it's rural, remote. But it's not socially remote."

And Gulliford was impressed that although she could lead on the front lines if necessary, she preferred to lead from behind and not be concerned with getting all the plaudits she may have deserved. Part of that leadership meant fostering engagement and commitment. "She epitomized that for many people," Gulliford said. "It wasn't enough just to watch. We needed to be involved."

Morley served as president of the FLC Foundation from 1999-2001, as the Center was built, giving Rochford Figgs even more insight into her style. "She was a real taskmaster. Better meet your deadlines. Better be on time. Better not have any excuses. I learned that very quickly," Rochford Figgs said. "She was a tremendous leader. So many women that I know – and the list is long – consider her a mentor, consider her a friend, consider her someone to whose level they would like to rise."

While she kept people on task, Morley was thoughtful and a good listener who paid attention to other people's ideas. "It wasn't just her way or the highway," Rochford Figgs said. "She wanted to be part of the group. ... One of the things I appreciated about her, was it wasn't like she expected to be treated like a queen bee."

As she had demonstrated many times, if people wanted a project or idea to succeed in Durango, one nearly surefire method was to have Morley Ballantine involved. If there was one thing that most endeared her to everyone who lived in and loved Southwest Colorado, it was

Morley's staunch advocacy of anything beneficial to the area and its people.

Linda Mannix was relaxing with then-husband Terry Fiedler one afternoon at their house on East Third Avenue. It was the fall of 1978, a Sunday, and the Denver Broncos were on TV. In came John Murrah, an advertising salesman at *The Durango Herald*.

Murrah had been talking with Morley about the need for something to stimulate the local economy during the slow winter months. The town needed it, and the *Herald* could use it to increase advertising dollars. Someone had suggested that a few days of celebration might be the panacea, and Murrah figured his nutty and creative friends Linda and Terry might be able to help. As they watched the Broncos and shared a twelve-pack of Bud, the concept jelled.

"We sat around the living room and dreamed up Snowdown," Linda Mannix said.[386] Morley had agreed to put up seed money. Fiedler, as event director, would organize the inaugural event. It was very loosely modeled after other winter events in places such as Aspen, where Mannix had briefly lived and which had held its annual Winterskol for several decades. Durango had discontinued its own winter carnival years earlier.

The Durango Chamber of Commerce formed a committee to get the project rolling. Bob Lieb, the thirty-seven-year-old former clothing manufacturer who'd just moved from California, was new to his job as chamber director. He was still feeling his way around town. He'd met a lot of people, but he hadn't gotten around to meeting Morley Ballantine. For whatever reason, Morley thought twice about donating the seed money, and word got to Lieb. Although a bit apprehensive, Lieb decided it was time to introduce himself to her and suggest she reconsider putting up the vital cash.[387]

As they talked, Lieb could sense Morley sizing him up. She asked a few questions: What are your plans? What will make this a success? But Lieb sensed she was simply judging his commitment, and whether this newbie West Coast bikini maker was real or a flake. He also sensed that Morley was looking out for the community:

"What's good for the town?" Lieb heard her saying between the lines. And as he got to know her better he came to understand that was her constant thought. "If it improved the town then she was all-in and became an advocate for it."

Lieb said the meeting went well. He emphasized that the chamber was fully behind it, and the town had built-up energy raring to go. "I did as great a sales job as I possibly could. She said, 'OK, I'm back in, and I'll commit $1,500,'" which, Lieb said, is like $50,000 today.

The first Snowdown was held on a cold and snowy February 1-4, 1979, and it was a rousing success. Several events were held at the in-town ski area, which had recently been renamed Chapman Hill following the death of local ski pioneer Colton Chapman in October 1978.[388] Morley praised the new festival in a February 1 editorial:[389]

> It certainly is appropriate that Snowdown ... begins this evening. One complaint that John Murrah, Bob Lieb, and Terry Fiedler can NOT make is that nature has been uncooperative. As organizers of the event, they've worked hard the past six weeks and already are looking forward to next year.
>
> The events are mostly free, they're designed for all age groups, and they'll all be just as much fun as we make them. So dispel the winter blahs by getting out and joining in.
>
> Maybe, after it's all over, just maybe, the snow will stop falling.

The event's success meant Morley got her $1,500 back, and Durango began what would quickly become the region's largest wintertime party. Morley's seed money spurred an annual celebration that continues to bring locals and tourists – and former Durangoans – to town for five days of contests, shows, parades, races, fun, and, yes, a bit of drinking. It reached forty-two consecutive years before the COVID-19 pandemic forced its cancellation in 2021. It made a successful return in 2022.

The Ballantines continued to support Snowdown, and every so often enjoyed some of the events in person. Mannix co-created the Fashion Do's and Don'ts in the mid-1990s, and offered Morley four complimentary tickets to the first event. Morley enjoyed the off-color proceedings at the VFW Hall – locals cavorting in bizarre and sometimes suggestive themed costumes – with a glass of wine. The second year Mannix again offered the complimentary tickets, then was stunned on event day as the suddenly popular venue filled to capacity. Morley showed up near start time with Nancy Whitson, then the manager of the Ballantine Family Fund.

"Aagghh!!" Mannix realized at the arrival of this VIP. "I forgot to save a table!" Quickly, she dashed into the VFW bar, grabbed a small table, returned and crammed it into the morass of people. "Gotta take care of Morley."

MCB fondly recalled Snowdown in a 1999 column: "There's some feeling that participants in Snowdown are aging, along with the event itself. Those of us who were involved from the start know that we *are* twenty-one years older just as is Snowdown. Terry Fiedler, the first organizer, remains the best one. His management style – laid back – complements the institution. … You don't know how glad we all are that you are back in charge."[390]

Lieb, who went on to found clothing company Durango Threadworks, become a county commissioner, and serve alongside Morley on the First National Bank board of directors, is tickled every year the event comes back around. "My ultimate belief is that Snowdown wouldn't have started that year, which was the perfect year to start it, without Morley Ballantine getting behind it."

Stories are similar for many other now-established Durango causes and institutions. Morley would offer advice, funding, and her name to things she wanted to succeed. For one newcomer, the cause was a rodeo.

Jeff Mannix, a former New York City advertising media buyer with Benton & Bowles and fashion model with the Ford Agency, moved west to Ketchum, Idaho, in the 1980s to write a book. He landed in Durango in 1989 when he bought the pro rodeo. A stranger in town, he was looking to make connections that would aid in finding sponsors. After the *Herald* wrote a story on the rodeo transition, Morley, curious about this newcomer, invited Jeff in for a visit. They had a nice chat in her office.[391]

Soon after that, Morley invited Jeff to escort her to a fundraiser for Bandanas & Boots, a local charity started by horsewomen. For Jeff, walking around with Morley among 300 locals, many of them influential or potential advertisers, the opportunity was inestimable. "That was my coming out party," he said. "That probably kicked me off pretty well when I started to look for advertisers."

Later, Jeff also experienced how to lose favor with Morley. When running in a county commissioner primary in 2002, he showed up for a *Durango Herald* editorial board meeting about five minutes late. For whatever reason – Jeff thinks he knows why – the *Herald* ended up picking a different candidate.

"I must have ticked her off by being late," Jeff said, admittedly still licking his wounds twenty years later. He lost the race. "She got me back by not endorsing me." They would come around to be friends again.

Morley's status as a Durango VIP put her in deep water one year.

Those who have ever volunteered for a dunk tank know that there is nothing highfalutin about it. You take a seat above a tank full of water and wait for the inevitable splashdown to occur. This happens when someone, who pays for the opportunity to "get you," throws a ball and hits a target, thus unlocking the seat and plummeting the volunteer down into the often-ice-cold water.

Dave Spencer was looking for help with a fundraiser not long after he established the nonprofit Adaptive Sports Association in 1984 at Purgatory Resort. Spencer, an energetic and still-young man, had lost a leg to cancer and had dedicated his life to helping others with physical and mental disabilities enjoy the sport of skiing.

Spencer was good at getting people to help him, recalled Beth Lamberson, who would later become the association's director.[392] But even Spencer was nervous the day he asked Morley Ballantine if she would volunteer for the dunk tank, which was being set up during an event at the La Plata County Fairgrounds. Could one really ask the esteemed owner of *The Durango Herald*, nearing age sixty, to do the dunk tank?

For whatever reason – maybe it was an inability to turn down an earnest man with one leg – she said yes. And Morley did indeed get wet that day, attested her son Richard, who was there. If anyone ever needed proof that Morley was willing to "take one for the team," this was it.

A year or two later, Lamberson was whining to Spencer about dreading a call she had to make to a sponsor. "Hey," retorted Spencer, who would die of cancer in 1986, "if I can get Morley Ballantine in a dunking booth, then you can do anything."

Lamberson never forgot Spencer's words. "That story has carried me," Lamberson said. "How much harder can this be than asking Morley to be in a dunk tank?"

As Adaptive Sports director, and later as director of KSUT Public Radio, Lamberson got to know Morley fairly well and over time began speaking to her in sound bites. Maybe Morley's children should have figured this out? "I learned that when she asked a question it would likely appear in a column."

Moreover, Lamberson came to regard Morley as an encouraging mentor who not only gave to her causes but raised her abilities as a nonprofit fundraiser. "I looked at her not to write a check, but that she would empower me to go get those checks from other people."

Honored and Esteemed

For influencing the world around her, more specifically the people, the 1980s and 1990s were Morley's zenith. Her dauntless opinions were highly respected, her support valued – whether by word or pocketbook – and thus her community of admirers expanded. She was most revered locally, but known by first name in certain state and even national circles as well. She continued to break barriers. The magnitude of her impact on a broad spectrum elicited honors on multiple levels.

In 1990 she received her most significant community honor, being named Citizen of the Year by the Durango Area Chamber Resort Association (DACRA). This was the first time a woman had received the award, in its tenth year. It was given to her during ceremonies at the Red Lion Inn, now the DoubleTree, in January 1991.[393] At that time she was chairman of the board of *The Durango Herald*, kept regular office hours, and continued to write editorials and a weekly column. She was sixty-five, and she'd lived in Durango for thirty-eight years. The *Herald* wrote:

> It is fitting that Ballantine is the first woman to garner DACRA's highest honor. Taking the reins of the *Herald* as publisher and editor for eight years after her husband's death in 1975, Ballantine provided a model for women leaders. Today she supports women's issues with contributions of time and

money to Planned Parenthood, the Women's Resource Center, the Mothers' Center, the Southwest Safehouse, and the Four Corners Chapter of Women in Communications Inc.

In November 2000, among 100 nominees for various awards, she was named Colorado's "Outstanding Philanthropist of the Year" by the Governor's Commission on National and Community Service and the Association for Healthcare Philanthropy.[394] The award recognized Morley's support for an array of charitable and humanitarian-based institutions.

In October 2000, US Rep. Scott McInnis, of Grand Junction, paid tribute to Morley Ballantine in remarks to Congress.[395]

> Mr. Speaker, I wanted to take this moment to recognize a woman who has exemplified extraordinary dedication to philanthropic work, my friend Morley C. Ballantine, who currently serves as editor and chairman of *The Durango Herald*. … Morley's robust efforts to make her community, state, and nation a better place make her more than deserving of this distinction. … This, friends and colleagues, is a truly remarkable legacy of service.

Morley received the Bonfils Stanton Foundation's Arts and Humanities Award for 2001 for her work in supporting arts and culture in Southwest Colorado.[396] In 2002 she was inducted into the Colorado Business Hall of Fame.

It was a bit of a surprise when the national president of Planned Parenthood, Gloria Feldt, visited Durango in July 2004. It was an even bigger surprise when, at a fundraising lunch at the Strater Hotel downtown, Feldt handed Morley Ballantine the Margaret Sanger Award for Planned Parenthood of the Rocky Mountains.[397]

Receiving this recognition for her local and statewide work surrounding women's productive rights was a high honor for Morley. And it brought back memories of her mother, Betty, who after meeting Sanger back in the 1930s had been inspired to start Planned Parent-

hood of Iowa. Sanger was a pioneer in family planning beginning in the early twentieth century, who battled against laws and mores that criminalized abortion, birth control, and sex education.

Richard and Mary Lyn Ballantine were among the seventy-one in attendance along with two Durango city councilors and a state senator. Morley had supported the local Planned Parenthood clinic from its opening in 1981. Feldt called her "one of the most highly regarded individuals in the state of Colorado," adding, "We want you to know how much we appreciate the work you have done daily to make life better for other human beings."

In thanking Feldt for the award, Morley said, "I hope we will all continue to keep up the good fight."

Morley received Durango's 1997 Athena Award

in January 1998. To her this was a most meaningful honor, given to a woman involved in public service. She received the honor at the DACRA awards banquet "for her tireless efforts to promote social and gender equality, expand the arts, and strengthen education," the *Herald* wrote.[398]

The history of the Athena Award parallels in many ways Morley's story of how women came to be accepted and take charge in the business world. The Athena Award was the brainchild of Martha Mertz, a Michigan real estate developer who, in 1982, as a new member of the previously all-male Lansing Regional Chamber of Commerce, discovered that the chamber had honored only one woman in its seventy-five-year existence.[399]

Mertz created a women's honor she dubbed the Athena Award, after

the revered Greek goddess of wisdom, war, and crafts.[400] Mertz acquired the sponsorship of Oldsmobile. The Athena grew, with Oldsmobile's help, into an award given by chambers of commerce across the country. The Athena goes to those who excel professionally, contribute time to improve the lives of others in their community, and assist others in realizing their leadership potential.

Morley holds the Athena Award, which she won in 1997. Sheri Rochford Figgs, seen here, and other Athena winners unanimously agreed to rename the honor as the Morley Ballantine Award in the mid-2000s.

As the head of Morehart Chevrolet-Oldsmobile in Durango, Jim Morehart eagerly latched on to local sponsorship of the award. The first local Athena Award went to Shari Chrane, a local insurance agent and community leader, in 1990. Morley Ballantine received the award seven years later.[401]

When Oldsmobile became defunct in 2004, "we wanted to continue to sponsor [the Athena]," Jim Morehart said. So his local dealership took over the financial obligations. Morehart graciously put the award in the hands of previous recipients to decide on the annual winner, with his rubber-stamp approval. At that time, "It was suggested we make it the Morley Ballantine Award."[402]

The suggestion apparently came from Shari Chrane (now Shari Jones) and Laurel Waller, two of the first three Athena Award recipients.

"It was unanimous," said Sheri Rochford Figgs, the 1993 Athena Award recipient. "We wanted it to become the Morley Ballantine award." Morley wasn't all that thrilled with the idea, but was honored and finally relented.

Ellen Roberts, a Durango lawyer who served as state legislator from 2006-2016, received the Athena Award in 2003. She said there was barely any discussion about changing the name to the Morley Ballantine Award. "Oh sure, that makes sense," was the consensus. "It really grounded that award here locally as well as being a tribute to her."[403]

The change occurred in 2005, and the first Morley Ballantine Award honoree was Karen Langhart, co-owner of the Red Snapper restaurant. Joanne Spina, assistant county manager at the time, received the 2006 "Morley." (Winners began referring to themselves as "Morleys.")

"You just felt so honored to be given an award named after her," Spina said, "and all that she represented in terms of her leadership in the community."

As a former Fort Lewis classmate of Morley's, Pam Patton was ecstatic to receive the third Morley Ballantine Award in 2007. "She lived in a man's world" for much of her life, Patton said of Morley, "but she really championed women."

Meetings to decide winners were held at Morley's house to make it easier for her to attend. By this time she'd been battling cancer and was less than energetic. In the late 2000s Morley was in a hospital bed in her living room as the recipient was chosen. Always, she was present and paying attention.

"We'd all be talking at the same time about the names that were under consideration, and all of a sudden Morley would stop us and she'd say something ... and we'd all stop and listen," Rochford Figgs recalled. "I think we all felt she had been a mentor to us in many ways."

One anecdote reveals how deeply Morley wanted to remain involved in the Athena Award, despite her illnesses. Helen Healy was in Durango taking care of her mother one year when the Athena Award committee was scheduled to gather at the West Park house. Morley was not feeling well, so Helen made the decision that Morley was not up to the meeting. Helen told the committee to meet somewhere else. "OK, we'll be down at the Palace Restaurant," Helen was informed. Then Morley found out.

"My mother just exploded. She was so mad," Helen recalled. "She got out of bed [in the living room], threw on clothes, made me take her down to the Palace ... insisted on paying for everything and told me, 'Don't you ever do that again.'"

For Ellen Roberts, who grew up in an upstate New York town frequently inundated by what she perceived as wealthy and sometimes snobbish tourists, Morley's frequent travel columns and well-to-do background felt like a barrier. But over the years, Morley won her over. It began, interestingly enough, with a George Winston concert.

Winston, a nationally renowned pianist, played at Durango's Miller Middle School auditorium in the early 1990s. He took the stage shoeless and played that way. Roberts thought it was strange, and Morley not only thought it odd, but didn't appreciate it. In a review, Morley ripped Winston, saying basically, "How dare you!" No, it wasn't Carnegie Hall, but he showed disrespect for the audience by being so cavalier. Morley was sticking up for her fellow citizens.[404]

"She was direct and honest," Roberts said. "She didn't mince words."

Roberts learned from Morley: "Figure out who you are, honor that, and follow through on it. Don't cave in because other people are pressuring you to cave in."

Karen Zink, a Durango native, is a nurse practitioner involved in the community in myriad ways. She serves as a volunteer, and on boards at the local and state levels. In 1991 she was the second-ever Athena Award recipient.[405]

Morley first came to Zink as a patient, and asked Zink to see her through "to the end." "I will," Zink promised.

As Morley's primary health provider, Zink had insight into the physical struggles Morley endured during the 2000s, particularly following her diagnosis of throat cancer in 2003. Zink also witnessed Morley's intellectual curiosity. When she couldn't read, she kept up by asking others to read to her.

"She stayed extremely sharp with the news until the very end," Zink said. "No one could pull the wool over her eyes as far as what was going on in the world, or regionally. She had a very, very keen mind."

In one way or another, Durango women became "Morleys" just by getting to know her.

Morley had experienced first-hand the difficulties of women being accepted in the business world, and at a time – the 1950s and '60s – when women's presence was much less common. Later, particularly in the 1980s and '90s, she invested profuse energy into helping other women in business. She mentored them too, often quietly, sometimes without them even realizing it. She placed importance on developing the next generation of women leaders.

Diane Wildfang arrived in Durango in 1992 with her husband, Fred Wildfang, and children Kirk and Kara Komick. The family purchased several dilapidated buildings in the 700 block of East Second Avenue and, under Diane's vision, set about restoring them. Diane got involved in the Women's Resource Center and met Morley at a board meeting.

On more than one level, Morley was excited to learn about Diane's project. Morley was for anything that would beautify a run-down section of town. Also, she was eager to help a woman entrepreneur.[406] The Wildfangs and Komicks started with restoring the Leland House and two other buildings. Soon, they also took on the Rochester Hotel, directly across the street from the Leland.

Morley invited Diane to her office to talk about the work. The two became good friends, and Morley took to visiting the Leland on her strolls about town. "She was always checking on my job, and asking me how it was going, and how I was doing," Wildfang said. "[For me as] a newcomer in town, she just really expanded my world. … She introduced me to people, both men and women, she thought it was important I know. Morley had a lot of connections, and she was very generous with her information."

When the work was completed, Morley and Richard held meetings at the Rochester and planted out-of-town guests at both the Leland and Rochester. A year after Morley received the Athena Award, Diane Wildfang received it in 1998.

Nancy Whitson worked for *The Durango Herald* and Ballantine Family Fund for twenty years, first as the *Herald's* director of human resources beginning in 1994. Starting in 1999 she worked closely with Morley as executive director of the Ballantine Family Fund. As part of her role, Whitson joined Morley at social affairs – anything from the rowdy Snowdown Follies to the more staid Music in the Mountains – and at meetings.

"It was always heartwarming as it was clear she was loved and very respected," Whitson said.[407] "She always treated everyone the same, so

I never really knew the movers and shakers at events until after the fact. ... Everyone treated Morley like she was their dear friend and she just made everyone so comfortable that I never had the chance to feel intimidated."

Morley encouraged Whitson to become involved in local and women's issues, so Whitson participated in a local leaders' conference and joined the Women's Foundation of Colorado board. "I never believed that my voice could make a difference," Whitson said. "She supported and encouraged me to voice my opinion, especially if it wasn't popular."

When Sheri Rochford Figgs retired she began an endowed scholarship at Fort Lewis College. "Morley inspired me to be that kind of person," Rochford Figgs said.

Stephanie Moran, a longtime educator, respected Morley for several reasons. Although she came from wealth, she took seriously the expectation that with privilege comes responsibility. Wherever she settled, she was determined to make a difference. Circumstances had landed Arthur and her in Durango, and the town had benefitted. "I think she was taught early on, you're not privileged because you have more than other people," Moran said. "They picked their place and made it better."[408]

There was a toughness to men and women of Morley's era, and a strong work ethic. Growing up during the Depression and World War II meant making sacrifices. So Moran made it a point to befriend Morley Ballantine and Mary Jane Clark, both born in 1925. These two didn't complain or whine, although at the other end of the spectrum, neither laughed easily either.

"You could get a chuckle out of Morley," Moran said, "but you weren't going to get a big guffaw. She took life seriously."

Moran spent the final two decades of her career as program manager at Durango's Adult Education Center. Moran had come to know Morley in 2000 through the Center of Southwest Studies, where her husband, Andrew Gulliford, was director. She attended the salon gatherings of influential locals at the Ballantine home. She and Morley shared a belief in the importance of literacy, that literacy and education should be available to all, that literacy opened doors to people of all means. Morley encouraged anyone, whatever sex, race, or means, who sought to improve Durango.

"The community's vibrancy was so important to her," Moran said. "And so everybody had a part in that."

However serious she might be, Morley kept her sense of fun and spontaneity. Rochford Figgs felt that, as a staff person at Fort Lewis College, she wasn't quite in Morley's league socially. So it was a surprise when they were toiling on a project one day and Morley, out of the blue, said, "Let's go get a facial!"

"So we did," Rochford said with a chuckle. "It was nothing I expected."

Morley's Travels

Morley's love of travel did not wane after Arthur's death. Before she got too old, she was fine with roughing it a bit, allowing her to take in some exotic settings.

In 1979 she joined several friends, including Claude and Anne Maer of Denver, on an adventure to India, Nepal, and Pakistan.[409] The group was trapped in bad weather in Gilgit, Pakistan, at the foot of the Karako- rums. Mountains around them towered to 25,000 feet, and planes could not fly out. The Muslim-dominated town was officially dry.

"Things were going along fairly well until we ran out of booze," Claude Maer wrote in 2009. "Being Pakistan, liquor was not served, but I was appointed to find a bootlegger (at the risk of getting my hands cut off)." Maer consulted their tour guide and a hotel manager, snuck down a dark alley or two late at night, and finagled four bottles of Pinch Scotch. "After a few swigs, no one cared whether we ever got out or not."

The group drove up Khyber Pass to look into Afghanistan, which at that moment was on the verge of being invaded by the Soviet Union. The trip included a twenty-four-hour journey from Kathmandu, Nepal, to Agra, India, "arriving about 6 a.m. after being up all night on a small, uncomfortable bus bumping along the back roads of India."

Antigua was an annual trip for Morley, usually accompanied by other family members. She continued visiting into the 2000s, despite the difficulty of travel as her health declined. The getaway at the Mill

Reef Club was a place to relax, to warm up after Colorado's winter chill had set in, to dig one's toes into the white sandy beaches.

Antigua is the jewel of the Caribbean islands nation of Antigua and Barbuda. Since the Cowles arrived and built their home in the early 1950s it has morphed into a major destination resort, and tourism is the economy's backbone. At 108 square miles, it is one-fifteenth the size of Rhode Island, the smallest US state. Its population is ninety percent black, the result of British settlers importing African slaves in the seventeenth and eighteenth centuries to work the sugar cane fields. The official language is English.

Antigua was described in a 1961 *LOOK* magazine story as "a small, contented, solidly British member of the West Indies Federation. It is a place that attracts visitors and settlers to whom the larger Caribbean islands seem too fast, too bouncy, too glittering. Antigua is quiet, unruffled, restrained, and those who know the island prefer it to remain that way."[410]

More from the *LOOK* story:

> Stone sugar mills rise among the bluish-green, tall cane fields; the foliage dazzles the eye with those tropical colors,

which always appear brighter than bright; the rudest house is charmingly surrounded by an English garden; hazardous and curvy roads wind through coconut groves and fields of sea-island cotton; and almost everywhere one can glimpse the flashing sea.

In 2001 Elizabeth Ballantine co-authored a book on the history of the Mill Reef Club, where Ballantine and Cowles families still own homes.

It is "a tiny, arid island at the southern end of the Leeward Islands in the Lesser Antilles, which form the barrier between the Atlantic Ocean and the Caribbean Sea," according to the book, *A Vision of Paradise*.[411] The Mill Reef development, founded in 1947, includes forty-eight homes spread along a small section of Antigua's eastern coastline. The Cowles family house, which Morley inherited from her parents, stands atop a rocky point called Friar's Head.

The weather is generally warm and mild, but Antigua stands exposed to the Atlantic, and big storms – including an occasional hurricane – sometimes batter the island. Storms come with a warning. Late in the evening in January 1982, just after Morley and three family members had bid farewell to a dinner guest and the subject had turned to the merits of a nightcap, the unexpected occurred. Morley wrote:[412]

> We heard a sound, an indescribable one. At first I thought it was a rogue wave in a cavern not far from the house. ... It wasn't so much that it was loud as that it seemed to fill the universe. It was impossible that it was man-made. I considered the forces of good and evil. The Second Coming, perhaps (such was its power), or the start of a nuclear war?
>
> Then the concrete floor beneath our feet began to tremble. The lamps swayed crazily. One, a big, heavy one on the desk, reminded me of a clown in a circus who teeters so far to one side that just as the audience expects him to fall, he recovers and teeters just as far in the opposite direction. ...
>
> Earthquake! ...
>
> Then there was utter silence, not even the constant wind blowing from the sea. We looked at one another, abashed, un-

easy. One had moved to position himself in the door frame in case the ceiling fell. We laughed nervously as we noted nothing had been damaged. We agreed for sure to have the nightcap.

Morley served two three-year terms on Mill Reef's Board of Governors from 1985-1991. That responsibility meant showing up for four yearly meetings – held around Thanksgiving, Christmas, spring break in March, and the Fourth of July. Her children took turns accompanying her, and she invited other guests.

Durango friend Mary Jane Clark was a frequent visitor who went several years in a row at Thanksgiving time. She recalled flying to Antigua from Durango on the Cowles family's private plane, and arriving just after a hurricane had hit. Water was everywhere, but damage was minimal. They enjoyed the beaches almost every day, and Mary Jane said both Morley and Arthur were excellent swimmers.[413]

Many of Mill Reef's inhabitants annually spent most of the winter there, so over the years Morley made many longstanding friends. The family furthered its social connections as members of St. Philips Anglican Episcopal Church. For those seeking social encounters, the club was the perfect place to hang out.

One of the Cowles family's special Antigua friends was Archibald MacLeish (1892-1982), a renowned poet and writer who earned three Pulitzer Prizes. The Cowleses and MacLeishes apparently first crossed paths when both Gardner "Mike" Cowles Jr. and "Archie" MacLeish served the US Office of War Information during World War II.[414] Both John Cowles Sr. and MacLeish bought into the Mill Reef Club in its first few years of existence, and their plots faced each other across a small bay along the coastline.

When Arthur Ballantine died, Archibald penned a letter to Morley co-signed by his wife, Ada. A short excerpt: "It just doesn't make sense that you of all people should have to bear so great a loss. You know – you must know – how much we love you and how much your sorrow hurts us – and most of all – because we think we can guess the depth of that sorrow."[415]

Gerald Ford honored MacLeish in January 1977 with the Presidential Medal of Freedom. Others honored that day at the White House included artist Norman Rockwell, Army Gen. Omar Bradley, baseball star Joe DiMaggio, writer James Michener, and, interestingly, Arthur Ballantine's old friend Nelson Rockefeller.[416]

Morley used a part of MacLeish's 1968 *New York Times* essay about astronauts' perspective of the Earth in a 1980 commencement address at Simpson College, referring to him as "an old and dear friend, one of the wisest men I know."

> To see the Earth as we now see it, small and blue and beautiful in that eternal silence where it floats, is to see ourselves as riders on the Earth together, brothers on that bright loveliness in the unending night – brothers who SEE now they are truly brothers.

Generally, Morley's fellow adventurers to several continents became her children, and later her grandchildren.

In April 1981, with newlyweds Elizabeth Ballantine and Paul Leavitt, she traveled to Kenya for two weeks. It was her wedding present to them. In a Leisure section story for the *Des Moines Register*, Elizabeth described how they "traveled by small airplane and van in four of Kenya's game reserves, ending our tour on the beaches of Lamu, a small island archipelago off Kenya's coast."[417] In a van, with a handy sunroof for taking photos, they were "able to mingle among herds of impala, or approach a lioness and her cubs, or wander among giraffes eating tree-tops."

In December 1982, Morley ventured for a week with son Bill to the Soviet Union to visit Elizabeth, who was spending a year at Moscow State University as part of an academic exchange program. Elizabeth, joined by husband Paul, was researching for her doctoral dissertation on nineteenth century jurist and writer Anatoly Koni, a leading Russian liberal of his day.

Morley and Elizabeth wrote stories about the Soviet Union for *The Durango Herald*, while Paul wrote several for the *Des Moines Register*. Arriving in Leningrad at dusk on a Russian Aeroflot plane, Morley and Bill were greeted by light snow, and – as they stepped off the plane onto a snow-packed runway – "Russian soldiers, including several women, in high boots, great coats, and fur hats. They looked like characters out of Tolstoy."

The Cold War (approximately 1945-1991) was an era of intrigue and suspicion. Americans traveling in the Soviet Union, or any Soviet bloc country, would be closely scrutinized and likely watched to some degree. Certain luxury items Americans carried were coveted by Soviet citizens, who would either use them or sell them on a lucrative black market. But selling to or buying from the wrong person – a Soviet agent or informant – could land one in big trouble.

This backdrop made it a fascinating but fearsome time to travel to the other side of what Americans had dubbed the "Iron Curtain." Morley was a well-experienced globetrotter, but this was something new for her.[418]

> Because our baggage was lost, we were at the end of the line going through customs. This meant the young, male, uniformed inspectors could leisurely rummage in our hand luggage. They were particularly interested in our reading material and passed around a copy of *Time* and of *Newsweek* and a book of Bill's about Russia today. They slowly pieced together the captions under the pictures and looked at the index of the book. ... Eventually, there was general agreement among them that nothing was subversive and all was, albeit reluctantly, returned to us.

MCB wrote about tipping a waiter with a mystery novel, being approached by youths looking to exchange money (West German marks and US dollars were valued highly), and others wanting to buy Bill's corduroy pants "at practically any price (in rubles) or his sweater."

> Tipping? In the Soviet Union where tipping is banned because all are equal? Nonsense! No country more vividly illustrates George Orwell's *Animal Farm* where some are more equal than others. Ahead of time we'd been told to tip with ball point pens and postcards of the United States, but the Russians who deal with [tourists] have become more sophisti-

cated than that toward the holders of hard currencies, such as Western Europeans and Americans. From us, the women want cosmetics, the men razor blades. It doesn't matter what kind, for all have barter value.

Morley, with children Elizabeth and Bill, returned to Russia in 1992, post-Soviet Union collapse. They traveled along the Baltic Sea coast by train and cruise ship. Under Russia's new, slightly more democratic regime, Leningrad had taken back its traditional name, St. Petersburg. She wrote to *Herald* readers:[419]

> We went into the Astoria, the Leningrad Intourist hotel where we'd stayed in 1982. We couldn't believe our eyes. The dirty, dark building interior, then divided in two and one part used only (and secretively) by Communist party officials was now an airy white with a piano player in the lobby and a gift shop selling ties and perfumes from Paris.
> It was exhilarating to see history in the making. The determination to make freedom work was inspiring. Frequently we were told, "we want to be like you." Humbling. What a trip it was.

In January 1995 she traveled to Kirkland, Wash., to meet her ninth and final grandchild, two-week-old Hunter Ballantine, son of Bill and Mary.

Then it was time to gather the grandchildren and show them the world, as her children had been shown. This generation didn't have Glendalough, where family would gather every summer, and where the sixteen grandchildren of John and Betty Cowles became well-acquainted. As a substitute, Morley planned trips and invited along anyone who was able.

She was excited to travel with her grandchildren. These vacations meant two to three weeks of sharing rooms, bus rides, and meals. Morley would quiz the youngsters on events and highlights of the day. She wanted some depth; responses such as "Oh, I liked the fish" were entirely insufficient.

One of the first such trips was to Scotland in May 1995, followed by South Africa in March 1996. All the grandchildren – except Hunter, who was just learning to walk – went to South Africa.

Turkey was the destination in June 1998. Morley was joined by Richard and Mary Lyn and their two boys, Elizabeth and Paul and their two children, and Helen and Ed and their four children.

Morley and Elizabeth took a mother-daughter trip in October 1998 to France, Spain, and the Basque region between them. Durango, Spain, lies in that Basque region, and Morley wrote about visiting the sister city of both Durango, Colo., and Durango, Mexico. Leaders of the three Durangos had made official visits every three years for a decade to the triad of like-named cities.[420]

> We had not been aware of the extent of the Basque terrorism on the part of those who want independence from Spain. It may be that peace will come to the Basque country as the standard of living rises. We were glad we'd seen that part of the world. Too, we hope the sister cities come together once again.

The destination in March 2000 was Egypt, with a short stay in Jordan. Again, eight grandchildren made the trip.[421]

> We ... have traveled together frequently and know the routine: finding backpacks, counting the luggage, cooperating on tipping, being on time for meals and departures. They all, without being asked, help their vision-impaired ancestor (me) up and down steps and across tricky terrain.

Sarah Healy-Vigo recalled that the grandchildren were all on their best behavior for these trips, and not for fear of reprisal. "Every interaction with our grandmother was special," she said. "We always wanted to give her the respect she deserved."[422]

Accommodations and sights varied between posh and crude, forcing the grandchildren to be prepared for just about anything. There was a luxurious Nile cruise, visits to the famous temples of Luxor and Karnak, then a look at a cruder setting before a return to the posh.[423]

Our family group of fifteen, with the youngest, Sarah (Leavitt, age eleven), and me the eldest, by now knew how to keep moving together. We'd toured the two temples and the two valleys this morning and now were on our way to visit a rural family. The family home was made of adobe. The "garage," as it was called with great humor, next to it, housed a donkey. Alongside was a bathroom but without benefit of running water. The toilet was chemical.

In the Sinai we met an extended Bedouin family. … The Bedouins, though camped out in the middle of nowhere not far from a paved two-lane highway, were surprisingly close to an elementary school. … At Sharm El Sheikh in Sinai we stayed at a beautiful resort hotel on the banks of the Red Sea. The hotel's beauty spa featured a cucumber mash massage but the place was too booked to take us.

At the time, MCB called Egypt both "fascinating" and "safe," but just eighteen months later the world would change with the events of 9/11.

From her first visit there with Arthur in 1955, posing on camels in front of Egypt's Great Pyramids became a family tradition. Here, Morley is joined by three of her children and their families. From left, Sarah Leavitt, Akmed (guide), Will Leavitt, Morley Ballantine, Morley Healy, Richard Ballantine, Helen Ballantine Healy, Elizabeth Ballantine, Mary Lyn Ballantine, Justin Healy, David Ballantine, Katherine Healy, Chris Ballantine, Ed Healy, and Paul Leavitt.

Importance of Family

To the people of Durango, Colo., and the country, Morley Cowles Ballantine had become, simply, Morley. But to her grandchildren, she was Mamama, with an accent on the first "ma." The name "Mamama" was what she had called her favorite grandmother, Florence Morley Bates (1878-1945).

Morley took her role as grandmother seriously. When with her grandchildren – particularly on world travels – she made sure they were learning, that they were paying attention to the history and culture surrounding them. And the grandchildren understood almost from the get-go that Mamama valued each of them, yet had expectations regarding manners and responsibilities.

Morley was twenty-seven when the last of her four children was born. Her children all demonstrated the customs of a new, liberated era that no longer placed such great expectations on women, or men, for that matter, to start families early. The four children of Morley and Arthur Ballantine got advanced degrees, traveled, tried out different career paths. Marriage and/or children generally came next. Morley's first grandchild didn't come until Helen, who married youngest at twenty-two, had turned thirty. Elizabeth was thirty-five, Richard was forty, and Bill forty-five when their first children were born.

Morley's first grandchild, the daughter of Helen and Ed Healy, was a living tribute. Named Morley Anne, she was born May 26, 1982, in

Wichita. Morley had turned fifty-seven five days previously.

Will Cowles Leavitt, son of Elizabeth Ballantine and Paul Leavitt, was the second grandchild, born April 3, 1984. Katherine (Morley Healy's sister) arrived just ten days later, April 13, 1984.

Two sets of twins followed: Chris and David, who were adopted not long after their April 7, 1986, birthdate by Richard and Mary Lyn, and Sarah and Justin, born March 11, 1987, to Helen and Ed. The group of nine cousins was rounded out by Sarah Leavitt on July 12, 1988, and Hunter Ballantine to Bill and his third wife, Mary, on December 27, 1994.

The grandchildren became a big part of Morley's life, but because they were spread out around the country and she had her own busy life to lead, she generally saw them just a couple of times a year. Morley's children were drawn to Durango four times a year for board meetings, but the grandchildren were busy with school, sports, and other activities. So Mamama would demonstrate her devotion whenever possible.

Note that "devotion" is a different word than, say, "affection" or "sentimentality." The love was there, but she didn't slather them with it. Instead, she would challenge them to express ideas.

"There was no question that you would participate in the conversations, and have an opinion," said Katherine Healy Dougan. Morley would have her evening gin-and-tonic, relax on the couch, invite the grandchildren to sit around her, and ask some probing questions.[424]

"They weren't, 'How was your day.' They were, 'What do you think about the presidential election.' You could be twelve, but … she wasn't going to assume because you were young you didn't have an opinion."

The Healys regularly traveled to Durango for Christmas. Elizabeth and Paul often took their children to join Morley in Antigua. Richard's children, of course, didn't have far to travel to see Mamama. She went to see Bill's son, Hunter, in Washington state when he was just a couple of weeks old.

Morley with Richard and Mary Lyn's sons, Christopher and David.

Mamama had standards, displayed a "regal formality," and could be intimidating, said Sarah Leavitt. But get beyond that, and you had a grandmother itching to have fun. Sarah got some quality time with her grandmother, accompanied by an "entourage of nurses," during the less chaotic summer season on Antigua.

"Interspersed with discussions of current events were honest debates and fits of laughter," Sarah wrote.[425] "It's [in Antigua] where Mamama taught my teenage self to mix cocktails beyond my parents' normal gin and tonic or rum punch. She taught me that knowing the state of the world is one thing, but forming an opinion is far more important."

"We played charades after dinner and laughed until bedtime."

The grandchildren became accustomed to the black bag that accompanied Mamama on overseas travel. This semi-secretive bag contained her many medications, but also a bottle of vodka.

Morley encouraged her grandchildren to grow, to be thoughtful. She impressed upon them the importance of manners, of being considerate, of writing thank you notes. Said Katherine, "What was really important to her was our education, our ability to think and be good people."

Her grandchildren listened. Almost all of them have advanced degrees. For example, Katherine graduated from Duke University and the

Wharton School of Finance at the University of Pennsylvania, and now works in private finance for families in the tech industry. Sarah Leavitt, a graduate of the Judge Business School at the University of Cambridge, is a marketing director for high-growth technology companies. Sarah Healy holds a BA from the University of San Diego and an MBA from the University of Kansas, and is an insurance broker in Broomfield, Colo. Morley Healy Stalnaker is a BS and MHC graduate of Trinity University in San Antonio, Tex. She is a senior health care executive for a large regional hospital in Wichita, Kans.

Nine grandchildren scattered around the country is a difficult bundle to get together in one spot, and it didn't happen often. "Mamama was the only one with the power to bring us together in the same place," Morley Healy read at her grandmother's memorial in Durango on October 16, 2009.

Indomitable to the End

Life was not without its struggles for Morley. The first in a line of health issues that she would battle as she aged was her vision.

Her eyes were never good. Glasses had sufficed for a couple of decades (she wore them by the early 1950s), but as happens with age, her vision became progressively worse. In 1979 she had her first cataract surgery, and the next year her second at Northwestern Hospital in Minneapolis. Post-op, her first order of business was reading.

"Now, twenty-four hours after surgery, I'm at my father's comfortable house," she wrote in an editorial titled "Hospital Care" in September 1980.[426] "Unable to read from either eye eight-point [newspaper body] type, I've two magnifying glasses and a variety of large-type books. My handwriting I'm practicing to make it large enough for me to read."

The cataract surgery helped to a small degree, but vision remained a struggle the rest of her life. Several surgeries followed. After a sudden case of blurred vision due to a retinal problem, another procedure in Minnesota helped somewhat restore vision in her right eye in early 1983.

By the time she'd reached her fifties, Morley's eyes were failing. Those unaware sometimes mistook her vision problems as inattentiveness, a lack of focus on discussion and events happening around her. That was particularly evident during her years on the First National Bank of Durango board. Steve Short, who had worked his way from

senior lending officer to bank president said he had not initially realized the extent of her visual impairment. "It made more sense to me why she was such an audio person," he said.

"Not a whole lot of people understood how very blind she was," daughter Helen Healy said. The text on Morley's work computer was magnified so much that eventually the screen showed only a half-line of type. In her living room she read the newspaper with a magnifying glass, her constant companion. "I remember being amazed at how she had to work through all this stuff. And she really didn't complain at all," Helen recalled.

After a couple of decades, during which she was very hesitant to undergo further procedures, she had a cornea transplant in her left eye in July 1999 at the University of Iowa's Carver College of Medicine. Suddenly she could see better, and that held for most of the rest of her life.

Various ailments continued to hound her. A bathroom fall in October 2001 led to back surgery, a kyphoplasty, to repair a fractured vertebra. "Never, ever, have I experienced such pain," she wrote. "Backs must have a life of their own. ... More details will be forthcoming next week. No flowers, please, but all the prayers you can muster."[427]

In 2003, age seventy-eight, she was diagnosed with throat cancer. It's not hard to draw the connection between that and her cigarette habit. That diagnosis began a six-year struggle during which Morley showed a bottomless supply of grit.

"Resilient," Karen Zink, Morley's medical provider, described her.

Friends continued to visit regularly, including Bob Beers. On one occasion Beers invited Sheri Rochford Figgs with him to see Morley.

Beers, in his nineties at that time, had started taking violin lessons. And as was their tradition, both drank cocktails not unlike Arthur's "Ballantine Bombs." "One of the things I learned about Robert and Morley, they had strong cocktails," Rochford Figgs said. "Finally, I had to say, 'Do you have any wine?'"

Morley and Beers had a great time telling stories, particularly about Durango's development, and Beers played the violin. A few days before turning ninety-five, Bob Beers reflected on his friend at Morley's memorial. "Everybody loves to talk about Morley. It's because she was a gem," he said at the service.[428] "Morley had a gentle sense of humor. I think that's primarily why she loved life so much, and everyone loved Morley."

Throat cancer surgery made it hard, almost impossible, for Morley to swallow. A "PEG tube" to supply nutrition was inserted through her abdomen and into her stomach.

"It was quite a struggle for her," Zink said.[429] "I mean, just imagine one day you're diagnosed with throat cancer and then you have radiation treatment and then you can never eat again." Her interest in current events didn't flag a bit, said friend Katherine Barr. But it was extremely tough for Morley not to be able to enjoy her afternoon cocktail or fine food. She loved going to restaurants. The two had often dined at downtown Durango establishments such as Seasons Bar & Grill.[430]

Years earlier, after selling his rodeo, Jeff Mannix had begun writing arts and entertainment reviews for the *Herald*. He decided to drop by Morley's house one day while his new tires were being installed nearby. He phoned and got the okay to visit.

He'd been reading a book at the tire shop and brought it with him to the West Park house. Morley, reclined on a couch, inquired about the book, J.M. Coetzee's *Disgrace*, a highly influential novel that takes place in post-apartheid South Africa. He started reading it to her that day, and returned each week until the book was finished. He would keep coming to read to her for several years.

"It got to be such a ritual," Mannix said. Her nurses had strong coffee and a plate of cookies prepared for his visits. Morley's strength waned, and eventually she was limited to a bed in the living room.

Mannix kept coming to read. When it seemed she was dozing off, he would stop. A few minutes would go by and she'd respond.

"And after he walks through the door then what happened?" Morley would inquire.

"She did that over and over and over again," Mannix marveled. "She remembered where it was left off. … Every single time."

Stephanie Moran wondered if the eyes-half-closed trait was a trick Morley used to learn if *you* were paying attention. "You only made the mistake once, if you made it at all, that she wasn't listening," Moran said.[431] "You learned that half-closed did not mean half-asleep."

Moran read short essays to Morley, or short stories such as E.B. White's "Once More to the Lake." Or Ernest Hemingway, because that was from Morley's era and easy to read. (A year before she retired as an educator in 2018, Stephanie Moran was extremely honored to receive the Morley Ballantine Award. "It was very meaningful for me," said Moran, who lost her mother in 1980 and valued older women who served as role models. When Morley died, "It was like losing another piece of my mom.")

By 2005 no one was sure how much time Morley had left, how long her ailing body would hold together. So when her eightieth birthday rolled around on May 21, the family put together a special tribute: a two-page special section printed by the *Herald*, but distributed privately.

Judith Reynolds, a *Herald* arts critic and political cartoonist – the latter a rarity for a small-town newspaper – wrote a long biography of Morley that was truncated for the special section and served as the main story. Several "letters to the editor" from family and friends served as odes to the octogenarian. Elizabeth, who choreographed this section, also contributed with a story bylined "Daughter and Self-appointed Scribe."

From Elizabeth's story:

> Morley is both a very private matriarch in a closely knit family and a public persona. She is one of a handful of people whose life is a measuring stick for others. Asked recently about her greatest satisfaction, Morley responded "raising my chil-

dren." We – not only her children but all apprentices to her vision – thank her on her eightieth birthday for the lessons (not easy) that she has taught us by example.

From friend and fellow writer Ray Parker:

> Congratulations on her eightieth birthday to Morley Ballantine, publisher, writer, and one of the most caring human beings this town has ever seen. … She has given her time and money unceasingly to lighten and brighten the lives of all Durangoans. She is a citizen activist who would seem to be everywhere at once, concerned and caring, a friend to everyone. What the world needs most, it seems to me, are more Morley Ballantines.

Does staying engaged and interested lead to a longer life? It definitely requires a commitment. This from her sibling, Sally Cowles Doering:

> I offer greetings to Morley, and all my love and admiration. A lot of energy, perseverance, and patience with plowing through adversity are required of anyone who reaches their eightieth birthday. But to accomplish so much along the way with grace and generosity – that is something else. Congratulations, Morley! From your little sister.

Yet, Morley was far from finished. With the help of a team of nurses, she continued to attend board meetings and entertain at her home. She traveled an astonishing twenty more times to Antigua during her final six years, always accompanied by two nurses.

Nancy Whitson became engaged to Robert Whitson in April 2006, by which time Morley was cared for constantly by a private nurse. She requested the wedding, originally scheduled for June 2007, be moved up to October 2006.

"She really wanted to be there," Whitson said. "I was happy to oblige her."

Whitson was one of many who cared for Morley in her final years. She brought mail from the *Herald* to the West Park house. She read letters, *Herald* articles, and *New Yorker* magazine stories she thought Morley would enjoy.

"Morley was the first person in my life that I was close to who experienced physical decline and taught me empathy and patience," Whitson said.

Morley endured pneumonia, during which the pastor at St. Mark's anointed her, as if she were nearing death. "This is not her time," Karen Zink insisted, understanding her inner strength. "You can stop anointing her."

Others came to visit and read to Morley as well: family, friends, *The Durango Herald* employees. Her nurses were always at hand. "She let people into her life when she got ill," Karen Zink said, "and it was such a gift to them and a gift to her."

Some felt they were intruding by coming to visit, but many whose lives she had touched came to the house and were surprised at her lucidity, even reclined in a chair or bed in the living room at the West Park house.

Mischa Semanitzky, longtime director of Music in the Mountains – which Morley helped get off the ground in 1987, then attended and supported – and his wife Jenny St. John saw her every summer in Durango. St. John wrote in a condolence letter to the family:[432]

> Even on our last visit she asked about all the details of the festival ... and was more current and able than many of the people we see every day. Mischa visited her this last summer [2009], and again marveled at her quick mind!
>
> She held a special place in the heart of Music in the Mountains. ... Mischa would not have considered an important move without talking with her. There are just a few people who appreciate the difference between average and excellent music. You all are among those people. We will miss Morley's wise, human touch.

Helen, her daughter, periodically spent multiple months helping Morley during health crises in her final years. At one point earlier in her life, Helen uncritically adored her father and blamed any problems she had on her mother. Morley had a strong personality and could be tough to be around. Arthur finally sat Helen down and convinced his youngest child that her problems didn't all stem from her mother. Helen took the message to heart. Over the years, with maturity and mellowing, Helen developed an even stronger bond with Morley.

Although Helen resisted the siren call to journalism that her parents heard, she did not ignore the family calling to public service. After settling into a career as tax accountant and consultant in Wichita, Helen involved herself in myriad community improvement efforts as her mother had. The boards she joined include the Greater Wichita YMCA, Rainbows United Charitable Foundation, and Far Above, a campaign for the University of Kansas.

"I'm sure we all went through our rebellious stages as children," Helen said. "She and I got to know each other pretty well in those last many years."

Sherry and Charles Manning came to visit in the early fall of 2009. Looking back at the thirty-two years they'd known each other, Sherry marveled at how Morley had taken advantage of the final third of her life, how she'd redefined herself after Arthur's death. Morley had become a distinguished figure and leader in her community, the state, the nation. She was a fount of knowledge regarding education, water rights, women's issues, newspapers, and much more.

"Her standards of newspapering and hard work, of connecting individuals and building relationships in pursuit of sometimes very specific goals, and organizing times and places to make things happen, were legion," Manning said.[433] "I cherish that visit. I miss her."

By then, Morley was fading.

In the morning of October 10, 2009, a Saturday, she died of respiratory failure. Her iron will could take this wasted body no further.

Enduring Influence

Morley Ballantine descended from a strong line of Cowles women who were not afraid to speak up, to challenge the status quo, and to write about it. Her grandmother, Florence M. Call Cowles, traveled from Algona, Iowa, to attend Northwestern University in 1884, when few women even dreamed of a college education. She earned a degree in literature, wrote long letters about her experiences, and composed the class song. Later, Florence traveled around the world and published a book entitled *Foreign Skies through Mother's Eyes: Round the World Letters to My Children* (Rand-McNally & Co., 1924), as well as numerous articles on Iowa history. Morley's mother, Elizabeth Bates, attended Smith College, traveled to China in 1921, and founded a women's healthcare organization in Iowa that led to what is today Planned Parenthood. As if grassroots community building weren't already in the family's blood, Morley's mother enrolled all of her children and their spouses as lifetime members of the NAACP. Her sister, Sarah, was a graduate of Radcliffe College and founded an influential organization to support Buddhism in the US.

The men in her family had a strong influence beyond just journalism, as evidenced in Morley and Arthur's children. Richard took over running the Ballantine businesses, including *The Durango Herald*. Elizabeth became a lawyer and college professor, part of a long line of Ballantines involved in higher education. Helen, a CPA, followed

numbers like her great-grandfather Gardner Cowles, who managed finances at the *Des Moines Register* with a steely eye. Bill joined the legion of many art collectors in the Cowles family, influenced further by his ancestor Russell Cowles (1887-1979), an American painter whose works are in major museum collections today.

Morley clearly had grown up with an understanding of economic and political power. It allowed her to hold her own in business discussions and serve on powerful boards of directors. Having the knowledge that her opinion was as important – and as well-formed – as anyone's in a room gave her confidence to voice it.

Morley greatly enjoyed the town she called "home" for fifty-seven years. She formed a multitude of deep friendships, and through her writing and advocacy helped shape the community.

Knowing that her grandmother was heard and respected in high-power, and often male-dominated, realms has given granddaughter Katherine Healy Dougan inspiration. She holds that same confidence to make sure she's heard in her financial career, which has included the still-male-dominated finance and oil-and-gas industries.

"I can't imagine what she dealt with in that regard," Katherine said of her grandmother.[434] "She never hesitated to voice an opinion. I do think a lot about that."

Katherine, in her mid-thirties, appreciated that she's been encouraged to attempt to thrive in any career she chose. Although gender equality has not been achieved, it's within striking distance. Women such as Morley Cowles Ballantine helped pave the way for Katherine and her generation.

"I guarantee there wasn't anyone saying, 'Yeah, go run a paper. Go do these things.' No one was telling her that," Katherine said.

There is a photo of Morley wearing her big, round glasses, taken at her work desk, with piles of books and papers behind her. She is staring at the camera, bold, unafraid, as Athena recipient Ellen Roberts sees it. "'I belong here,' Morley seems to be saying with her expression. 'I have something to say, and I'm going to say it.'"

Community leader Don Mapel said that since he arrived to stay in 1970, and for several decades before that, there has been a core group of influential leaders who dedicated themselves to bringing positive changes – in business as well as culturally and civically. These changes have brought an impressive reign of prosperity to Durango and to Southwest Colorado.

"I would have to put the Ballantines at the top of that list of influential people who had a vision beyond 'today,'" Mapel said.

Jim Joyce was a newcomer when he met Morley, not long after Arthur's death. The two became fast friends, despite an almost two-decade age difference. Joyce reflected on his friend in his book, *The Guys in the Gang*, "For all her wealth and accompanying power, Morley was unpretentious, gracious, polite, and interested in you, no matter who you were."

Even after her death, accolades continued for Morley Ballantine.

Susan Lander, the former Women's Resource Center director, became a member of the Colorado Women's Hall of Fame nominating committee in 2012. One of the hall's goals at the time was to incorporate Southwest Colorado, a region sometimes forgotten in the Front Range-dominated state. Morley's name was the first to surface among Durangoans, and in March 2014 she was inducted posthumously. Several tables' worth of Durango-area residents traveled to Denver for the ceremony, attended by 500 at the Marriott City Center hotel. Many Denver friends were there too.

"She made such a difference. I just loved her. She was amazing," Lander said.[435] "Everything is different and unique about her. Like her name. She's like Cher. She only needed a first name."

As Helen Ballantine Healy accepted on behalf of her mother, she felt the impact Morley had made throughout Colorado.

"This is such an honor for her, coming from such an isolated part of the state," Helen said at the banquet.[436] Morley's contributions, the boards she'd served on, were listed. But there was more. After Morley's death, countless women came up to Helen and other family members and told them how much she'd advised and encouraged them.

"Along with all that [philanthropy and board service], her big job, she felt, was mentoring," Helen said. "And I didn't fully understand that until my mother died."

Rochelle Mann, former head of the Fort Lewis College Music Department, was part of the effort to apply for Morley's induction. "Morley was always one of my mentors, not that she knew that," Mann said.[437]

Eleven days later, a Durango reception for Morley's induction was hosted by Diane Wildfang in the garden area of the Rochester Hotel.[438] About sixty people attended, including Morley's granddaughter Sarah Healy, who had begun a stint working for Ballantine Communications in Durango.

In April 2018 Morley was inducted into the Colorado Press Association Hall of Fame. In a ceremony in Colorado Springs, she was recognized for her long dedication to journalism in Colorado.[439]

She was far ahead of her time championing civil rights, cultural awareness, and social justice in Southwest Colorado, press association officials said in bestowing the honor. "In an era when so many women journalists were relegated to society and home and garden coverage, she rallied for equal pay for equal work, reproduction rights, and protection from workplace harassment."

From Arthur and Morley, and on to the children, the family has left an indelible mark, and continues to do so.

"They're always going to be a real cornerstone of Durango," said Elizabeth Ballantine's childhood classmate and native Durangoan, Barb Eggleston Conn.[440] "Just like other people throughout history have been, there are just certain names that will always be out there."

Local attorney and longtime family friend Denny Ehlers wrote in a sympathy card to Richard and Mary Lyn: "Communities, like great structures, rely on the strength of their most important pillars. Morley's strength and breadth of interest and caring have touched more people than you will ever know. Her character is reflected in the unique, special town of Durango. Bringing an intellectual and critical sophistication uncommon to the cowboy West without spoiling its sense of place is my perception of her gift. For that we should all be grateful."

Former *Herald* reporter Deborah Uroda said, "I know they really cared about Durango and the community, yet they were solid journalists and really believed in the mission of the *Herald* to be the watchdog of the community. That's who Morley was."

Morley's influence continues to be felt in myriad ways by the many whom she affected. Granddaughter Sarah Leavitt, the daughter of Elizabeth Ballantine, conjures her grandmother's image regularly. "I've often said to my mother, 'What do you think Mamama would advise?' while weighing various decisions. I would love to talk to her today. Her advice would not necessarily be heartwarming, but it would be honest. She wouldn't hesitate to say bluntly the pluses and minuses of any scenario, and because of that, she made those around her stronger."

Joel Jones' term as Fort Lewis College president, from 1988-1998, benefitted immensely from one of the school's most illustrious graduates. He wrote in a tribute:[441]

> Why did I grow to love this woman? As a surrogate big sister? Mother-mentor? Book-loving reader? And having written that question, I can see Morley's face with that singular smile-grin which says, "You've got to be kidding – but go on."
>
> Succinctly, what struck me as so admirable – and lovable – about Morley was her absolute honesty, her bedrock integrity, her ever-present intellectual curiosity, her passionate commitment to certain causes, and her guarded modesty, even humility, about both her extraordinary family history and her myriad achievements, appointments, and awards.
>
> With reference to the Fort Lewis College Foundation, our causes and campaigns, Morley's (and her family's) generosity, counsel, and energy were absolutely critical, from the Community Concert Hall and Center of Southwest Studies to the current Student Union project. Were I to say to her face that for me, personally and professionally, and for Fort Lewis College – as well as for many, many other nonprofit organizations

– she was, and is, our angel, she would deck me with that look – but then, perhaps, she would smile, and say, "Go on." And her legacy will go on, and on, and on.

Morley's influence survives in myriad ways. Her name lives on in the newspaper itself, appearing on the Opinion page masthead next to Arthur's: Morley C. Ballantine (Mrs. Arthur A. Ballantine): Chairman and Editor, 1952-2009.

Arthur and Morley's names are just below the words of Kansan William Allen White (1868-1944), a progressive newspaper editor and contemporary of Gardner Cowles, Morley's grandfather. It was Morley's idea in 1985 to add White's pithy yet charming aphorism:[442]

There are three things that no one can do to the entire satisfaction of anyone else: make love, poke the fire, and run a newspaper.

Part IV

CONTINUING THE LEGACY

Richard Gale Ballantine

Morley kept a presence and unquestioned influence, but the task of keeping the *Herald* afloat, on task, and technologically up to date had fallen into Richard Ballantine's hands. It did not take long for him to settle into a comfortable leadership role after assuming the position of publisher in 1983.

Richard grew up around newspapers. As a child he had a delivery route, which he completed on a bike or motor scooter. He also partook briefly in other *Durango Herald* tasks, and he learned plenty from osmosis, just by being around the business daily and listening to Morley and Arthur's post-work chats.

He began public schools in Minneapolis. Just as he was turning seven, the family headed west and his Durango schooling began in the fall of 1952. For second grade he walked to Needham Elementary School, heading straight down West

Richard tours the *Minneapolis Star and Tribune* printing plant with grandfather John Cowles in September 1959.

Third Avenue, still a gravel road at that time.

His first journalistic endeavor came while an eleven-year-old sixth grader. He wrote an editorial deploring the seemingly endless road work between his house and Needham. The April 23, 1957, piece was titled, "What's Durango Coming To?"

Reading was a common pastime for Morley, and the Ballantine children were highly encouraged to always have something to read handy, particularly when traveling. "We learned very quickly that you're frequently waiting in life, and how helpful it is to have something to read that you could just pull out," Richard said.

After elementary and junior high in the Durango public school system, Richard headed for New England. He spent two years at Phillips Exeter Academy in New Hampshire, where he was on the soccer team, and then finished his primary education with two years at Fountain Valley School, in southeast Colorado Springs. He wrote sporadically for the school paper, *The Dane*.

His soccer career reached its zenith at Fountain Valley, where an assistant coach told Arthur that "Richard had been the star of the weekend's two games. ... FV won both by lopsided scores."[443]

Richard loved machinery and tinkering. His sister Elizabeth recalled that when he got to driving age, Richard often had a car taken apart in the front yard. He later collected and raced Alfa Romeos, Italian sports cars.

He graduated from Fountain Valley in 1964, then after a summer in Durango went to the West Coast to attend Stanford University. Richard avoided journalism courses at Stanford because he'd been counseled that they wouldn't be particularly helpful to someone who had been involved in running a family newspaper. He did utilize his *Durango Herald* experience while serving as night editor of the *Stanford Daily* as a freshman, which he found was a great way to make connections and learn about campus. Richard graduated from Stanford in 1968 with a history degree.

Not long after leaving Stanford, Richard volunteered for duty in Vietnam. He spent forty-seven weeks at a training course learning Vietnamese to serve with a US advisory squad called an MACV – Military

Assistance Command Vietnam – Team. MACV Teams were small groups that worked with Vietnamese military leaders.

Richard's group, stationed then in Quang Ngai, south of Da Nang, provided intelligence and more to a Vietnamese infantry division. Richard was there in September 1970 when he turned twenty-five. Interestingly, his brother Bill, who volunteered for duty as a paratrooper with the Army's 173rd Airborne Brigade, dropped in on Richard in Quang Ngai in early December 1970.

"I admired his ingenuity in getting up here," Richard wrote to his parents. "Bill was surprised to see what luxury I have here – he borrowed a pair of civilian clothes for the first time and we had a hamburger snack in the evening from the [malt shop] stand just outside my door. But Bill made it clear that he didn't think much of my boring 'desk' job, and he was eager to get out and around."[444]

Richard accompanied Bill via helicopter on the fifty-minute flight back to Bill's quarters down the South China Sea coast. "We both agreed," Richard wrote, "that the best feeling will be to be discharged in June."

Not long after his military service, Richard had a full-time go at agriculture, purchasing a farm in the Longmont area north of Denver. His siblings weren't surprised. During his childhood he had often spent parts of summers at his biological grandparents' 250-acre Wickham farm in Mound, just west of Minneapolis. Dick and Isobel Gale raised crops, beef cattle, sheep, pigs, and horses. This introduced Richard to farming, and got him tinkering with the machinery used – tractors, hay bailers, and such.

Notwithstanding his later devotion to *The Durango Herald*, Richard has been a farmer ever since. As Arthur put it in a 1974 interview:[445]

> He is now living quite happily in Longmont, Colo. He has a ... ranch and is raising pigs and cattle and has become foreman of the grain elevator in Longmont. Morley and I are extremely proud of that because he just started at the bottom and came to the top.

Mary Lyn and Richard Ballantine, 2015.

The trials of farming were underscored by a small item in a February 1977 family letter from Bill Ballantine, who referred to his brother at that time as "Dick" rather than "Richard."[446] "Alas, the latest report from Longmont is that Dick's sow, (Bertha? Katherine??) died after giving birth to a litter of piglets."

Following Arthur's death, Morley solicited estate tax advice from Holland & Hart. Firm co-founder Stephen Hart, who had a Yale connection with Arthur Ballantine Jr., introduced Morley to Claude Maer, an estate tax expert with the firm. Claude Maer would become her good friend and traveling partner.

But more important, the paralegal assigned to the clients was Mary Lyn. She would be the one organizing the proper paperwork. "I was dazzled," Richard said of meeting Mary Lyn.

Mary Lyndale Allen was raised in a small town in northeastern Pennsylvania, on the New York border. She ventured to Philadelphia for paralegal school. No huge fan of the big metropolis, she left there and moved to Denver in 1971 – her family had vacationed in Estes Park – and took a job with Holland & Hart, one of Denver's premier law firms. She would work there for nine years. The Denver metro area was much smaller then – one million population in 1970, compared with 2.8 million in 2020. Metro Philadelphia's 1970 population was four million.

In the summer of 1976 they went out for Chinese food on their first date. On the farm, "Richard put me through a few tests," Mary Lyn joked.[447] She hopped on a tractor and disked a field (breaking up dirt clumps) and fed a few pigs.

They were married October 4, 1980, at Church of the Redeemer in Sayre, Pa. They lived briefly in Longmont, but two months after the wedding, moved to Durango. After nine years in the Denver area, Mary Lyn was ready for a change. She had visited Durango once with her family and liked what she saw. The couple lived for a short time at the West Park house, rented for a while following that, and then bought farmland on the Florida Mesa in 1982. On the mesa they lived in a double-wide trailer until construction was completed on their Spanish Colonial farmhouse.

In December 1980, a new set of initials appeared on editorials: RGB for Richard Gale Ballantine. Morley welcomed the family help, just as she had been grateful for Elizabeth's presence on the staff after Arthur's death in 1975. Richard was named assistant publisher, and he ventured into various newspaper departments, brushing up on tasks with which he was familiar, and learning about those still foreign to him.

"I'd always expected to be part of operations at the *Herald*," Richard said. "I was glad to come back."[448]

The Newspaper

Richard spent time working in accounting, filling out the daily deposits and running them to the bank. Writing never came easily for him, and it helped to have a long stint in the newsroom.

One of the crucial issues of the early 1980s was finding a place for the uranium mill tailings that had been abandoned at the foot of Smelter Mountain alongside the Animas River. Richard wrote about possible burial places for the potentially hazardous tailings. He learned how to make maps to accompany his story, using the typewriters then in use (not long before computers were the norm).

In a way, he said, working in coordination with his mother was a continuation of how Morley and Arthur ran things. Morley had her social circles, Richard had his, and they compared notes, shared ideas, and generated concepts for *Herald* stories and columns.

In 1983, Morley was preoccupied with boards and meetings around the country, and Richard was now thirty-seven and ready for a new challenge. The family board members named him publisher.

In the June 1, 1983, *Herald* story announcing the change, Morley wrote, "I've seen too many members of older generations refuse to step aside to give the younger ones a chance to make their own mistakes. Richard's bright and quick and, above all, he has common sense."

His official first day as publisher was October 1, and he would hold that title for almost thirty years.

Richard made no drastic changes. Most tweaks at first were subtle, such as ending the use of writers' initials on *Herald* editorials. This minor alteration fit with Richard's personality – to not relish the spotlight – but also was in step with the times. Papers around the nation decided it was best to present a unified position, not one that might look like it was just Morley's or Richard's.

Like the rest of his family, he had to change his staunch Republican stance as the party crept, or leapt, farther to the political spectrum's right. Ballantine positions remained, in general, fiscally conservative and socially liberal. In this, Richard was very similar to his mother.

If the issue was promoting local business, readers could pretty much count on the *Herald* to be on board. And when it came to a core handful of social issues – women's choice, gay rights, racial and gender equality – the *Herald* almost unfailingly supported those, too.

If employees and the public expected standards to dip with the new guy in charge, they were mistaken. Technological updates were happening, and the news staff only continued to grow.

Awards continued to pile up under Richard's leadership. The newsroom, advertising, designers, and web department all garnered multiple honors annually. Scores of trophies and plaques came during the annual Colorado Press Association awards in February in Denver, and were displayed proudly in a glass case in the *Herald* foyer.

The newsroom staff was consistently stocked with top-notch reporters, many of whom would hone their talents in Durango, then step up to larger markets. Those included Dave Curtin, who worked as a *Herald* reporter and photographer from 1984-1987, then three years later won a Pulitzer Prize – the most prestigious award a journalist can receive – for feature writing for the *Colorado Springs Gazette-Telegraph*.

Barry Smith worked as a *Durango Herald* reporter and city editor from 1980-1990, won several awards for his stories, and recalled that "some of the best journalists in Colorado came through the *Herald's* newsroom – some drawn by Durango's charms, some because they knew the *Herald* could be a bit feisty."[449]

Smith and a local radio newsman in 1980 refused to reveal their sources when reporting on a murder case. Preliminary court hearings had been closed to the public despite objections from the *Herald* and KIUP-AM. Smith and Dave Tragethon, the KIUP reporter, were found in contempt of court and spent forty-eight hours in La Plata County Jail.

"The *Herald* and the Ballantines had the guts to challenge the courts in the first place in support of open government, publish the story that told what was really going on, and then defend me in court through a rather lengthy and expensive process," Smith recalled. "It showed a commitment not only to journalism but to civic responsibility."

Smith won more awards after settling in Nevada. He became a member of the Nevada Press Association Board of Directors, took over as executive director from 2006-2018, and helped craft legislation that reformed the state's public records laws. In 2021 he was inducted into the Nevada Newspaper Hall of Fame.

After retiring from journalism, he returned to the Four Corners to live. "The Ballantines had a reputation as real newspaper people, and they were respected by folks across the country who worked in the industry at much bigger, metro-level newspapers," Smith remembered from his decade in Durango. "The Ballantines were proud of the *Herald*. It had character, and that character reflected on them."

Other special awards came to the newspaper.

In 1991, with a circulation of about 8,500, the *Herald* beat out other statewide newspapers for major honors from the Colorado Press Association: best daily newspaper sweepstakes awards for both general excellence and community service. General excellence is an overall award judged on quality of reporting, headline writing, page design, and advertising.

The *Herald* had been publishing an afternoon paper since the Ballantines' purchase in 1952. For most of the history of newspapers, it had made sense to gather the latest news each morning and deliver an up-to-date product to readers at about the time they were heading home from work. But the advent of the TV evening news, then CNN, and copycats with their round-the-clock broadcasting, had changed Americans' news consumption habits.

Many big-city media companies, including the Cowles-owned Des Moines Register and Tribune Company, had phased out their afternoon papers as early as the 1970s and 1980s. The afternoon *Des Moines*

Morley and Richard celebrate the debut of the morning edition of the "Daybreak Daily," April 4, 1995.

Tribune ceased publication in 1982, and the *St. Petersburg Evening Independent* closed in 1986, just two examples of many. Other papers such as *The Denver Post* switched from evening to morning publication. The *Post* did this in the early 1980s even though that meant direct competition with its rival, the *Rocky Mountain News.*

Richard began to consider a change. He came to realize that the afternoon paper, delivered in the early afternoon, had a "short window," particularly in newspaper racks or retail outlets that closed at 5 or 6 p.m.; the next morning it was yesterday's paper. He had a gut feeling the morning paper would be more successful.

When Richard and others from the *Herald* began approaching advertisers about the potential major change, many replied, "You bet we're supportive. Then our ad will be visible all day."

On April 4, 1995, *The Durango Herald* switched to morning delivery. Simultaneously, it dropped the Monday edition and added Saturday, continuing to publish six days a week.

As Richard said, the benefits were numerous: "We had an hour at night when it was possible to fix the press. We found more time in the day. Public reaction arrived early in the morning instead of the evening. We were in contact with our readers mid-morning. We accelerated the debate."[450]

In October 1998, Richard added a Monday newspaper and the *Herald* began publishing seven days a week.

Not that there was competition between them, but Richard's statewide influence began to rival his mother's. He became involved with the Colorado Press Association and was named Colorado Newsperson of the Year in 1997. Two years later he served as president of the association.

An Ever-Changing Business

To support local writers working on projects involving regional history, Richard and Morley began publishing books. Morley really wanted to help the writers print their works, and the *Herald* had the resources to help.[451]

The first book, in 1995, was former *Herald* associate editor Ian Thompson's *Houses on Country Roads: Essays on the Places, Seasons, and Peoples of the Four Corners Country.* At the time, Thompson was director of research at Crow Canyon Archaeological Center just west of Cortez. He died of cancer in 1998 at age fifty-seven. (Ian's son Jonathan Thompson is a former newspaper writer and highly regarded regional journalist whose book *River of Lost Souls* is the authoritative look at the 2015 Gold King Mine disaster that turned the Animas River orange and made national headlines.[452])

In 2003 the Ballantines officially took the name Durango Herald Small Press for their book-publishing activities. Under the leadership of Robert Whitson, DHSP published books by authors including Fort Lewis College history professor Duane Smith, prominent Southwest US archaeologist Florence Lister, the Mesa Verde Museum Association, and the San Juan Mountains Association.

The Small Press was never envisioned as a big money-maker, which was good, because it never was. But it served an important purpose for many. Editor Elizabeth Green and graphic artist Lisa Snider, along with an editorial board that included Suzy Garrison Meyer (publisher of the *Cortez Journal,* by then a Ballantine newspaper) and Andrew Gulliford, worked with authors to craft multiple acclaimed books about people, places, events, and institutions in the Four Corners.

One of the Small Press's highlights was a seven-book series published about the history of Mesa Verde National Park, launched in 2006, the year of the park's 100th anniversary. The series won the Colorado Historical Society's Josephine H. Miles History Award, given annually to a project that makes a major contribution to advancing knowledge of Colorado history.[453]

In 2011, the Small Press book *Landscapes on Glass: Lantern Slides for the Rainbow Bridge-Monument Valley Expedition,* written by Jack Turner, won the Colorado Book Award in the Pictorial class. The awards are presented annually by the nonprofit Colorado Humanities. DHSP books also earned multiple Colorado Independent Publishers Association EVVY awards every year. DHSP's final publications were the Detours walking tour series, including *Walking Durango, Walking Silverton,* and *Walking Telluride.* Produced in cooperation with local historical societies, which shared in royalties, the books remain very popular today.

Under Richard's leadership, the *Herald* in April 1999 purchased the *Cortez Sentinel* and *Montezuma Valley Journal,* with a combined circulation of 6,500. The *Mancos Times* came along as part of the deal.

"We were looking for a new project," Richard said in a June 2003 interview.[454] "There are certainly a lot of similarities between these two communities. ... We thought we could strengthen the *Herald* and the *Journal* as well."

The *Herald* then purchased the *Dolores Star* in 2000. The *Herald*-owned papers shared some news content and advertising, but the Cortez and Dolores papers remained editorially separate.

With the presses aging at both the Durango and Cortez papers, the Ballantines decided it was time to modernize with a new one. So a major change occurred in September 2002 when printing ceased in the Durango Herald basement and moved to the newer plant in Cortez. The old *Herald* press was shipped to Rapid City, S.D., to print the *Lakota Journal,* then the largest independent Native American newspaper.

Technological changes came fast and furious between the 1980s and 2000s. *Herald* reporters began writing on computers in the 1980s, and editors began designing pages on computers in the mid-1990s. The switch to computers made it easier for the press to print consistent plates and to align color photos, which greatly expanded the use of color in both news photos and ads. The *Herald* had printed its first color photo on July 25, 1977, of a Comanche war dancer, George Woodgee Watchataker. But newsroom use of color photos was rare until the 1990s.

Always trying to think ahead, the *Herald* went online in July 1996. Its web presence was at first rudimentary, and many people weren't even using email or the internet yet, but it was a start. The technology was brought to fruition mainly by in-house talent led by news editor Lewis McCool and a high school student.

The internet greatly influenced news delivery, with a new devotion to the rapid dissemination of stories. Unfortunately for newspapers, these developments, and the addition of web readers, did not lead to an increase in profits. Web content brought in little revenue.

Another innovation was WebDurango, a separate department begun in 2000 to maintain the company's websites. It also built and maintained sites for other regional businesses.

The *Herald* newsroom was the largest and at its prime under the guidance of managing editor David Staats, who led the news department from 1997-2004.[455] Staats demanded a lot from his staff, and those who were willing to take his incisive critiques and were willing to work hard flourished. During his reign he created an invaluable *Durango Herald* stylebook, which reporters and editors referenced for everything from writing obituaries to reporting the police beat to the proper spelling of Ridgway.

When a Cortez policeman was murdered in May 1998 by machine-gun-wielding local men, Staats directed comprehensive coverage of the 1998 desert manhunt. That included multiple trips to remote sections of the Four Corners by reporters Amy Maestas, Joshua Moore, Bret Bell, John Peel, and others, and photographers Jerry McBride and Nancy Richmond. The protracted manhunt in the Utah desert brought national attention for the next two months, increasing web traffic exponentially. News media from around the country constantly contacted *Herald* editors and reporters for local insight into the manhunt, which dragged on for weeks, then months, and years.

Website "hits" ballooned again in 2002 when a massive wildfire ravaged the San Juan National Forest and private lands, threatening hundreds of homes in subdivisions on the forest border. The *Herald's* coverage of the Missionary Ridge Fire was crucial to the community. The tireless staff kept readers up to date on the fire's progress and path, letting them know instantly, through the website, who needed to evacuate their homes and who should be prepared to do so.

With Staats overseeing the newsroom, and Moore as city editor, a reporting team that included Jim Greenhill, Shane Benjamin, Melanie Brubaker Mazur, Jennifer Kostka, Tom Sluis, and others stayed on top of hourly developments. McBride and Richmond again provided photography, often traveling with "Nomex" fire-resistant coveralls into the vicinity of the blaze. Relying on the *Herald's* constant web updates, both locals and second-home owners in other states kept track of the Missionary Ridge Fire, which charred 73,000 acres and destroyed eighty-three structures over thirty-nine days.

Herald staffers helped put together a keepsake book about the Missionary Ridge blaze, featuring text by reporter Jim Greenhill and extensive photographs by Jerry McBride and Nancy Richmond. The book was published by Durango Herald Small Press.

For its extensive and vital work during the fire, the *Herald* earned the 2002 Sigma Delta Chi Award for Excellence in Journalism in public service from the national Society of Professional Journalists. The *Herald*, circulation around 10,000, competed with papers up to 100,000 circulation for the prestigious honor.

The award ceremony in July 2003 in Washington, D.C., was attended by several Ballantine and Cowles family members, who rubbed elbows with winners from *The Oregonian, Washington Post, Chicago Tribune,* and *Arizona Republic,* among others. The *Herald* threw a post-award party at the International Spy Museum, and with about two dozen in attendance, John Cowles Jr. was among those who spoke in honoring his sister's newspaper.

A Different Style

Although he maintained a busy schedule of meetings and travel, as well as managing the farm on Florida Mesa, Richard was pleased to sit down and chat with visitors or staff during his untethered time. His main-floor office looked east toward Buckley Park, a small but oft-used public gathering point. If some hubbub or protest was occurring at the park, the publisher was the first to know, and he'd make sure the newsroom was on the spot to investigate.

A first-time visitor to his office might take a look in, see the three-foot-high cascade of papers on his desk, and wonder when this loose, unarranged pile of material might become unmoored and drop in a sudden, life-threatening avalanche. And, oh my gosh, was that balding head *behind* that stack or buried within it?

Richard hadn't read all that material on his desk, but he had read some. (Much of it he planned to get to later.) Whether it regarded farming, or nice sports cars, or a brainstorm about a potential improvement at the newspaper, ideas were constantly roiling in his head. And he was happy to help people see and even experience his point of view.

In one instance, when the *Herald* newsroom misidentified alfalfa hay as grass hay in a photo caption, Richard brought both into the office. He held a clinic in the conference room, where he taught city folk that, even if they couldn't tell the difference, they would know there *was* a difference.

Ellen Roberts, who had written a rotating column in the *Herald* called "On the Law," ran for state legislature in 2006. Richard suggested that to serve constituents properly she needed a hands-on course in rural living.

"He told me I needed to get on a tractor, and I said I'd love to, but I don't have one," Roberts said.[456] She went out to Richard's farm and spent several hours baling hay. "I didn't do a very good job of getting the bales lined up correctly, but I really appreciated his helping me appreciate agriculture."

Richard gave his time to causes, some in continuation of what Morley and Arthur had begun, others on his own. In the 1990s he took a spot for several years on the Cowles Media Company board, necessitating trips to Minneapolis. Later his sister Elizabeth became a board member, and Richard resigned.

After Morley left the First National Bank of Durango board of directors at the end of 2001, Richard took her spot. Steve Short, First National president from 2000 to 2011, came to value Richard's advice and mentorship, and found him to be both accessible and genuine. The two periodically met for breakfast, where they'd have serious discussions, usually on a specific topic.

"I certainly picked his brain on things going on at the bank, and what the community reaction might be," Short said.[457] "I always trusted Richard's advice. … I have really looked at Richard over the years as being a strong mentor for me in terms of thoughtful community thinking."

When Richard left the Fort Lewis College Board of Trustees in December 2011, Short took his spot and heeded his counsel. "He was extremely helpful to me as an incoming trustee."

Richard kept his finger on the pulse of many Durango happenings, whether it was the railroad, or business development, or the schools, or even the ranching community. After Morley died in 2009, Richard and Mary Lyn continued the salons – the gatherings of local influencers – at 175 West Park. Short noticed the house decorations, from classy furniture to unique artwork, had been left largely intact, and it was still called "Morley's house." That felt like a nice memorial to her.

After dinner, the ten to twenty salon attendees would gather in a circle in the living room, and Richard would conduct a community forum.

Not unfairly, participants would be put on the spot, and asked to discuss a specific community topic of interest. "He is so good at stimulating intellectual thinking. ... He has this way of drawing out a variety of salient topics within the community and then getting group engagement," Short said. "I think that is a special knack that somebody has. Not just anybody could do that."

Peter Decker (1934-2020), a former Fort Lewis trustee, came to know both Morley and Richard, and fought higher education battles alongside them. "Richard knows how difficult it is to create personal integrity and a personal reputation," Decker said. "He also knows how quickly it can vanish with a dumb statement or foolish act."[458]

As much or more than his mother, Richard enforced the separation between the editorial board and the newsroom staff. The latter were free to report the news as they saw fit.

Richard continues to be involved regionally and statewide, serving on several boards, including Colorado Humanities, Crow Canyon Archaeological Center, and the Center of Southwest Studies.[459] And as his mother had done, Richard joined the Colorado Forum, the powerful, idea-sharing organization that meets periodically and takes positions on issues of statewide importance.

Gail Klapper, Colorado Forum president and a good friend of Morley's, described Richard as having a quiet influence. "He doesn't make his case in a way that puts people off; he makes it with good information and with a smile."[460]

Some reporters and editors had lengthy careers at the *Herald*. While they didn't get rich, they were supported by a fine health plan and a few perks that developed, such as free passes to the local sports club and hot springs. For a time, a part-time masseuse came in for quick employee massages during work hours. While some newsroom staffers moved up to larger city journalism jobs, several stayed in town in public relations, or as spokespersons, or in jobs that had nothing to do with media.

The Durango Telegraph, a free, independent weekly, was co-created by former *Herald* newsroom staffer Missy Votel in 2002. It provides news and features and appeals to a somewhat younger and hipper audience, although it does not cover the community as comprehensively as the *Herald* does and provides no school sports coverage.

The Ballantines always made a case for press freedoms, and for continuing to exercise those freedoms so they will not be forgotten or lost. The Fourth Estate's right to access public information is a journalistic cornerstone. If, for instance, the city government or courts balked at turning over documents that reporters believed to be open records, or closed a meeting that should be open, the *Herald* was prepared for a fight. The family kept a First Amendment attorney, Tom Kelley of Denver, on retainer for when the need arose.

In September 2010 the Colorado Freedom of Information Council awarded the Ballantine family the prestigious Jean Otto Friend of Freedom Award. This honor is given sporadically, only when a worthy candidate arises. Richard, Elizabeth, and Helen all proudly accepted the special honor at the Strater Hotel in Durango.[461]

As part of this battle, Elizabeth Ballantine became an integral member of the Inter American Press Association, a consortium of newspapers in the Americas from Alaska to Argentina. It has many goals, with the first "to defend freedom of the press."[462] Elizabeth and editorial page editor Bill Roberts, also an IAPA member, traveled several times to the "General Assembly," held in alternating venues in North or South America. Elizabeth served a term as IAPA president, and as of 2022, remains involved as a consulting member to the board of directors.

Morley and Arthur, and later Richard with help from his sister Elizabeth and her husband Paul Leavitt and connections, took pride in encouraging young journalists. They did this in myriad ways, whether it was hiring interns or hosting a regional media day that brought high school students from Southwest Colorado and Northwest New Mexico to Fort Lewis College.

Almost since the day the Ballantines purchased the Durango papers they welcomed interns. Sometimes they were family members, such as Tilly Lorentz Grey in the late 1950s, or a worthy friend of the family, such as Jim Rousmaniere in 1965, or the irrepressible Chase Olivar-ius-McAllister in 2011. Under Richard and Managing Editor David Staats, the *Herald* began an internship program with Fort Lewis College. During some summers in the 1990s and 2000s, the newsroom would have both a photographer intern and news reporter/editor intern. Sometimes high school students would be put to work.

In the 2000s, the *Herald* began an intern program with the School of Communications at American University in Washington, D.C. This was the brainchild of Gary Hook, who retired from his position as newsroom executive at *USA Today* in 2008 and spent the next five years overseeing web-related changes at *The Durango Herald*.

The partnership "is unique among family-owned newspapers," said Hook, also a former Ballantine Communications director. Hook still interviewed and selected those interns as of 2022.[463] The partnership has provided "valuable and important real-world experience" for more than thirty students.

Remarkably, working for a small-town paper in Southwest Colorado became a plumb year-round internship among American University's communications students. "The internship has become quite competitive," Hook said. "Such a special legacy for Richard."

A Brand New Day

For years, Editorial Page Editor Bill Roberts stored a small, faded, wooden peach crate in his work cubicle. Whenever Richard had an important announcement – a major purchase, a death, the annual awards to staff who'd hit career milestones at the *Herald*, or the hiring or departure of a department manager – Bill would drag the crate to the center of the main floor between advertising and the newsroom. Richard, remaining remarkably nimble, would step up on the rickety crate and raise his voice to get everyone's attention.

Sometimes these announcements came as a shock. But when Richard took to the crate for the last time on July 31, 2013, everyone knew what was coming. The search for a new company leader outside the family had begun in February. It was a bittersweet moment when Richard announced that he was stepping aside as publisher, and Douglas Bennett was stepping in as chief executive officer.

It was sixty-one years and two months since the purchase of the *Herald-News* and the beginning of the Ballantine era. And it was thirty years and two months since Morley's announcement that she was turning the publisher's reins to her oldest son. The role of publisher existed now in memory only. Richard remained deeply engaged in his role as chairman of Ballantine Communications Inc., or BCI, the new name for the business holdings with the *Herald* as its centerpiece.

The family continued sole ownership of the company. Richard also continued to write editorials.

At that moment, Ballantine Communications owned four newspapers – the *Herald*, the *Cortez Journal*, the *Mancos Times* and *Dolores Star* – as well as *Directory Plus*, Ballantine Digital Media, and Durango Herald Small Press. Just a few months later, in January 2014, the company purchased the *Pine River Times*, Bayfield's weekly paper.

Bennett was handed a difficult charge. He'd need to lead this Durango-based company into a digital age unkind to many forms of printed media. He was tasked with making cuts where necessary and trying to stem the bleeding of cost overruns produced by each of Ballantine Communications' newspapers. He was asked by a unanimous vote of the board of directors to explore any and all possibilities of creating new media platforms – within the company's limits.

"Digital distribution and digital interactivity is where communication is and is going," Richard Ballantine said in an interview that day.[464] "We felt we had to have a leader who knows how we can play a role in that."

Elizabeth Ballantine and her siblings are very grateful for Richard and his ability to steer the *Herald* and Ballantine Communications.

"As a family, we had a long-term vision for the newspaper. Richard managed it successfully for my generation. We don't know what impossible challenges will face our children. Regardless, a core Ballantine family value is the belief that a healthy press is critical to US democracy and to all our lives."[465]

Company employees looked at this new era with excitement and trepidation. The newsroom, guarded of its independent role and the value of its separation from advertising and outside influences, was particularly concerned.

Board members – as well as anyone understanding economic realities – knew there would have to be cuts to the newsroom, and these soon began. The printed product was costly, and in 2017 the painful decision was made to end the production of a daily printed newspaper. This was cut to four days a week – Mondays, Wednesdays, Fridays, and Saturdays. Within a year the Monday newspaper was also discontinued. Readers could continue to get daily stories online.

The Ballantines' belief in the newspaper as an important community watchdog never wavered. If not the *Herald*, then who would keep an eye on city planning and development, the school board, the forest, the environment? Who but the *Herald* could possibly provide such a forum? Other family-owned papers around the country also stood calm in the storm, dreading the alternative for the towns they love and support.

Said Francis Wick, president and CEO of the family-owned Sierra Vista, Arizona-based Wick Communications: "Our biggest concern is that, if there's not local professional journalism taking place, we don't know what the alternative is to that."[466]

The *Herald's* saving grace is its link to the community. For local stories, there is one daily source. For airing your views to the greatest audience, readers still rely on the newspaper. The back-and-forth among readers on the *Herald's* opinion page and online continues with vitality and passion.

The newspaper is a service that first Morley and Arthur, and then Richard, have provided to the community. The *Herald*, with the backing of altruistic owners who steadfastly took positions and encouraged whatever they believed was in the region's best interest, has helped create a place where people continue to flock.

Citing these contributions and others, the Colorado Press Association inducted Richard Ballantine into its Hall of Fame in 2019.

Some may hold grudges against the Ballantines, some may even have legitimate beefs. After all, no one can run a newspaper to the satisfaction of everyone. Bill Roberts said the "overwhelming feeling" he was left with after twenty-seven years at the *Herald* is that Richard is a "profoundly decent man."

Richard was philosophical about the curtailing of his role. Would he miss the daily interaction with the team he had helped assemble? Oh yes. But at age sixty-seven he was ready to step aside and let people with new ideas take charge.

"I've had two things in my life that I really enjoyed doing – journalism and farming," he said.[467] "And I've gotten to do both of them. Many people don't get to do even one."

Digital Challenge

Starting in earnest in the mid-1990s, the publishing business – books, magazines, educational materials, and newspapers – came to grips with digital competition. Many concluded that to maximize profits, their content should be available digitally. From floppy disk to CD-ROM to the internet, changes occurred at a staggering pace. Traditional print newspapers were losing subscribers as people increasingly sought news and information online. The *Herald* would have to adapt to the growing digital demand, a field that required someone with experience beyond journalism.

Doug Bennett

Doug Bennett was in the middle of these developments, and when it came time in 2013 for Ballantine Communications to hire someone to bring digital expertise, consolidation, financial stability, and potential growth to BCI. Bennett's portfolio stuck out. Several aspects of his background and experience were attractive.

Bennett grew up on a farm in Pontiac, a small town in central Illinois. He could talk with Richard about the agrarian lifestyle. Bennett was an all-state basketball player recruited by Coe College, a Division III school in Cedar Rapids, Iowa. So he had an Iowa connection to which all the Ballantines could relate.

He had graduated with business administration and economics degrees, become an expert in software and internet publishing, and worked his way up in the business world. He became president of Indianapolis-based Macmillan Computer Publishing in 1998. Wanting to be part of the dot.com world, he moved to the Bay Area, and became president of two start-ups, including digital content company iUniverse in 2001.

In 2008 he was named to head up Freedom Interactive, a division of Freedom Communications, which owned thirty-one daily newspapers, including the *Orange County* (Calif.) *Register*, then the nation's eighteenth-largest daily. Bennett led an effort to shift the paper to a "digital-first" mentality, converting newsrooms toward this goal with up-to-date technology and a new perspective on content delivery. That gave him some insight into the newspaper world that was vital to BCI.

The *Orange County Register* was in the midst of a tumultuous bankruptcy and sale to a hedge fund. Bennett watched the brutal transformation and was ready to try his hand in a different company. The Durango job intrigued him, and his family a decade earlier had purchased property in Avon, in the Vail area, giving him a Colorado tie. Bennett met the BCI search committee in Denver, then came to Durango for a final, probing interview. He assured them that he valued news and information, or "content," which he had come to realize was "king" to a successful business.

He was confident that his digital skills as a change agent would provide new channels of advertising growth. "I've always come to companies and started transformation," Bennett said in a 2021 interview.[468]

His task in Durango would be just that: leading and transforming a print-based company into a digital world. But his first surprise, as he began the job August 1, 2013, came when he looked at revenues and expenses.

"I had to spend all this time cutting expenses, because expenses were way out of whack," he recalled. "The only thing that was working was *Directory Plus*, and [it was] going down. And I learned really quickly directories [were] funding the entire operation."

The digital transformation had to come after expenses were properly aligned, he said. Bennett was chagrined that, in a time of digital growth, BCI had invested in the Cortez printing plant not long before his arrival. As someone who'd spent his last twenty years making digital transitions, he had expected more progress in Durango. The printing costs had to be chopped, and he wanted to charge for content, not just give it away on the web.

He trimmed workers from several departments, and, as is the nature when a new leader arrives, some didn't care for the change of regime and left on their own.

As much as it might have pained the Ballantines to watch these changes, they knew it was necessary. Richard, who continued as chair of the BCI board of directors, didn't see eye-to-eye on Bennett's urgency to create new stories and post them immediately on the internet, to "feed that beast." He favored more thorough stories that were verified and carefully edited, and preferred to save at least some stories for the print version.

However, from a media revenue perspective, Bennett's goal was no longer increasing print circulation. Instead, he focused on getting website "hits." To emphasize this, Bennett had large TV screens placed around the building that displayed the current number of visitors on the *Herald* website.

As the Ballantines had done for sixty-plus years in Durango with their hired staff, Richard allowed Bennett to do his thing. When Bennett heard, "Did you run this by Richard?" he would ignore the question. As difficult as it was at times, Richard refused to get in the way of the new CEO.

Bennett, for his part, did not tell the newsroom what it could and could not cover. He became part of the editorial board, however, along with Richard and the editorial page editor. As such, he took part in decisions to support various issues and candidates, but did not write editorials. The links he developed with the community were mainly on the business side of BCI, not on the editorial side. If there was a face of the *Herald* in the Bennett era, it remained Richard's.

Bennett was brought in to deal with a situation familiar to any newspaper owner in the twenty-first century.

Revenue was suffering on many fronts. Auto dealers and real estate agents who had been purchasing full-page ads in the *Herald* were now taking a half page. Classified advertising, which at many newspapers once contributed a quarter of all revenue, dropped precipitously as the country began shifting its "want-ads" to Craigslist and other online competitors. The number of print subscribers fell.

Industry figures show that total newspaper advertising revenues in the US dropped eighty-two percent from 2006 to 2020. Figures also reveal that nationally, digital advertising accounted for thirty-nine percent of newspaper advertising revenue in 2020.[469] That number was seventeen percent just nine years previously.

With numbers like those, it is not surprising that the United States has lost 2,100 newspapers since 2004, when advertising, circulation, and employment were at or near their peak.[470] That's about one-fourth of the country's newspapers, including seventy dailies and more than 2,000 weeklies or non-dailies, according to the University of North Carolina journalism school. (*The Durango Herald* shifted from a daily to a non-daily, published fewer than four times a week, in 2019.) Among the casualties was Denver's venerated *Rocky Mountain News*, which ended its 150-year run in 2009. Family-owned newspapers have been especially hard hit.[471]

Just as troubling for newspaper owners: the University of North Carolina noted that print readers are disappearing even faster than print newspapers, and the pace appears to be accelerating. Over the past fifteen years, total weekday circulation – which includes both dailies and weeklies – declined from 122 million to sixty-eight million.

To combat these trends, Bennett tried myriad methods of attracting the younger, digital audiences, and new ways of bringing business to BCI. He knew that not all would work, but believed some would stick.

The new ventures included two magazines, one geared toward outdoor adventures in the Four Corners, and one toward "refined living and big adventures," targeted to Texas and the Southwest. A new company division called Adsperity helped businesses with their mobile device advertising.

A younger digital audience was targeted with 4 Corners TV, an online TV format that featured short, fun stories about people and events around the area.

Sarah Healy, one of Morley Ballantine's grandchildren, came to Durango in 2014 to work for 4 Corners TV. The Wichita, Kans., native was twenty-five by then and had developed performing skills and marketing knowledge from a college education and a budding career that included work in China.

"I saw an opportunity to be part of navigating BCI through the modern digital age," she said.[472] "Doug Bennett saw the potential for short-form video to match the short attention span of millennials, myself included."

Millennials, those born between 1981 and 1996, are generally not print newspaper readers. They go online for news, and generally don't stay long on a story or on a particular site.

Bennett's 4 Corners TV offered this audience irreverent, comedic, less newsy, two- to five-minute videos that were also informative. Story topics varied widely, and included subjects from the suddenly thriving marijuana business to motor sports.

As a producer, Healy's role was to make things interesting, "Ask questions, see if I can get people to think on the spot and be goofy."

They were attempting something that had been successful in a larger market. While 4 Corners TV "created a lot of wonderful shows," they needed more advertisers to make it economically feasible in the long-term, and the venture ultimately folded. Healy left BCI in 2017, returned to the Midwest, and earned a master's in business administration from the University of Kansas in 2018.

Bennett noted that 4 Corners TV "was really a success when it came to people watching those videos. It was a failure when it came to people being willing to pay for it." Advertisers were accustomed to paying rates based on thousands of viewers, 4 Corners was getting hundreds. Bennett said he was "humbled that my ideas were not working from a revenue perspective."

He acknowledged he had failed to grasp how to make his ideas work in a smaller market than he'd had at Freedom. "Probably the thing that was hardest for me to learn when I got here was scale," he said.

While experiments like 4 Corners TV eventually were curtailed, the

Bennett-created BCI Media Services survived and continued to build clientele. The subsidiary helped businesses with digital marketing, using social media, video, websites, search-engine optimization (SEO), and more. BCI Media Services was growing at a thirty-five percent annual rate, Bennett said in 2021, with offices from Billings, Mont., to Las Cruces, N.Mex.

The changes had not been easy, but no one argued that none were necessary. "Where we ended up getting to was where we needed to be," Bennett said, adding, "It wasn't without pain."

On October 5, 2021, the Ballantine Communications Inc. board decided it was time to find a new leader. Although a couple of Bennett's innovations and investments were a success, most lost money, with costs far outstripping revenue. For example, a regional magazine called *Dorado* was of top quality and lasted two years, but never generated sufficient revenue to justify its steep costs.

Community journalism was not a chief concern of Bennett's, and the BCI board was ready to reaffirm its commitment to the town. Officially, Bennett stepped down from his role as CEO and his employment ended that day. Richard Ballantine, board chair, made the written announcement, and spoke twice to groups of employees the following day.

"Over the past [eight] years, Doug's knowledge, vision, and contributions have been instrumental in taking BCI through some key transformations, and we thank him deeply for bringing his strengths to BCI," the announcement said.[473] "He has honed our focus and added efficiencies, while creating a digital presence that's the envy of large communication companies."

In May 2022, Carrie Cass, former director of finance and administration and acting CEO, was named CEO of Ballantine Communications Inc.

The summer of 2022 marks seventy years since Arthur Ballantine, a thirty-seven-year-old East Coast man with a law degree, and Morley Cowles Ballantine, a twenty-seven-year-old Midwesterner with newspapers in her DNA, looked to the West. Their arrival in Durango with a full caravan of children drastically altered not only their own lives, but that of their adopted community as well.

Rich Past, Hopeful Future

Through persistence, resilience, hard work, and no small amount of courage and idealism, the Ballantines turned *The Durango Herald* into an honored journalistic enterprise, a valued community resource, and a successful business. Durango – with the Ballantines contributing to its leadership – paved its streets, turned a struggling junior college into a respected four-year institution, and created arts, entertainment, and recreational offerings that have made the town an attractive place to live and a popular place to visit.

What was once a more rural community is now filled with telecommuters, second-home owners, and outdoors enthusiasts. Every aspect of Southwest Colorado is shifting, and the newspaper is no different. The *Herald* remains a valued community resource, reporting on local people, politics, and events. But like almost every other community newspaper in the United States, the *Herald's* daily circulation has suffered at the hands of Facebook, Twitter, and a host of other social media outlets, losing much of the revenue that pays for such coverage.

The *Herald's* newsroom staff now is down by about a third of what it was a decade ago, said Richard Ballantine, adding, "We're still covering the community quite well, but editors and reporters are working really hard."

Richard estimated in late 2021 that roughly half of the *Herald's* 9,000 subscribers took the print version of the newspaper with the other half reading an online version. That percentage of online subscribers is higher than what most newspapers can boast these days.

As the Ballantines prepare to celebrate their seventieth anniversary in Durango, they confront new challenges, just as Arthur and Morley did upon their arrival.

What does the shifting of reader habits foretell?

With the migration from print to digital readership, Richard Ballantine worries that the ability of citizens to understand their communities may suffer. Readers of digital news sites may look at the top six to eight items, but miss the broad range of community events and happenings – the social gatherings and clubs such as Rotary and garden, or what is happening at the local grade schools and college.

"Those are not being seen and used," he said. "They're the glue of a community. I love the fact we can communicate on so many platforms, but readers have only so much time."

As for the economic future of community newspapers like the *Herald*, options are emerging, though none is what sports fans would call a home run.

There is the public radio and television example, which depends partly on loyal and appreciative readers to make contributions. The *Herald* certainly has loyal readers. In this vein, a few small, community newspapers in Iowa have formed a nonprofit foundation that allows readers to make tax-deductible contributions that support local newspapers. As another example, the massive Knight Foundation has funded media-related research projects, funded nonprofit news sites, and paid salaries of reporters at scattered newspapers.

In Colorado, a local and national funding consortium formed in May 2021 has facilitated the purchase of a network of twenty-four weekly and monthly newspapers to preserve local coverage under local control. This network, the Colorado News Conservancy, is jointly owned and operated by the National Trust for Local News and *The Colorado Sun*, and backed by a coalition of local and national investors. Among the investors is the Denver-based Gates Family Foundation.

"News shouldn't be owned by private equity firms and hedge funds that put profits before journalism," the Conservancy stated on its website, echoing something the Ballantines might say. *The Colorado Sun*, a journalist-owned digital news outlet formed in 2018, provides stories of statewide interest. The *Herald* runs many of the *Sun's* stories in print and on the web to supplement its coverage.

"Our goal is not to turn a profit," the Denver-based *Sun* says. "Our goal is to produce the best possible journalism. ... Every dollar we take in goes directly toward the journalism we produce."

The run of success begun by Arthur and Morley has been maintained by a second and third generation of Ballantines, some more directly than others, but all concerned and connected to the future of Ballantine Communications, Inc. Helen's daughter, Morley Healy Stalnaker, is on the BCI board. So are Richard's sons, Christopher and David Ballantine, and Elizabeth's daughter, Sarah Leavitt.

BCI remains determined to continue its community role. It has helped that the family has been willing to forgo large profits and instead invest revenue in a robust news department that remains much larger than those of nearly every similarly sized newspaper, even after newsroom cuts. That, too, is a family tradition, begun by Arthur and Morley Ballantine.

"We have always supported the newsroom," Richard says. "We've allowed it to be larger than a paper our size normally would have. In content, the *Herald* has delivered more than you might expect."

Sarah Healy-Vigo, in reflecting on her time at BCI, said the solution to providing community journalism in a financially viable method is not obvious. "I wish I had an answer. I would love to hear what my grandmother would do," she says. "People are going to have to take a step back and really reflect on how to go forward with traditional news in the modern age. ... I think [Morley] would agree it has taken a buy-in, a trust, a sense of loyalty from her community."

Richard and Elizabeth are hopeful that having the third generation on the board will keep the company steered in the right direction. Following a November 2021 board meeting, this "third generation" issued a statement to BCI employees:[474]

> As we enter our seventieth year, we wanted to reassure all of you that BCI is not for sale; not any part of it. Morley and

Arthur Ballantine bought the Durango papers in 1952 and the Ballantine family remains committed to what has been built over the years: the papers, directories, and many links to the community.

The challenge is to have a day-to-day leader who shares the principles and values that have guided seventy years of Ballantine ownership.

For one, this person must be curious. "We were raised in a family that was always curious," Richard said. "Why were events happening? What does it all mean?"

Successors also will be expected to have the courage to call out public malfeasance, even if it means getting popped in the nose by an unhappy politician, as Arthur once was.

"We're fortunate to live in a community that is heavily transparent and forthright," Richard says. "There are not a lot of shenanigans. But our government is aware that if something pops up, we'll grab ahold of it."

A democracy works best with a free flow of information. How that information is delivered may be in question, but its value is not. To participate fully in the type of community envisioned by the US Constitution's framers, and reinforced in decisions by the US Supreme Court, citizens must have a means of airing their views, as well as access to credible news about public happenings.

Said Thomas Jefferson, "Where the press is free, and every man able to read, all is safe."[475]

Supreme Court Justice William Brennan wrote that there is "a profound national commitment to the principle that debate on public issues should be uninhibited, robust, and wide-open, and that it may well include vehement, caustic, and sometimes unpleasantly sharp attacks on government and public officials."[476]

If not for local news sources, how do people stay in touch with their community? Without the *Herald*, without local ownership dedicated to serving its readers, who would provide valuable, and regular, local news?

For seventy years the Ballantine family has championed this philosophy in Durango, making certain the town was informed of events, achievements, important issues, and malfeasance, shining light, and creating a better community.

Owning a newspaper is certainly not the best method of attaining wealth. Neither is a career in journalism, as any reporter will attest. But women and men willing to work for less pay than their peers, who are willing to stand up for the rights of a free media, who are willing to take the criticism that honest journalism engenders, still exist and will remain an important cog in a properly functioning republic.

The Ballantines will always back people who, like Morley herself, aren't afraid to look out at the world boldly, through big, round glasses, put aside their prejudices, talk amongst their peers, and dig into the nuances of the day's important issues. People who are willing to say "yes, no, and maybe" before coming to a conclusion.

Morley's message to a group of college graduates more than four decades ago still resonates: Keep learning, stay engaged, never stop asking questions.[477] And despite all the sometimes seemingly overwhelming change, don't fear the future:

> Change … should evoke in us a sense of wonder, of excitement. Truly, what next?

Notes

ARTHUR

1. Nelson A Rockefeller (1908-1979) was the grandson of oil baron John D. Rockefeller. He was considered a progressive Republican, which matched the Ballantine family's politics. Rockefeller served as vice president from 1974-1977 for Gerald Ford, after Ford became president with Richard Nixon's resignation in 1974. Interestingly, the other two candidates Ford considered for vice president were Donald Rumsfeld, who became his chief of staff and later secretary of defense under George Bush, and George H.W. Bush, who later became vice president and president.

2. From memorial tribute written by Harvard classmate George S. Franklin, taken from the Century Memorials, 1976, "The Century Association," appears in memorial booklet printed by *The Durango Herald*.

3. Brooklyn Daily Eagle, September 15, 1941, P. 6. After joining Sullivan & Cromwell, the story about his engagement to Sue Barbara Headington says, "He later was with the office of the co-ordinator of Inter-American Affairs, Washington, and more recently has been with the State Department in the Division of World Trade Intelligence."

4. Arthur A. Ballantine Jr., transcribed interview with David McComb, June 10, 1974, at *The Durango Herald*. This was part of the Oral History of Colorado Project, which included multiple interviews with prominent Coloradans in various fields.

5. US Navy muster rolls, *SC-691*, P. 71.

6. US Navy muster rolls, USS *Migrant*, November 27, 1942.

7. US Navy muster rolls, *SC-691*.

8. US Navy muster rolls, *SC-691*, March 31, 1944, P. 8.

9. Arthur A. Ballantine Jr. diary from April-October 1944 while aboard *SC-691*.

10. Arthur A. Ballantine Jr., interview with McComb.

11. US Navy muster rolls, *SC-691*, stamped July 28, 1943.

12. Arthur A. Ballantine Jr., interview with McComb.

13. Ibid. Tilly Grey said that Arthur talked about the friendly-fire incident on more than one occasion.

14. Arthur Ballantine wrote this for the December 16, 1943, edition of a service letter printed by Sullivan & Cromwell, Arthur's former law firm, which tracked its former employees.

15. Letter, Barbara to Arthur, November 26, 1943, Ballantine family archives.

16. Letter, Arthur Sr. to Arthur Jr., August 14, 1944, Ballantine family archives.

17. Letter, Helen to Arthur Jr., August 14, 1944, Ballantine family archives.

18. Arthur A. Ballantine Jr., interview with McComb.

19. Arthur A. Ballantine diary, April-October 1944.

20. Henry Kaiser's shipyards are said to have revolutionized shipbuilding, completing ships in two-thirds the time and a quarter the cost of the average shipyard. See Arthur Herman, "Freedom's Forge: How American Business Produced Victory in World War II," (New York: Random House, 2012).

21. Letter, Arthur Sr. to Arthur Jr., July 20, 1944, Ballantine family archives.

22. Tim O'Brien, *The Things They Carried*, (Boston: Houghton Mifflin Harcourt, 1990). "The Things They Carried" is among the short stories in the book by that name. The renowned story is a list of what ground soldiers portered during the Vietnam War.

23. From copy of inventory sheets that Arthur Jr. kept, Ballantine family archives.

24. Arthur A. Ballantine Jr. diary.

25. Ibid.

26. Arthur A. Ballantine Jr., transcribed interview with David McComb, June 10, 1974.

27. Arthur A. Ballantine Jr., interview with McComb.

28. Arthur Ballantine Sr. and both John and Mike Cowles traveled in similar circles, particularly among the Republican party. All knew President Hoover, and candidates Wendell Willkie and Thomas Dewey, for instance, on a first-name basis. It couldn't have been too difficult for Arthur Jr. to contact the Cowles and ask to give him a shot as a reporter.

29. A search for Arthur Ballantine's byline in the Minneapolis papers on newspapers.com found his earliest story was written for the May 10, 1946, *Minneapolis Morning Tribune*, P. 12.

30. Arthur A. Ballantine Jr., interview with McComb. Kenny was often referred to as "Sister" Kenny, but that was an Australian nursing corps title bestowed upon her during World War I.

31. *Minneapolis Morning Tribune*, March 29, 1947, P. 10.

MORLEY
32. *Des Moines Tribune*, December 28, 1932, P. 1. The house was built for Henry C. Wallace, secretary of agriculture from 1921-1924. Edwin T. Meredith, who preceded him as ag secretary from 1920-1921, bought the house after Wallace died in 1924. Meredith died in 1928.

33. *Des Moines Register*, May 20, 1935, P. 11. Interestingly, this production occurred on Morley's 10th birthday, May 21.

34. A *Des Moines Tribune* story, April 10, 1932, P. 25, shows that Betty Cowles was hosting a membership drive for the Des Moines Civic Music Association. In 1935 she served as association vice president.

35. *Des Moines Tribune*, March 17, 1937, P. 11. The story by Wendell Erickson mentions that Anderson was staying at a suite at Hotel Fort Des Moines. Anderson had just arrived after a long train ride from Winnipeg, Manitoba.

36. *The Durango Herald*, October 11, 2009, "Herald Editor Morley Ballantine Dies," P. 1.

37. Ibid. The football anecdote came from Morley's daughter, Helen Ballantine Healy.

38. *Time* magazine, July 1, 1935, P. 26.

39. *Minneapolis Star-Journal*, July 6, 1938, P. 6.

40. *Minneapolis Star-Journal*, July 25, 1940, P. 23.

41. *Minneapolis Tribune*, February 11, 1940, P. 27.

42. *Minneapolis Star-Journal*, January 28, 1940, P. 26.

43. *Minneapolis Star-Journal*, June 9, 1940, P. 33.

44. History of Glendalough State Park on Minnesota Department of Natural Resources website, dnr.state.mn.us/state_parks.

45. Judith Reynolds, "Morley Cowles Ballantine: On the Occasion of Her 80th Birthday," P. 4. Reynolds based the story on research and interviews with Mor-

ley and other family members. This statement was based on John Cowles letters, which his granddaughter Elizabeth Ballantine (Morley's daughter) made into books.

46. John Cowles Jr., from interview for video "The Cowles Family Weekend: July 29-31, 1994," produced by Julie Gammack.

47. Sally Cowles Doering, from interview for "The Cowles Family Weekend: July 29-31, 1994."

48. *Des Moines Register*, July 24, 1940, P. 13.

49. *Minneapolis Star-Journal*, January 14, 1939, P. 11. Morley is pictured with two fellow Northrop Collegiate girls carrying a toboggan up the steps at the Minikahda club snowslide.

50. *The Rosemary Question Mark*, December 1941, Vol. 32, No. 2, PP. 21-22.

51. The year of this honor is uncertain. A letter acknowledging the award, found in Ballantine family archives, appears to be from the 1960s or 1970s.

52. *Minneapolis Star-Journal*, November 19, 1943, P. 17.

53. "Letters from John Cowles to His Family, 1943-1976: 1944," (Durango: Durango Herald Press, 2004), edited by Elizabeth Ballantine, PP. 14, 23.

54. "Letters from John Cowles: 1944," P. 44.

55. A *Minneapolis Star-Journal* social column from December 15, 1940, P. 32, shows they were both among those planning a junior dinner-dance at Minikahda on December 21. Morley was on Christmas vacation from Rosemary Hall.

56. The connections were numerous. Richard Gale Sr. and John Cowles families belonged to the same clubs. Both were well-acquainted with Gov. Harold Stassen and other public figures, and John Cowles certainly would have made it a point to get to know a neighbor who was a US Congressman. The Stassen connection is talked about in a *Minneapolis Tribune*, December 5, 1973, P. 14, obituary for Richard P. Gale.

57. From interview with Richard Gale Ballantine, August 13, 2020. Richard Ballantine worked the farm several summers in his youth and acknowledges this probably led to his future endeavors in farming.

58. *Minneapolis Star*, December 5, 1973, P. 3, obituary for R.P. Gale.

59. *Minneapolis Morning Tribune*, August 9, 1923, P. 10.

60. Mrs. Richard Gale is featured in multiple stories about horse riding and horse shows, including the *Minneapolis Star*, September 3, 1938, P. 21.

61. A *Minneapolis Star* feature story of September 1, 1943, about Richard Gale Sr. says that son Alfred, 16, is in Washington. Richard Jr. had joined the military by then.

62. US World War II enlistments, 1938-1946, accessed via ancestry.com.

63. "Letters from John Cowles: 1944," PP. 59-60.

64. *Minneapolis Star*, September 1, 1943.

65. "Letters from John Cowles: 1944," PP. 59-60.

66. Ibid.

67. *Minneapolis Sunday Tribune*, July 2, 1944, P. 24. Sister Sally Cowles was maid of honor, with friend Lucia Heffelfinger and cousin Sue Cowles Kruidenier as bridesmaids. Richard's brother Alfred Gale was best man, and Morley's brother John Cowles Jr., Lt. William R. Strong, Wheelock Whitney Jr., Pvt. Ross Hanson, and Navy man James Freeman Hield as ushers.

68. From receipt found in Ballantine family archives.

69. Documents in Ballantine family archives show Morley was at Stanford during the 1944 autumn quarter and 1944-45 winter quarter.

70. "Letters from John Cowles to His Family, 1943-1976: 1944," (Durango: Durango Herald Press, 2004), edited by Elizabeth Ballantine, P. 130.

71. Morley lived for a while in Belvedere, just south of San Rafael.

72. According to *The Pacific War Online Encyclopedia*, pwencycl.kgbudge.com, there were 111,606 US soldiers killed or missing in Asia and the Pacific, and 253,143 wounded, as well as 21,580 prisoners of war.

73. Among the notes found in Richard Gale Jr.'s car after his death was a reference to Bataan. *Boston Globe*, April 10, 1946, P. 1-2. Very likely he talked to prisoners of war who'd been freed in the Philippines after undergoing torture during the Bataan Death March and subsequent imprisonment.

74. Ballantine family archives.

75. "Letters from John Cowles to His Family, 1943-1976: 1944," P. 139, December 26 letter to Mother and Father.

76. Right, there's always a war somewhere.

77. US World War II Draft Card, accessed via ancestry.com, shows Richard P. Gale Jr. as a "discharged serviceman," dated December 20, 1945.

78. An Associated Press story on the account of Richard P. Gale's death was used by many publications on April 10, 1946, including the *Minneapolis Star-Journal*, P. 21 (front page of the second section). The details are unsettling, so we won't go into them here. He kept a journal of the final moments before his death.

79. "Letters from John Cowles to His Family, 1943-1976: 1946," P. 30.

80. "Letters from John Cowles to His Family, 1943-1976: 1946," P. 54.

81. Ibid. P. 54.

82. Ibid. P. 62.

CHURCH AND FAITH
83. *Durango Herald*, September 19, 1966, P. 2.

84. Ripon College 1875-76 Catalogue of the Officers and Students, accessed via ancestry.com.

85. Ibid.

86. Ibid, PP. 15-16.

87. "William Gay Ballantine: Biographical Notes …," PP. 16-17.

A NEW BEGINNING
88. *Minneapolis Morning Tribune*, March 29, 1947, P. 10.

89. *Minneapolis Sunday Tribune*, June 1, 1947, P. 46.

90. United Kingdom Incoming Passenger Lists, Southampton, England, 1878-1960, accessed via ancestry.com.

91. "Letters from John Cowles, 1946," August 14 entry.

92. *Minneapolis Morning Tribune*, December 12, 1947, P. 15.

93. *Minneapolis Morning Tribune*, February 6, 1949, P. 26.

94. Morley from interview with Judith Reynolds in 2005 for a story "Morley Cowles Ballantine: On the occasion of her 80th birthday – May 21, 2005," P. 8 of fourth draft.

95. Otis Carney, *New Lease on Life*, (New York: Random House, 1971), P. 8.

96. The Resors' Snake River Ranch was listed in the National Register of Historic Places in 2004. Stanley B. Resor (1879-1962) led the famous J. Walter Thompson advertising firm in New York City in the 1940s and 1950s.

97. Morley from 2005 interview with Judith Reynolds.

98. Arthur A. Ballantine Jr., transcribed interview with David McComb, June 10, 1974, at *The Durango Herald*, P. 13. This was part of the Oral History of Colorado Project, which included multiple interviews with prominent Coloradans in various fields.

99. Associated Press story, *Delphos* (Ohio) *Daily Herald*, April 22, 1952, P. 1.

SETTLING IN
100. Arthur Ballantine Jr., *Durango Herald-News*, June 1952, exact date unavailable from clipping in Ballantine archives.

101. Ibid. Excerpts from two editorials, "New Management" and "Building the Community."

102. *Durango Herald-News*, August 5, 1952.

103. *Durango Herald-News*, August 1952 (exact date unknown), from family scrapbook.

104. Ibid.

105. *Durango Herald-News*, September 1952 (exact date uncertain), from family scrapbook.

106. From file of Durango League of Women Voters documents on the 1953-54 water issue at the Center of Southwest Studies, Fort Lewis College. Airport Hill – there was once an air strip there – would later be renamed College Mesa.

107. *Durango Herald-News*, March 1953 (exact date uncertain), from Ballantine family scrapbook.

108. *Durango Herald-News*, March 25, 1953.

109. *Durango Herald-News*, March and April 1953, several issues.

110. *Durango Herald-News*, February 21, 1954.

111. *Durango Herald-News*, February 22, 1954.

112. Duane A. Smith, *Condemned by Many, Read by All: Durango's Newspapers, 1880-1992*, (Durango: *Durango Herald*, 1992), P. 20.

113. *Rocky Mountain News*, November 12, 1967, Festival Section, story "Durango Publishers Make Mark" by Al Nakkula.

114. Duane A. Smith, *Condemned by Many*, P. 20.

115. From Percy Villa's "Almost About Everything" column, *Minneapolis Spokesman*, August 1, 1952. Villa simply reprinted a letter he received from Arthur Ballantine Jr.

116. *Durango Herald-News*, May 15, 1953, MCB editorial titled "Editorial Page."

117. *Durango Herald-News*, May 15, 1953, MCB editorial titled "Editorial Page."

118. *Durango Herald-News*, May 17, 1953, ABJr. editorial titled "Job of a Newspaper."

119. *Durango Herald-News*, May 31, 1953, ABJr, editorial titled "Market Place."

THE PAPER FLOURISHES
120. Duane A. Smith, *Condemned by Many*, P. 1.

121. Arthur A. Ballantine Jr., transcribed interview with David McComb, June 10, 1974, at *The Durango Herald*. This was part of the Oral History of Colorado Project, which included multiple interviews with prominent Coloradans in various fields.

122. *Durango Herald-News*, April 1953 (exact date uncertain), from family scrapbook. The Wells Group realty company is at 1128 Main and Carver Brewing Co. is at 1022 Main as of 2020.

123. *Durango Herald-News*, November 4, 1953, P. 1.

124. Ibid, P. 2.

125. *Durango Herald-News*, April 13, 1954.

126. From spring 1955 newspaper story in Ballantine family scrapbook, likely

Denver Post or *Rocky Mountain News* judging by the story's statewide angle.

127. The editorial originally appeared in the *Durango Herald-News* on January 26, 1954. Awards are often based on the previous calendar year, thus the 1955 awards were for 1954 stories.

128. *Durango Herald-News*, February 20, 1956.

129. *Durango Herald-News*, April 16, 1956, P. 2.

130. *Durango Herald-News*, October 6, 1957, P. 2. An Editor's Note explained that "the substance of this editorial supplied the basis" for a talk Arthur had delivered October 3 at a Kiwanis club meeting in observance of Newspaper Week.

131. *Durango Herald-News* house advertisement, October 1956, from Ballantine family scrapbook. Ralph Crosman, after whom the award is named, was the first head of the CU Journalism Department and College of Journalism.

132. Their 1967 Outstanding Journalist Award certificate notes they won the Crosman in 1956, 1957, 1961, and 1966, and the Parkhurst in 1956, 1957, and 1966.

133. *Durango Herald-News*, June 15, 1956.

134. *Grand Junction Sentinel*, October 5, 1959, P. 2.

A DISTINCT STYLE
135. *Durango Herald-News*, spring 1954, undated MCB editorial in family scrapbook.

136. *Durango Herald-News*, December 1952 (exact date uncertain), Señora San Juan column from family scrapbook.

137. *Durango-Cortez Herald*, June 30, 1963, P. 3.

138. Ibid.

139. *Durango Herald-News*, September 20, 1957.

140. Duane A. Smith, *Condemned by Many*, pp. 20-21.

141. *Durango Herald-News*, August 4, 1953.

142. *Durango Herald-News*, late summer or early fall 1953 (exact date uncertain), MCB editorial in family scrapbook.

143. Colorado is divided into a "Western Slope" and "Eastern Slope" by the Continental Divide. Durango is on the Western Slope.

144. Selection from *Ant Palaces and other stories about life: A collection of editorials by Morley Cowles Ballantine and Arthur A. Ballantine,* (Durango: Durango Herald, 1992), PP. 19-21. Originally appeared in the *Durango Herald-News* on January 29, 1957.

145. *Durango Herald,* November 22, 1966, P. 2.

146. *Durango Herald,* January 26, 1962, P. 2.

147. *Durango Herald,* February 19, 1962, P. 2.

148. *Durango Herald,* May 20, 1968, P. 2.

NEW NAME, NEW LOCATION
149. Duane A. Smith, *Condemned by Many,* P. 20.

150. Calculation made at usinflationcalculator.com.

151. Duane A. Smith, *Condemned by Many,* P. 21.

152. From notes on plant dedication program, October 8, 1965. (Printed on the Herald Chief 15 offset press.)

153. Ibid.

154. *Durango Herald,* October 8, 1965, P. 1.

155. The Supreme Court justice was Edward Pringle. Among the notable attendees was Roy Romer, then a state senator, who would go on to serve three terms as Colorado governor (1987-1999).

156. *Durango Herald,* October 8, 1965, P. 1.

157. Recollections of Richard Ballantine, from interview December 3, 2020. Quote from *Durango Herald,* October 8, 1965.

158. "*Herald* evolves as Durango changes: A letter from the Ballantine family," *Durango Herald,* April 1, 2017.

159. Arthur A. Ballantine Jr., transcribed interview with David McComb, June 10, 1974.

160. *Durango Herald*, September 28, 1967.

161. Ibid.

162. *Durango Herald*, April 13, 1999, P. 4.

163. Duane A. Smith, *Condemned by Many, Read by All: Durango's Newspapers, 1880-1992*, (Durango: *Durango Herald*, 1992), P. 22.

164. Ibid.

165. Ibid.

166. Duane A. Smith, *Condemned by Many*, P. 23.

167. Ibid, PP. 23-24.

168. Outstanding Journalist Award certificate, dated April 14, 1967, in Ballantine family scrapbook "A.B.-M.C.B. 1966- 1968."

CONNECTIONS

169. From letter Arthur Jr. wrote to Arthur Sr., dated July 31, 1960, and written on *Durango Herald-News* stationery. "This was the first convention I had attended since 1936 when you and Mother took us to the Landon convention," he wrote.

170. Joseph Kennedy was US ambassador to Britain from 1938-1940. He was among those, like British Prime Minister Neville Chamberlain, who believed in appeasing German leader Adolf Hitler in 1938, a policy that in hindsight completely backfired.

171. See footnote 2, this chapter.

172. *Rocky Mountain News*, June 23, 1962, P. 5.

173. Ibid.

174. *Durango Herald*, June 25, 1962, P. 2.

175. *Durango Herald*, June 24, 1962, P. 2.

176. The Cuban Missile Crisis occurred October 16-28. Russians had placed nuclear missiles in Cuba, and the US established a naval blockade to prevent more Soviet transports. Kennedy and Soviet leader Nikita Khrushchev reached a deal: the missiles were removed, and the US agreed not to invade Cuba and also to dismantle its missiles in Turkey.

177. *Rocky Mountain News*, October 23, 1962. Arthur Ballantine is quoted as saying, "The imposition of a naval blockade was the right course. The only question in my mind is whether it went far enough."

178. *Durango Herald*, November 1, 1964, P. 2.

179. One example is a story Arthur Ballantine Jr. wrote about Mayor Humphrey's appeal to the state legislature for financial relief. *Minneapolis Tribune*, April 19, 1947.

180. *Durango Herald*, October 29, 1968, P. 2.

181. *Durango Herald*, January 23, 1978, P. 2.

182. John Cowles Sr. letter to Morley (Mrs. Arthur Ballantine), dated January 27, 1978, from Elizabeth Ballantine's family archives.

183. *Durango Herald*, February 1, 1979, P. 2.

LENDING SUPPORT
184. *Durango Herald-News*, August 5, 1953.

185. *Durango Herald-News*, February 7, 1954, column by Arthur Ballantine Jr. called "Fort Lewis Branch Called 'Last Chance' for Survival."

186. Duane A. Smith, *Rocky Mountain Boom Town: A History of Durango, Colorado*, (Boulder: University Press of Colorado, 1980), P. 173. Smith was a longtime history professor at Fort Lewis College, starting in 1964.

187. Duane A. Smith, *Rocky Mountain Boom Town*, P. 172.

188. Faith Conoley, Feature Editor, (Fort Lewis) *Smoke Signals*, October 3, 1958, Vol. 24, No. 1, P. 1.

189. *Smoke Signals*, October 3, 1958, P. 5.

190. *Denver Post*, February 1962 (exact date uncertain), from clipping in Ballantine family archives.

191. The Four Corners is the general area where Arizona, Utah, Colorado, and New Mexico meet. It includes the Navajo, Hopi, Southern Ute and Ute Mountain Ute reservations; Monument Valley; the canyon country of Utah; Durango and the San Juan Mountains; Chaco Canyon in New Mexico; and a great deal more, often depending on how the area is defined.

192. *Fort Lewis Independent*, July 17, 1964, Vol. 30, No. 26, P. 1.

193. *Durango Herald*, October 11, 2009, P. 1, story following Morley's death.

194. *Fort Lewis Independent*, March 1, 1968, Vol. 34, No. 18, P. 1.

195. *Fort Lewis Independent*, January 13, 1970, Vol 37, No. 1, P. 1.

196. Durango was surveyed and platted in September 1880, but officially became an incorporated town in April 1881.

197. The railroad tracks were constructed from 1880-1882, and the first train arrived in Silverton in July 1882.

198. Arthur A. Ballantine Jr., interview with David McComb, June 10, 1974.

199. *Durango-Cortez Herald*, December 6, 1959, P. 2.

200. The Nomad, called the Fairplay until around 1950, is still operable and used for special occasions.

201. *Denver Post*, December 5, 1959, P. 1. Presidents William Taft, John Kennedy, and Gerald Ford also rode on the Nomad at various times.

202. Ibid.

203. *Durango Herald*, December 6, 1959, P. 2.

204. Mickey Hogan, *Hogan's Story: Here's My Story, And I'm Sticking To It,* (2019), P. 130.

205. *Denver Post*, March 31, 1963, "San Juan Basin Plans For 5 Million Visitors," story based on interview with Arthur Ballantine.

206. Ann Butler, *Durango Herald*, December 31, 2013, P. 1. Accessed at durangoherald.com.

207. Ibid.

208. From estimate from Durango Area Tourism Office.

THE BALLANTINE WAY
209. *New York Times*, September 26, 1958, story in Ballantine family scrapbook. It's easy to see the link between Eisenhower and the Cowles/Ballantine family, and thus, Arthur's chairmanship. However, it may have been the Colorado governor, Steve McNichols, who had more of a say in the committee membership.

210. *Denver Post*, February 20, 1959, P. 1.

211. *Fort Collins Coloradoan*, September 8, 1959, P. 1.

212. *Durango Herald-News*, September 10, 1959, P. 2.

213. Arthur Ballantine, "A Layman's View of Public Education," *Durango Herald*, January 10-16, 1972. From printed booklet with the series of six editorials. Arthur continued to serve on education commissions for several more years.

214. Many of these dates and commissions are from Judith Reynolds, "Morley Cowles Ballantine … 80th birthday," P.10. It's possible that exact dates are off by a year or two.

215. *Durango Herald*, March 1960, P. 2. Exact date uncertain, but probably between March 22 and 28.

216. *Durango Herald*, January 19, 1975, Associated Press story. She was officially appointed on January 31.

217. *Durango Herald*, February 2, 1975, Associated Press story.

218. *Rocky Mountain News*, May 10, 1971.

219. *Aspen Times*, February 27, 2011, obituary on William R. "Bil" Dunaway, born 1923. Story accessed at aspentimes.com.

220. Interview with Don Mapel, October 27, 2020.

221. The first line of the original agreement establishing the Ballantine Family Charitable Fund says it was entered into on December 23, 1957.

222. From Ballantine Family Fund files. The seed money is mentioned in the founding papers.

223. For a list of recent grantees and other information, visit ballantinefamily-fund.com.

FAMILY AND FRIENDS
224. Phone interview with Tilly Grey, September 16, 2020.

225. Email from James Rousmaniere to Elizabeth Ballantine, January 16, 2021.

226. Interview with William "Bill" Ballantine, February 4, 2021.

227. Interview with Richard and Mary Lyn Ballantine, January 21, 2021.

228. Interview with Helen Ballantine Healy, January 26, 2021.

229. James A. Alcott, *A History of Cowles Media Company*, (Minneapolis: Cowles Media Company, 1998), P. 240.

230. Elizabeth Bates Cowles letter to Elizabeth Ballantine, postmarked July 25, 1968, from Ballantine family archives. Russell and John are her two boys, and Gretchen and Sage their wives, respectively.

231. Morley letter to family, dated June 30, 1989, on *Herald* stationery, from family archives.

232. *Minneapolis Star Tribune*, April 22, 1990, P. 3B.

233. John Cowles Jr. letter to siblings, July 1, 1993, Ballantine family archives.

LIFE AT HOME
234. From undated video interview with Morley Ballantine, retrieved on video made for her 2014 induction into the Colorado Women's Hall of Fame.

235. From a talk Elizabeth Ballantine gave at a gathering in August 2002 celebrating the 50th anniversary of Ballantine ownership of *The Durango Herald*.

236. Ibid.

237. Interview with Mary Jane, Jackson II, and Antonia Clark at Toh-Atin Gallery, November 16, 2020.

238. Interview with Bobby Duthie (Robert C. Duthie III), February 22, 2021. The blackballing incident was related to Bobby by his father.

239. John Otis Carney, letter to Mr. & Mrs. Arthur Ballantine, dated March 20, 1961. The letter was tucked into a copy of Carney's book, *New Lease on Life*, in the Ballantine book collection.

240. Elizabeth Ballantine email, March 28, 2021.

241. *The Durango Herald* published a special commemorative section on the Ballantines' 50 years of owning the newspaper in December 2002. Elizabeth Ballantine wrote several stories, including one on Morley.

242. Elizabeth Ballantine email, March 28, 2021.

243. Beverly Neal Darmour letter to Richard, Bill, Helen and Elizabeth after Morley's death in 2009.

244. Toh-Atin Gallery operated out of the Pepsi plant until 1981, when it moved into its present location on Ninth Street downtown.

245. Program for the May 3, 1962 "Service of Confirmation" at St. Mark's Church in Ballantine family scrapbook. Arthur was one of 34 being confirmed that day.

246. Interview with Helen Ballantine Healy, January 26, 2021.

247. Some details of Ray's story from interview with Bill Ballantine, February 4, 2021.

248. Ibid.

SALONS
249. Thomas Jefferson did not travel to Paris until several years after he wrote the Declaration of Independence, but he borrowed from the ideas of Thomas Hobbes, Renee Descartes, John Locke, and Voltaire, among others.

GROWING UP A BALLANTINE
250. Harvard College Class of 1936, 35th Anniversary Report, 1971, entry for Arthur Atwood Ballantine.

251. Third Avenue Ski Hill was renamed Calico Hill in the 1960s and Chapman Hill in 1979 after Colton Chapman's death.

252. Morley letter to "Bets" (Betty, or Elizabeth, Ballantine), postmarked August 9, 1968, from family archives.

253. Smith College Class of 1947 Year Book, 10th anniversary, 1957, from blurb Morley wrote.

254. From Elizabeth Ballantine talk in August 2002 for 50th anniversary celebration.

255. John Peel, *Durango Herald*, March 9, 2009, P. 1. In 2009 Bowman wrote a book on the rise of women's sports in Durango, *Those Darlin' Demons: A Century of Girls Athletics in Southwest Colorado and the Effects of Title IX.*

256. Interview with Barbara Eggleston Conn, February 18, 2021. Conn spent her career as an administrator at Fort Lewis College.

257. *Durango Herald*, November 10, 1960, Morley column titled "Paging Elsa Maxwell." Maxwell, a syndicated gossip columnist, wrote advice on hosting parties.

258. *Morley Cowles Ballantine, May 21, 1925-October 10, 2009*, (Durango:

Durango Herald Small Press, 2009), excerpts from Morley's memorial service, related newspaper stories, and other tributes, P. 15.

259. From Elizabeth Ballantine talk in August 2002 for 50th anniversary celebration.

260. Interview with Richard Ballantine, January 21, 2021.

261. *Durango Herald*, September 19, 1966, P. 2.

TRAVEL
262. The *M.S.* (motor ship) *Saturnia* was an Italian liner built in 1927 and scrapped in 1965. It could take around 1,600 passengers.

263. *Durango Herald-News*, February 21, 1956.

264. *Durango Herald*, November 2, 1961, P. 2.

265. *Durango Herald-News*, March 7, 1960, P. 2.

266. *Durango Herald*, July 11, 1966, P. 2.

267. *Durango Herald*, September 8, 1967, P. 2.

268. *Durango Herald*, September 10, 1967, P. 2.

269. *Durango Herald*, October 1, 1967, P. 9, Southwest Colorado Life section.

A COLLEGE DEGREE
270. A quick recap: Morley enrolled at Smith College in fall 1943, attended for one year, and then married Richard Gale in July 1944 and headed with him to the West Coast. She then enrolled at Stanford University for the fall 1944 term and earned two quarters of credits. After the war, Morley briefly attended Radcliffe College. After her husband Richard died in April 1946, Morley returned to Minneapolis and enrolled at the University of Minnesota in fall 1946. But again she didn't get far in her studies, completing three more quarters while marrying Arthur Ballantine in July 1947 and having a second child, Elizabeth, a year later.

271. *Durango Herald*, July 3, 1963, P. 2.

272. Interview with Pam Patton, April 2, 2020.

273. Details from trip itinerary found in family archives.

A WELL-LIVED LIFE

274. Arthur A. Ballantine Jr., interview with David McComb, June 10, 1974, P. 27-28.

275. Ibid, P. 28-29.

276. Ibid, P. 35.

277. Telephone interview with Matilda "Tilly" Morley Lorentz Grey, September 16, 2020. Tilly and Morley were cousins, although Morley was thirteen years older. Tilly is the daughter of Sarah "Sally" Bates, who is the sister of Elizabeth Bates Cowles, Morley's mother.

278. As one example, Arthur Ballantine Jr. served as the escort to McGeorge Bundy, President Kennedy's assistant for national security, at a Harvard commencement ceremony in 1961. From *Durango Herald* newspaper clipping in Ballantine family scrapbook.

279. Columbia's Russian Institute was in 1982 renamed the W. Averell Harriman Institute for the Advanced Study of the Soviet Union, and the Harriman Institute now includes Russian, Eurasian, and East European Studies.

280. *Durango Herald*, November 12, 1975, P. 2.

281. The change happened in early August 1965 without explanation. On August 2 it was ABJr. and August 3 it was AB. It could have had something to do with his father's death, although that had come back in 1960.

282. Judith Reynolds, "Morley Cowles Ballantine: On the occasion of her 80th birthday – May 21, 2005," P. 11.

283. *Durango Herald*, November 16, 1975, p. 2

284. Ibid.

THE SHOCK

285. John Cowles Sr., letter to family, dated November 20, 1975, from family archives. John and Betty Cowles, Morley's parents, did not attend Arthur's service, due to Betty's declining health.

286. Ibid.

287. From interview at Mary Jane Clark's home on March 5, 2020.

288. From Associated Press story with Denver dateline, *Durango Herald*, November 16, 1975, P. 1. It appeared with Arthur Ballantine Jr.'s obituary.

289. George S. Franklin, from The Century Association's Century Memorials, 1976, and reprinted in a booklet printed and distributed by *The Durango Herald* as a tribute to Arthur A. Ballantine Jr. The Century Association is a social club based in Manhattan, New York City.

290. From "Arthur Ballantine 1914-1975," booklet printed and distributed by *The Durango Herald* as a tribute to Arthur A. Ballantine Jr.

291. John "Jack" Ballantine letter to family, December 1, 1975, printed in book, *Elizabeth Ballantine, 1948-2017, the Early Years*, by Elizabeth Ballantine and Paul Leavitt, 2017.

292. *Durango Herald*, November 23, 1975, P. 2, editorial "Growing up with Daddy," signed "by Richard, Elizabeth, William Ballantine and Helen Ballantine Healy."

293. *Durango Herald*, November 30, 1975, P. 2.

CARRYING ON
294. Judith Reynolds, "Morley Cowles Ballantine: On the occasion of her 80th birthday – May 21, 2005," P. 13.

295. John Cowles Sr. letter, November 20, 1975.

296. From interview at Mary Jane Clark's home on March 5, 2020. Jim Foster grew up in Des Moines and worked for the *Des Moines Register* while a college student at Drake University. He met Margaret Thatcher, giving his comparison even more credence.

297. From interview with Richard Ballantine, January 3, 2020.

298. *Durango Herald*, January 18, 1976.

299. Duane Smith, *Condemned By Many, Read By All: Durango's Newspapers, 1880-1992*, (Durango: *Durango Herald*, 1992), P. 21.

300. Interview with Richard Ballantine, January 21, 2021.

301. Morley Cowles Ballantine letter to Elizabeth and Paul, October 19, 1982, Ballantine family archives.

A NEW PARTNERSHIP
302. *Durango Herald*, June 1, 1983, P. 1.

303. Interview with Richard Ballantine, December 3, 2020.

304. *Durango Herald*, April 7, 1992, P. 4.

305. *Durango Herald*, September 5, 2000, P. 4.

306. *Durango Herald*, October 19, 1999, P. 4.

307. *Durango Herald*, December 15, 1998. When Mapel retired, Durango High School teacher Barbara McLachlan and her students "assumed responsibility" for the reviews, as Morley wrote on December 18, 2001.

308. *Durango Herald*, November 9, 1999.

309. *Durango Herald*, May 18, 1999.

310. Duane Smith, *Condemned By Many, Read By All: Durango's Newspapers, 1880-1992*, (Durango: *Durango Herald*, 1992), P. 24.

311. Interview with Katherine Barr, February 16, 2021.

312. *Durango Herald*, June 18, 2002.

313. Interview with Bill Roberts, November 24, 2020.

314. Recollection of *Durango Herald* reporter John Peel, December 14, 2020. Rep. R. Romer is on a four-page list of those attending a dinner after the noon plant dedication on October 8, 1965. He was actually a state senator by then, not a representative, and is identified correctly among notables listed in a *Herald* story that appeared the same day.

315. *Durango Herald*, January 26, 1999.

316. Jesse Jackson, as a black political activist, and Rosa Parks, as the black woman who famously broke the rules and sat in the white section of a segregated bus in Montgomery, Alabama, in 1955, were Clinton invitees to the speech. Clinton mentioned Parks during the speech, and she was given a long standing ovation. Parks lies in state at the Capitol rotunda, and a statue of her decorates the Capitol.

317. Duane A. Smith, *Condemned By Many*, P. 25.

318. From email interview with Nancy Whitson, November 18, 2020.

MINDING THE FAMILY BUSINESS
319. Alcott, *A History of Cowles Media Company*, P. 107

320. Alcott, *A History of Cowles Media Company*, P. 122.

321. Letter from Morley to "Dear Paul and Elizabeth," February 7 1983, from Minneapolis, from family archives.

322. Letter from Morley to "Dear E. and P.," dated May 3, 1983, on *Durango Herald* letterhead, from family archives.

323. Wayne Christiansen, "A Cowles Family Affair," *Washington Journalism Review*, 1983 (from family archives; exact date uncertain), P. 10.

324. N.R. Kleinfield, *New York Times*, "Looking Back at Look," February 6, 1983.

325. Thomas Moore, *Fortune*, April 4, 1983, P. 156-165.

326. William Friedricks, *Covering Iowa: The History of the Des Moines Register and Tribune Company*, (Ames: Iowa State University Press, 2000), P. 213.

327. Alcott, *A History of Cowles Media Company*, P. 131.

328. Friedricks, *Covering Iowa*, P. 218.

329. David Westphal and David Elbert, *Des Moines Register*, February 1, 1985, P. 1.

330. Friedricks, *Covering Iowa*, P. 221.

331. *Des Moines Register*, February 1, 1985, P. 1.

332. David Westphal, *Des Moines Register*, July 2, 1985, P. 5S.

333. Alcott, *A History of Cowles Media Company*, P. 141.

334. Alcott, P. 142.

335. Alcott, P. 146.

336. Interview with Richard Ballantine, December 3, 2020.

337. Alcott, P. 149-150.

ADVOCATING FOR WOMEN
338. In Morley's files is a document to "Dear New Member" of NOW, with Karen DeCrow listed as president. DeCrow was NOW president from 1974-77. After Congress passed the ERA in 1972, Colorado ratified it later that year. However, the ERA didn't get the 38 states needed for ratification by 1979.

339. Quotes from news release, dated November 28, 1976, from the International Women's Year Commission, part of the US Department of State. The 56 "states" included D.C. and several territories.

340. Morley Ballantine is on a May 1977 membership list of the Women's Forum of Colorado. There were 78 members at that time.

341. *Durango Herald*, June 22, 1977, P. 2.

342. Mary Hoaglund (1924-2020) is a founding mother of the Colorado Women's Bar Association. Mary, a year older than Morley, was attending law school at the same time Morley was finishing off her degree at FLC. The Hoaglands and Ballantines also were friends at the Mill Reef Club in Antigua.

343. A Republicans for Choice memorandum of June 26, 1984, outlined its and the White House's positions.

344. Werner Fornos (1933-2013) went on to head the Population Institute and gain renown as one of the world leaders in global population stabilization. His honors included the 2003 United Nations Population Award.

345. *Durango Herald*, March 10, 1986, P. 1. The front-page photo and story was from the Associated Press.

346. Interview with Pat Rustad, December 23, 2020.

347. *Durango Herald*, July 7, 1982, P. 2.

348. Interview with Deborah Uroda, February 22, 2021.

349. *Durango Herald*, October 25, 1983, P. 2.

350. Taken from Women's Foundation of Colorado website, wfco.org. The Foundation was formally launched in January 1987, but Morley had been active in its creation well before that.

351. *Durango Herald*, May 19, 1987, P. 4.

352. From interview with Susan Lander, November 17, 2020.

353. *Durango Herald*, October 13, 1998, P. 4.

354. *Durango Herald*, December 29, 1998, P. 4.

355. Interview with Joanne Spina, February 16, 2021.

PROMOTING EDUCATION

356. Colorado Women's College merged in 1982 with the University of Denver and now operates as one of eight undergraduate divisions there.

357. From a typewritten version of Morley's May 25, 1980, commencement address at Simpson College. It appears to be the edited version she used to deliver the speech.

358. Sherry Manning wrote out her "Thoughts About Morley Cowles Ballantine" for this project on January 3, 2021, and was also interviewed on January 5, 2021.

359. A search of *Durango Heralds* showed that Louis Newell, editorial page editor, was listed with the editors on October 17, 1978, but disappeared from the list on October 18.

360. From interview with Daniel L. Ritchie, December 1, 2020.

ORGANIZATIONS

361. There were 77 members as of fall 2020, with Gail Klapper serving as president. Durangoans at that time included Richard Ballantine, Don Mapel, John Wells, and Sidny Zink. Steve Parker is a member emeritus.

362. From interview with Gail Klapper, December 3, 2020.

363. Interview with Sherry Manning, January 5, 2020.

364. Interview with Russell Cowles, April 9, 2020.

365. *Durango Herald*, December 5, 2000.

366. *Durango Herald*, September 22, 1998, P. 4.

367. Ibid. Reynolds's story says she first joined in 1954, but Morley was speaking on behalf of the League by 1953.

368. Ibid, P. 16.

369. *Durango Herald*, October 7, 1981, P. 2. Ultimately the deal did not go through, and 30 years later the power plant would become the Durango Discovery Museum, and later the Powerhouse Science Center.

370. *Durango Herald*, September 29, 1998, P. 4.

371. Reynolds, "Morley Cowles Ballantine: On the occasion of her 80th birthday," P. 15.

WHAT'S GOOD FOR THE TOWN

372. Robert McDaniel, *Historic Durango*, a publication of the La Plata County Historical Society, 2010.

373. *Durango Herald*, April 6, 2011.

374. Interview with Bob Lieb, December 2, 2020.

375. Interview with Steve Short, February 17, 2021.

376. Interview with Sheri Rochford Figgs, April 7, 2020.

377. Ibid. Other original co-chairs of the committee included Fred Kroeger, Jan Roshong, and Susan Davies.

378. Interview with Don Mapel, October 27, 2020.

379. Taken from quotes by Charles Leslie, director of the Concert Hall, in 20th anniversary video:

380. Sadly, Robert Delaney did not live to see the Center's completion. He died November 10, 2000, age 82, at his home in Albuquerque, just two months before the dedication. He retired from Fort Lewis in 1986.

381. The original name was simply Southwest Room.

382. From "Timelines," Fall 2019. Timelines is a newsletter put out by the Center of Southwest Studies.

383. Tom Sluis, *Durango Herald*, June 28, 2001, P. 1A.

384. Chairman or chairwoman? Morley always preferred the title "chairman."

385. Betty Stevens, *Durango Herald*, May 8, 1999, P. 1A.

386. Interview with Linda and Jeff Mannix, April 17, 2020.

387. Interview with Bob Lieb, December 2, 2020.

388. It was Third Avenue Ski Hill originally, then renamed Calico Hill in the 1960s before the change to Chapman Hill. Colton Chapman (1903-1978) was one of four credited with pioneering the development of the small ski hill on what is now called Florida Road. The other three were Dolph Kuss, and brothers Arvo, and Wilho Matis.

389. *Durango Herald*, February 1, 1979, P. 2.

390. *Durango Herald*, February 2, 1999.

391. Interview with Linda and Jeff Mannix, April 17, 2020.

392. Interview with Beth Lamberson, September 28, 2021.

HONORED AND ESTEEMED
393. Amy Malick, *Durango Herald*, January 18, 1991, P. 1.

394. *Durango Herald*, November 10, 2000, P. 3. The award was given November 3 in front of 800 attendees, including two tables of Durangoans, at the Denver Renaissance Hotel. Bill Ballantine was an attendee.

395. Congressional Record, Proceedings and Debates of the 106th Congress, October 2, 2000. From a framed copy in Ballantine family archives.

396. The award is now called the Artist Award. https://bonfils-stantonfoundation.org/leadership/annual-awards- program/past-honorees/.

397. Patricia Miller, *Durango Herald*, July 16, 2004, P. 3A. Planned Parenthood of the Rocky Mountains includes Colorado, New Mexico, and southern Nevada.

398. *Durango Herald*, January 24, 1998, P. 8.

399. Mary Kramer, "Award marks 35 years of honoring women," August 7, 2016, Crain's Detroit Business website, crainsdetroit.com.

400. Described and often depicted as beautiful and stern, Athena was so revered that her powerful brother Ares feared her, and all the Greek male heroes asked for her help and advice.

401. This is sometimes confusing, but the chamber's awards ceremony is conducted in the January following the calendar year for which the recipient is being rewarded. So, Morley's 1997 Athena Award was given in January 1998.

402. From interview with Jim Morehart, October 26, 2020.

403. From interview with Ellen Roberts, March 31, 2020.

404. For the record, Winston often plays with his shoes off. It gives him better control of the piano pedals and minimizes the sound of his feet pounding the floor. Georgewinston.com/about/faq.

405. From interview with Karen Zink, May 14, 2020.

406. From interview with Diane Wildfang, November 30, 2020.

407. From email interview with Nancy Whitson, November 18, 2020.

408. From interview with Stephanie Moran, December 9, 2020.

MORLEY'S TRAVELS
409. Claude Maer Jr., letter to Mary Lyn and Richard Ballantine, dated October 21, 2009.

410. *LOOK Magazine*, "The Serenest Caribbean Isle," 1961, PP. 84-87. The undated short story about Antigua was found in a Ballantine family scrapbook among other photos and clippings from spring 1961.

411. Elizabeth Ballantine and Stephen S. Lash, *A Vision of Paradise: Robertson Ward and the Mill Reef Club*, (New York: The Derrydale Press, 2001), P. 11.

412. *Durango-Cortez Herald*, February 7, 1982, P. 2.

413. From interview with Mary Jane, Jackson II, and Antonia Clark, November 16, 2020.

414. Raymond Z. Henle, *Pittsburgh Post-Gazette*, July 11, 1942, P. 4. Mike Cowles was director of the Office of War Information's domestic operations, while Archibald MacLeish was head of the office's policy development branch in 1942.

415. Archibald MacLeish letter to Morley, dated November 28, 1975, from Conway, Mass. In family archives. The letter was co-signed by Archie and Ada, but obviously written by Archibald.

416. List of 22 medal winners, other notes on the ceremony, found at fordlibrarymuseum.gov. MacLeish was in Antigua during the January 10, 1977, ceremony in the East Room of the White House, but was represented by nephew Roderick MacLeish.

417. *Des Moines Register*, July 26, 1981.

418. Morley C. Ballantine, "Recollections of the U.S.S.R.," booklet of stories by Morley, Elizabeth, William Ballantine, and Paul Leavitt. This excerpt appeared in *The Durango Herald*, 1983.

419. *Durango Herald*, June 30, 1992, P. 4.

420. *Durango Herald*, November 10, 1998.

421. *Durango Herald*, April 11, 2000.

422. Interview with Sarah Healy-Vigo, September 28, 2021.

423. *Durango Herald*, April 25, 2000.

IMPORTANCE OF FAMILY
424. From interview with Katherine Healy Dougan, October 20, 2020.

425. Email from Sarah Leavitt, February 28, 2021.

INDOMITABLE TO THE END
426. *Durango Herald*, September 3, 1980, P. 2.

427. *Durango Herald*, October 30, 2001.

428. *Morley Cowles Ballantine, May 21, 1925-October 10, 2009*, (Durango: Durango Herald Small Press, 2009), excerpts from Morley's memorial service, related newspaper stories, and other tributes, P. 13.

429. From interview with Karen Zink, May 14, 2020. PEG is an acronym for percutaneous endoscopic gastrostomy.

430. Interview with Katherine Barr, February 16, 2021. Barr noted that during the interview she was toasting her friendship with Morley by drinking a glass of pinot grigio.

431. From interview with Stephanie Moran, December 9, 2020.

432. Jenny St. John and Mischa Semanitzky, letter to Richard and Mary Lyn Ballantine, October 2009.

433. Interview with Sherry Manning, January 3, 2020.

ENDURING INFLUENCE
434. From interview with Katherine Healy Dougan, October 20, 2020.

435. Interview with Susan Lander, November 17, 2020.

436. Joe Hanel, *Durango Herald*, March 21, 2014, P. 1A and 6A.

437. Ibid.

438. Ann Butler, Neighbors, *Durango Herald*, April 1, 2014.

439. *Durango Herald*, May 6, 2018, accessed online at durangoherald.com. The ceremony took place April 14, 2018, in Colorado Springs.

440. Interview with Barbara Eggleston Conn, February 18, 2021.

441. *Morley Cowles Ballantine, May 21, 1925-October 10, 2009*, (Durango: Durango Herald Small Press, 2009), excerpts from Morley's memorial service, related newspaper stories, and other tributes, PP. 45-46. This tribute originally appeared in the Fort Lewis College Foundation newsletter. Joel Jones died of brain cancer in 2016 at age 78.

442. The quote is dated 1917 in *The Durango Herald*, but William Allen White said it before that. He used it in a 1906 speech to the Los Angeles Chamber of Commerce. Source: *The Members' Annual of the Los Angeles Chamber of Commerce* (McKinney Publishing Co., 1906), P. 67.

RICHARD GALE BALLANTINE

443. Morley letter to Richard and Elizabeth, October 16, 1963, from family archives. Arthur ("Daddy") had talked to Mr. Perry, the assistant coach, who "was LYRIC about Richard on the soccer field."

444. Richard Ballantine letter to parents, dated January 7, 1971 from Quang Ngai, from family archives.

445. Arthur A. Ballantine Jr., transcribed interview with David McComb, June 10, 1974, P. 37.

446. Bill Ballantine letter to his mother, siblings, grandfather John Cowles, Uncle Jack Ballantine, and Aunt Peggy.

447. Interview with Mary Lyn and Richard, January 21, 2021.

448. Interview with Richard Ballantine, January 21, 2021.

THE NEWSPAPER

449. Email from Barry Smith, November 16, 2021.

450. From Elizabeth Ballantine story written for 50th anniversary special section, December 2002.

AN EVER-CHANGING BUSINESS

451. Interview with Richard Ballantine, January 21, 2021.

452. Jonathan Thompson owned and edited the *Silverton Standard-Miner* from 2002-2006 and was editor-in-chief of *High Country News* from 2007-2010.

453. From History Colorado website, historycolorado.org.

454. Interview for an updated version of Duane Smith's *Condemned By Many*, P. 27, published in 2008.

455. David Staats left Durango and took a job at the *Idaho Statesman* in Boise. He was business editor as of 2022.

A DIFFERENT STYLE
456. Mary McLachlin, "Richard Ballantine has left the building," *Durango Herald*, August 24, 2013.

457. Interview with Steve Short, February 17, 2021.

458. McLachlin, "Richard Ballantine has left the building," *Durango Herald*, August 24, 2013.

459. Richard Ballantine was serving on both Colorado Humanities and Crow Canyon boards as of 2021.

460. Mary McLachlin, "Richard Ballantine has left the building," *Durango Herald*, August 24, 2013.

461. *Durango Herald*, September 27, 2010, accessed online at durangoherald.com.

462. Inter American Press Association website History page at en.sipiapa.org.

463. Email from Gary Hook to Elizabeth Ballantine, March 11, 2021.

A BRAND NEW DAY
464. Emery Cowan, *Durango Herald*, August 1, 2013.

465. McLachlin, "Richard Ballantine has left the building," *Durango Herald*, August 24, 2013.

466. Gretchen A. Peck, "The Future of Journalism May Live on Through Family-Owned Newspapers," *Editor and Publisher* online, March 9, 2020.

467. McLachlin, *Herald*, August 24, 2013.

DIGITAL CHALLENGE
468. Interview with Doug Bennett, September 2, 2021.

469. News Media Alliance data through 2012, combined with Pew Research Center analysis of filings for publicly traded newspaper companies from 2013-

2020, accessed at pewresearch.org/journalism/fact-sheet/newspapers/.

470. Statistics from "The Expanding News Desert," an ongoing project of the University of North Carolina Hussman School of Journalism and Media study, led by Penelope Muse Abernathy, Knight Chair in Journalism and Digital Media Economics. The latest statistics were from the end of 2019. Accessed at usnewsdeserts.com.

471. https://en.wikipedia.org/wiki/List_of_family-owned_newspapers_in_the_United_States. Another paper on the list is *The Spokesman-Review* of Spokane, Wash., owned by a Cowles family that has remote genealogical ties to Morley Cowles Ballantine and her children.

472. Interview with Sarah Healy-Vigo, September 28, 2021.

473. Written announcement of the departure of Doug Bennett to BCI employees, from Richard G. Ballantine, Chair, BCI Board of Directors, October 5, 2021.

RICH PAST, HOPEFUL FUTURE

474. From letter "To All Employees of Ballantine Communications," issued November 13, 2021, by Chris Ballantine, Sarah Leavitt, Morley Stalnaker, and David Ballantine.

475. Thomas Jefferson, in a letter to Charles Yancey, dated January 6, 1816, retrieved at Library of Congress website, loc.gov. An expanded version: "The functionaries of every government have propensities to command at will the liberty and property of their constituents. There is no safe deposit for these but with the people themselves; nor can they be safe with them without information. Where the press is free, and every man able to read, all is safe."

476. William J. Brennan Jr., in 1964 US Supreme Court decision *New York Times* v. Sullivan.

477. Morley Cowles Ballantine, Simpson College commencement address, May 25, 1980.

References

BOOKS

Alcott, James A. *A History of Cowles Media Company*. Minneapolis: Cowles Media Company, 1998. *Arthur Ballantine 1914-1975*. Durango: *The Durango Herald*, 1975.

Ballantine, Elizabeth, and Lash, Stephen S. *A Vision of Paradise: Robertson Ward and the Mill Reef Club*. Lanham and New York: The Derrydale Press, 2001.

Ballantine, Morley C., and Ballantine, Arthur A. *Ant Palaces and other stories about life: A collection of editorials by Morley Cowles Ballantine and Arthur A. Ballantine*. Durango: Durango Herald Press, 1992.

Ballantine, Morley C.; Ballantine, Elizabeth; Ballantine, William; and Leavitt, Paul. *Recollections of the U.S.S.R.* Durango: *The Durango Herald*, 1983.

Ballantine, William Gay. *William Gay Ballantine: Biographical Notes Together With Selected Addresses, Essays and Miscellaneous Poems*. Stamford, Conn.: The Overbrook Press, 1939.

Carney, Otis. *New Lease on Life*. New York: Random House, 1971.

Cowles, Gardner Jr. *Mike Looks Back: The Memoirs of Gardner Cowles Founder of Look Magazine*. New York: Gardner Cowles, 1985.

Cowles, John, and Ballantine, Elizabeth, ed. *Letters From John Cowles to His Family, 1943-1976*. Durango: Durango Herald Press, 2004.

Friedricks, William. *Covering Iowa: The History of the Des Moines Register and Tribune Company*. Ames, Iowa: Iowa State University Press, 2000. *Gardner Cowles, 1861-1946*. Des Moines: Des Moines Register and Tribune Co., 1946.

Grey, Tilly. *On the Path With Heart: In Africa With Habitat for Humanity International*. Matilda Grey, 2006. *Harvard College Class of 1936, 35th Anniversary Report*. Cambridge: Harvard, 1971.

Hogan, Mickey. *Hogan's Story: Here's My Story, and I'm Sticking to It*. Durango: John Peel – Life Preserver, 2019.

Mills, George. *Harvey Ingham & Gardner Cowles, Sr.: Things Don't Just Happen*. Ames, Iowa: Iowa State University Press, 1977.

Morley Cowles Ballantine: May 21, 1925-October 10, 2009. Durango: Durango Herald Small Press, 2009.

Morison, Bradley L. *Sunlight On Your Doorstep: The Minneapolis Tribune's First Hundred Years, 1867-1967*. Minneapolis: Ross & Haines, 1966.

Smith College Class of 1947 Year Book, 10th Anniversary. Northampton, Mass., 1957.

Smith, Duane A. *Condemned by many, read by all: Durango's Newspapers, 1880-1992*. Durango: *The Durango Herald*, 1992.

Smith, Duane A. *Rocky Mountain Boom Town: A History of Durango, Colorado*. Boulder: University Press of Colorado, 1980.

NEWSPAPERS AND MAGAZINES

Ballantine, Arthur A. Jr. "A. Ballantine Jr. Uses Know-How Gained as Editor," *Harvard Crimson*, Jan. 30, 1948. thecrimson.com/article/1948/1/30/a-ballantine-jr-uses-know-/.

Ballantine, Arthur A. Sr. "When All the Banks Closed," *Harvard Business Review*," March 1948.

Christiansen, Wayne. "A Cowles Family Affair," *Washington Journalism Review*, 1983, P. 10.

The Denver Post, numerous references, accessed by family archives and via newspapers.com.

Des Moines Register and Tribune, numerous references, accessed via family archives and newspapers.com.

The Durango Herald and *Durango Herald-News*, numerous references, many available at the Durango Public Library.

Fort Lewis Independent and *Fort Lewis Smoke Signals*, numerous references, some accessed via coloradohistoricnewspapers.org.

Furlong, William Barry. "The Midwest's Nice Monopolists: John and Mike Cowles," *Harper's Magazine*, 1963.

Kleinfeld, N.R. "Looking Back at Look," *The New York Times*, Feb. 6, 1983.

LOOK Magazine. "The Serenest Caribbean Isle." 1961.

Minneapolis Star-Journal and Minneapolis Tribune, numerous references, accessed via family archives and newspapers.com.

Moore, Thomas. *Fortune*, April 4, 1983, PP. 156-165.

Peck, Gretchen A. "The Future of Journalism May Live on Through Family-Owned Newspapers." *Editor and Publisher* online. www.editorandpublisher.com/stories/the-future-of-journalism-may-live-on-through-family-owned-newspapers,1661?. March 9, 2020.

Rocky Mountain News, numerous references, accessed by family archives and via newspapers.com.

Time. "The Press: Iowa Formula." July 1, 1935.

WEBSITES

Bonfils-Stanton Foundation. "Leadership: Annual Awards Program: Past Honorees." https://bonfils-stantonfoundation.org/leadership/annual-awards-program/past-honorees.

Colorado Forum. "Members." www.coloradoforum.com/members.

Colorado Women's Hall of Fame. "Inductees. Women in the Hall. Ballantine." www.cogreatwomen.org/project/morley-ballantine.

History Colorado. "Miles-Bancroft. Past Awardees." www.historycolorado.org/miles-bancroft#past.

Inter American Press Association. "The IAPA. History." En.sipiapa.org/contenidos/history.html.

Minnesota Department of Natural Resources. "Glendalough State Park. About the Park." dnr.state.mn.us/state_parks.

Pew Research Center. "Research Topics. Newspapers. June 29, 2021." pewresearch.org/journalism/fact-sheet/newspapers.

University of North Carolina Hussman School of Journalism and Media. "The Expanding News Desert." usnewsdeserts.com.

Women's Foundation of Colorado. "Herstory: 1987 to Today." www.wfco.org/about/herstory.

MISCELLANEOUS

Ballantine, Arthur Jr., transcribed interview with David McComb, June 10, 1974, as part of the Oral History of Colorado Project.

Ballantine, Arthur. "A Layman's View of Public Education," series of *Durango Herald* editorials combined in printed booklet, written

January 10-16, 1972.

Center of Southwest Studies. "Timelines." Fall 2019.

La Plata County Historical Society. "Historic Durango." 2010 edition.

Reynolds, Judith, "Morley Cowles Ballantine: On the Occasion of Her 80th Birthday," written for family distribution.

Index

A

Adaptive Sports Association 211-212
Adult Education Center 220
Andrews, A.J. 40
Anesi, Pat 128
Animas Journal 64
Animas Museum 199
Antigua 90, 126, 151, 223-226, 235, 241
Athena Award 215-219, 247
Aydelotte, Gus 82
Ayres, Robert S. 42-43

B

Ballantine Communications 248, 271, 273-274, 277-279, 280-282, 285
Ballantine Family Fund 91, 181, 197, 199, 205, 210, 219
Ballantine, Ann 168
Ballantine, Arthur Jr. 3-11, 23, 25, 31-33, 37-48, 49, 50-53, 55-56, 58, 61-72, 75-76, 78-88, 90-91, 93, 95-97, 103-104, 107-111, 113-115, 119, 122-123, 125-129, 133-139, 143-149, 151, 156, 167, 172, 178, 201, 203, 206-207, 220, 226, 233, 243, 248, 253, 255, 259, 268, 270, 275, 282, 285, 286
Ballantine, Arthur Sr. 3-5, 9-10, 26, 32, 67, 114
Ballantine, Barbara 4
Ballantine, Christopher 93, 231, 234-235, 285-286
Ballantine, David 93, 231, 234-235, 285-286
Ballantine, Elisha Rev. 25
Ballantine, Elizabeth 32-33, 39, 44, 53, 79, 90, 92-93, 96, 98-100, 103, 105, 107, 109, 115-118, 120, 122, 125, 133, 137, 138, 146, 149-150, 198, 231, 238, 245, 254, 268, 270, 274, 285
Ballantine, Helen (Helen Ballantine Healy) 32, 39, 41, 53, 68, 79, 90, 92-93, 98-100, 110, 115-116, 118-120, 122-123, 127-129, 137-138, 146, 150, 167, 198, 203, 217, 230-231, 233-235, 238, 243, 245, 247, 270
Ballantine, Helen Graves 9-10, 32

Greene, Jack 45
Greenhill, Jim 266
Grey, Matilda "Tilly" Lorentz 95-96, 123, 137, 168, 270
Grossman, Dick 163
Gulliford, Andrew 114, 168, 206-207, 220, 264

H

Haas, Bob 126
Haas, Carolyn 126
Hamilton, Allan 158
Hannah, John A. 86
Harter, Hannah 158
Harvard Crimson, The see Harvard University
Harvard University 3-5, 11, 23, 39, 65, 67-69, 92, 97, 137, 145
Hawley, Philip 111
Headington, Sue Barbara 6, 8, 11
Healy-Vigo, Sarah *see* Healy, Sarah
Healy, Ed 230-231, 233-234
Healy, Helen Ballantine *see* Ballantine, Helen
Healy, Justin 231, 234, 286
Healy, Katherine 97, 231, 234-235, 246, 286
Healy, Morley 97, 231, 233-234, 236, 285, 286
Healy, Sarah 97, 230, 234, 248, 281, 285-286
Heartwood Cohousing 160
Heffelfinger, Lucia 24, 31
Hoagland, Don 96
Hoagland, Mary 181
Hook, Gary 271
Hoover, Herbert 3, 4, 67
Hull, Anne 68
Hull, Hadlai 68
Humphrey, Hubert 72, 73, 74

I

Ingham, Harvey 13, 177

LOOK 13, 71, 96, 224
Lorentz, Tilly *see* Grey, Matilda "Tilly" Lorentz
Love, Ann 63
Love, John 62-63, 89

M
MacLeish, Ada 226
MacLeish, Archibald 226, 227
Maer, Anne 223
Maer, Claude 223, 256
Maestas, Amy 265
Mancos Times 264, 274
Mann, Rochelle 248
Manning, Charles 191, 243
Manning, Sherry 189-191, 243
Mannix, Jeff 210-211, 239
Mannix, Linda 208-210
Mapel, Don 91, 203, 247
Mapel, Meredith 91
Mapel, Sandra 91, 158
Margaret Sanger Award 214-215
Matis, Arvo 115
Matis, Wilho 115
Maynes, Sam 116
Mazur, Melanie Brubaker 266
McBride, Jerry 265-266
McClatchy Newspapers 178
McCool, Lewis 265
McGrath, Nathan 158
McInnis, Scott 164, 214
McKean, Dayton D. 51
McLeod, Connie 133
McNicholas, Robert 40
McNichols, Steve 85, 127
Mertz, Martha 215-216
Mesa Verde National Park 83, 199, 264
Meyer, Suzy Garrison 264

Miller, Harry J. 55-56
Miller, Samuel 40
Minneapolis Star 15-16
Minneapolis Star and Tribune 12-13
Minneapolis Star and Tribune Company 171-172
Minneapolis Tribune 16
Missionary Ridge Fire 266
Montezuma Valley Journal 264
Moore, Joshua 265-266
Moran, Stephanie 220-221, 240
Morehart, Jim 216
Morley Ballantine Award 217, 240
Morrissey, Sally 166
Mountain Eagle 64
Murphy, Audie 103
Murphy, F. E. 16
Murrah, John 208, 209
Music in the Mountains 198, 219, 242
Myers, Lee 126
Myers, Virginia 126

N
National Association for the Advancement of Colored People 86
Neal, Bev 109
Neal, Tommy 109
Newell, Louis 64, 190
"News Buoy" 9
Nixon, Richard M. 34, 68-69, 72-73, 88
Noland, Helen 96
Noland, James 56, 91, 96

O
Olivarius-McAllister, Chase 97, 271
Orange County Register 278

P
Palmer, William Jackson 81

Parker, Ray 241
Parker, Steve 198
Parks, Rosa 164
Partridge, Dan 156, 162
Patton, Pam 114, 133, 158, 217
Peel, John 265
Peters, Joe B. "Kinky" 159
Pine River Times 274
Planned Parenthood 164, 181-182, 214-215
Purgatory ski area 91, 201-211

R
Rea, Dale 76-77
Reed, John 78, 206
Resor, Stanley R. 34
Reynolds, Judith 240
Richmond, Nancy 265-266
Riddle, Diane 153
Riddle, Hugh 153
Ritchie, Dan 192
Roberts, Bill 156, 162, 166, 270, 273, 275
Roberts, Ellen 216-217, 247, 268
Rockefeller, David 68
Rockefeller, Nelson 5, 68, 71, 74, 227
Romer, Roy 163
Roosevelt, Franklin Delano 3-4, 6, 67
Rosemary Hall 18
Rousmaniere, Jim 97, 271
Rustad, Pat 181

S
San Juan Journal 64
Sanger, Margaret 214-215
Schlichting, Don 56, 92, 121, 139, 165
Schratt, Hilda "Fraulein" 23-24
Scobie, Art 117
Scobie, Rose 117

About the Author

John Peel is a longtime journalist and writer who graduated from Drake University's School of Journalism in Des Moines, Iowa. His newspaper career has spanned four decades, leading him to Iowa, Wyoming, Florida and *The Durango Herald*, where he continues to contribute as a freelancer. He has written hiking and mountain biking guidebooks for Southwest Colorado, and currently operates a business, John Peel – Life Preserver, that creates books about people's personal and family histories.